THE PSYCHOLOGY OF REVOLUTION

Based on decades of psychological research and personal experience, Fathali M. Moghaddam presents a new and dynamic introduction to the psychology of revolution. He sets out to explain what does and does not change with revolution, using the concept of political plasticity or the malleability of political behavior. In turn, psychological theories of collective mobilization, the process of regime change, and explanations of what happens after regime change are discussed. This psychological analysis of the post-revolution period is pertinent because it explains why revolutions so often fail. General readers interested in learning more about the psychology of revolution, as well as students, researchers, and teachers in political psychology, political science, and collective action, will find this book accessible and beneficial.

FATHALI M. MOGHADDAM is Professor of Psychology at Georgetown University, where he served as Director of the Interdisciplinary Program in Cognitive Science (2016–21). He also served as Editor-in-Chief of the APA journal *Peace and Conflict: Journal of Peace Psychology* (2014–21). His extensive publications include about 30 books and 300 papers, and he has won a number of prestigious academic awards.

T0370787

THE PROGRESSIVE PSYCHOLOGY BOOK SERIES

This book is part of the Cambridge University Press book series, Progressive Psychology, edited by Fathali M. Moghaddam. As the science of human behavior, psychology is uniquely positioned and equipped to try to help us make more progress toward peaceful, fair, and constructive human relationships. However, the enormous resources of psychology have not been adequately or effectively harnessed for this task. The goal of this book series is to engage psychological science in the service of achieving more democratic societies, toward providing equal opportunities for all. The volumes in the series contribute in new and unique ways to highlight how psychological science can contribute to making justice a more central theme in health care, education, the legal system, and business, combatting the psychological consequences of poverty, ending discrimination and prejudice, better understanding the failure of revolutions and limits on political plasticity, and moving societies to more openness. Of course, these topics have been discussed before in scattered and *ad hoc* ways by psychologists, but now they are addressed as part of a systematic and cohesive series on Progressive Psychology.

THE PSYCHOLOGY
OF REVOLUTION

FATHALI M. MOGHADDAM

Georgetown University

Shaftesbury Road, Cambridge CB2 8EA, United Kingdom

One Liberty Plaza, 20th Floor, New York, NY 10006, USA

477 Williamstown Road, Port Melbourne, VIC 3207, Australia

314–321, 3rd Floor, Plot 3, Splendor Forum, Jasola District Centre,
New Delhi – 110025, India

103 Penang Road, #05–06/07, Visioncrest Commercial, Singapore 238467

Cambridge University Press is part of Cambridge University Press & Assessment,
a department of the University of Cambridge.

We share the University's mission to contribute to society through the pursuit of
education, learning and research at the highest international levels of excellence.

www.cambridge.org
Information on this title: www.cambridge.org/9781009433242

DOI: 10.1017/9781009433259

First published 2024

A catalogue record for this publication is available from the British Library

A Cataloging-in-Publication data record for this book is available from the Library of Congress

ISBN 978-1-009-43324-2 Hardback
ISBN 978-1-009-43322-8 Paperback

Cambridge University Press & Assessment has no responsibility for the persistence
or accuracy of URLs for external or third-party internet websites referred to in this
publication and does not guarantee that any content on such websites is, or will remain,
accurate or appropriate.

To
Abbas Milani
Visionary scholar and teacher

Look back over the past, with its changing empires that rose and fell, and you can foresee the future too.

Marcus Aurelius (121–180 AD)

Contents

Contents

Figures

Preface

I wrote this book because psychology is at the heart of revolutions, and psychological science has an invaluable and unique role to play in critically assessing, explaining, and even predicting revolutions. But this vast potential remains unfulfilled because the psychology of revolution is a neglected research topic. As I describe in the introductory chapter, the last book entitled *The Psychology of Revolution* was published in 1894.

In addition to undertaking essential and urgently needed research on the psychology of revolution, I am a psychologist who has experienced revolution in my country of birth, Iran. My personal experiences of living and researching for five years in post-revolution Iran, focusing particularly on the psychology of what takes place following the coming to power of a new revolutionary government, provides invaluable first-hand insights into the psychology of revolution. My argument is that in order to better understand revolutions, we must also concern ourselves with what happens *after* regime change and not, as has been the tradition, limit our attention only to what leads to regime change.[1]

The target audience for this book is students, researchers, teachers, and lay people interested in gaining a deeper understanding of the psychology of revolution. More specifically, this book will be of interest to teachers and students in courses in the areas of political science, political psychology, radicalization, collective mobilization, and group and intergroup behavior.

Acknowledgments

I am deeply indebted to the many people who have helped me to better understand revolutions, particularly during my time in post-revolution Iran. As a laboratory-trained psychologist, when I returned to Iran in the "Spring of Revolution" in 1979, I found I needed to become educated in a different, more worldly way – to become street-smart, with my teachers being ordinary people in the colorful neighborhoods of Tehran, in remote villages around Iran, in bazaars and mosques, in coffee houses, in shops and bus stations. Looking back, the lay people who educated me during those post-revolution years showed deep wisdom and considerable patience.

In the academic context, throughout the process of writing this book I have kept the analytic style of Hannah Arendt in my mind and used her as an inspiration. More specifically with respect to my indebtedness in the area of psychology, the ideas in this book have been shaped by a long line of researchers who have moved the psychology of group and intergroup relations forward since the 1970s, including Henri Tajfel, John Turner, Mick Billig, Winnifred Louis and, of course, Don Taylor and Rom Harré. I have also benefited greatly from discussions about revolutions and revolutionary movements with my dear and generous friend Duncan Wu.

I owe particular thanks to David Repetto of Cambridge University Press, who has been a true champion in support of the Progressive Psychology book series.

CHAPTER I

A Psychological Perspective on the Puzzle of Revolution

"Hurrah for revolution. . ." thus begins William Butler Yeats's poem "The Great Day," which ends with an image of a beggar on horseback and a beggar on foot changing places, but the "lash" continuing to fall cruelly on the back of the beggar on foot.[1] This dire, dark, and cyclical image of revolution contrasts sharply with the shining utopian dreams articulated by revolutionaries, particularly during the awe-inspiring days leading up to regime change, when so many people have to make life-and-death sacrifices in the struggle to topple the ruling regime. I enthusiastically reveled in these utopian dreams as Iranian society hurled itself into a mammoth revolution until Mohammad Reza Pahlavi (1919–80), the last Shah, was dethroned. But, as happens in so many societies after revolutions, life in post-revolution Iran proved to be very far from the open society for which tens of millions of people, holding many different religious and secular ideologies, had made sacrifices. My psychological research and everyday life experiences in Iran after the revolution led to a sobering reevaluation of the utopian dreams that propelled the Iranian revolutionary movement, as well as revolutions in general.

This book presents an adventurous new exploration of the psychology of revolution, based on my reassessment after about four decades of psychological research on this neglected topic. Psychology is at the heart of revolutions, and what I call the "puzzle of revolution" is best explained through a psychological lens. This puzzle is reflected in the expression "The more things change, the more they stay the same" ("*plus ça change, plus c'est la même chose*"). At the heart of the puzzle of revolution is the sense that after a revolution and regime change, a great deal has been transformed, but yet in the most important ways nothing of importance has actually changed.

On the one hand, major revolutions bring about what seems to be enormous and rapid radical change. Regimes are toppled, former rulers become powerless, new rulers rise to power; new governments are formed;

new constitutions are ratified; the rhetoric used in public and even private life changes; new forms of speech, dress, and fashion come to life; just about everything in the media, arts, and entertainment is transformed; and all forms of communications put on a new face. The names of institutions, universities, schools, streets, buildings, parks, and even entire cities and nations are changed in line with the ideals of the revolution. Monuments are torn down and new ones are erected. National holidays and their names are changed. Society adopts radical new images and ideals. Even the most popular names for newborn infants become "revolutionary."

On the other hand, even after the great revolutions, such as in France, Russia, and China, there was little change in central features of behavior such as the style of leader–follower relations and elite/non-elite inequalities in power and resources.[2] At a deep level, inequalities and injustices tend to continue after revolutions, even though the surface rhetoric about equality and justice indicates otherwise. Despite changes in rhetoric, the rulers and the ruled continue with their separate lives in their separate worlds, and their relationships continue to be characterized by chasms of inequalities. The beggars have changed places, but the cruel lash continues, as Yeats put it. Revolutions against dictatorships routinely lead to one dictator being replaced by another, as happened most recently in Iran and in the Arab Spring countries, and as had happened before in the great French and Russian revolutions: In France, Emperor Napoleon replaced the king; in Russia, Lenin, Stalin, and other dictators replaced the Tsar (and in the twenty-first century, Tsar Putin continues the same tradition of absolute, despotic rule). What explains this continuity? And, given the injustice of inequalities in power and resources in so many different societies, why are there so very few revolutions in human history? As Samuel Huntington has noted, "Revolutions are rare. Most societies have never experienced revolutions."[3]

I argue that these questions about revolutions are best explained through a psychological lens. This is because at the heart of every revolution is the challenge of bringing about psychological changes, in both collective and individual cognition and action. This is irrespective of the type of revolution being considered. For example, Jack Goldstone considers the following categories: republican revolutions, Marxist revolutions, revolutions against dictatorships, and revolutions against communism.[4] Later in this chapter, I shall return to this topic and explain how I chose to focus on particular revolutions for this project.

The goal of revolutionaries is to bring about the ideal society they have imagined and propagated through their revolutionary rhetoric. However, in order to create the ideal society, the revolutionaries must change behavior among both the masses and the elite; they must transform how people think and act. For example, after the 1917 revolution in Russia, revolutionaries such as Vladimir Lenin (1870–1924), Leon Trotsky (1879–1940), and Joseph Stalin (1878–1953) attempted to create conditions in which people would be motivated to work through collective rather than individual incentives and ownership. After the 1979 revolution in Iran, Khomeini and his extremist followers attempted to influence Iranians to abandon what they condemned as decadent Western values, ideals, gender roles, and behavioral styles, and instead to adopt what they claimed to be an authentic "Islamic" mode of cognition and action in both their private and public lives. The return to Islam was to create an ideal, ethical society, far removed from corruption and materialism. Behaviors such as theft and bribery would naturally disappear.

Thus, the first challenge confronting revolutionaries is to bring about behavioral changes in a society, moving toward achieving the goals of the revolution. Psychological science has a direct bearing on this behavioral change goal of revolutionaries. Psychological science illuminates the probability of successfully changing behavior in certain ways, and the conditions necessary for such possible changes. For example, reflecting on the goals of Lenin and other Russian revolutionaries, research on social loafing, social laboring, and human motivation casts light on the possibility of establishing a society based on collective rather than individual incentives and ownership under different conditions. Second, psychological science guides us to better understand the length of time and conditions required to bring about particular individual and collective behavioral changes. Under certain conditions, behavioral changes, such as in the areas of incentives, motivation, leader–follower relations, and the like, might require very long time periods to bring about, perhaps decades, centuries, or even longer. On the other hand, under certain conditions behavioral changes in some other domains, such as gender roles, can be achieved more quickly.[5] Third, in addition to helping to explain behavioral continuity before and after revolutions, psychological science can help explain why there are so few revolutions.

Despite psychology being central to revolutions, only one major book has been published on *The Psychology of Revolution*; this was authored by Gustav Le Bon (1841–1931) and first appeared in 1894.[6] The *Anatomy of Revolution* by Crane Brinton (1898–1968),[7] first published in 1938, also has a psychological theme. More recently, I served as coeditor of a collection of psychological discussions published in 2018 on radical social change and revolution.[8] However, there have been no published monographs on "the psychology of revolution" for well over a century. Nor do major handbooks on revolution include chapters on the psychology of revolution.[9] Perhaps the neglect of revolutions in psychology is not surprising, given that since the development of psychological science in Western societies in the late nineteenth century, there have not been any major revolutions in Western societies. Consequently, Western psychologists have not directly experienced or encountered revolutions during the development of their discipline. However, they have encountered collective movements, including the women's movement and various ethnic minority movements.

Although it is well over a century since a book on the psychology of revolution has been published, there is extensive theoretical and empirical psychological research on collective action and collective movements.[10] This research literature, which I discuss in the next two chapters, provides invaluable insights and perspectives on the conditions in which people participate in nonnormative collective action and mobilize against authorities and ruling regimes. However, getting to regime change is only one part of revolutions, and in a psychological sense it is the easiest part because it involves motivating people to topple a regime. The behavioral changes necessary for this type of collective action are relatively simple. A far more complex and difficult task is that of building the revolutionary society *after* regime change has been achieved.

In both Le Bon's pioneering book and in the more recent works on the psychology of collective action and radical change, a key insight is that a change of regime does not change the cognition and actions of the people.[11] As Le Bon noted, "Changing the name of a government does not transform the mentality of a people."[12] Numerous case studies of important revolutions highlight this same point, that a new regime and new rhetoric does not correspond with actual behavioral changes in society.[13] This insight has two important implications. First, it points to a gap between the idealistic narratives of revolutionaries, the constructed golden fictions used to inspire people to make sacrifices for the revolution, and the actual behaviors that take place among both leaders and followers, particularly in the post–regime-change period. The second implication, which has not been taken up, is that researchers must closely examine *what happens after revolutions*. Psychological science can help us to better understand not just what leads to revolutions, but also what happens in the post-revolution period. We must arrive at a more accurate picture of why so many revolutions manage to topple regimes and create different types of change, but fail to arrive at the ideal society envisaged by revolutionaries – or even something close to it.

The objective of the present work is to address this gap by examining the psychology of revolution through an exploration of both what leads to revolution and what happens in the post-revolution period. I present a new and dynamic account of revolution based on twenty-first-century psychological science, using as a central theme the concept of *political plasticity*, the malleability of political behavior: How much, how fast, and in what areas change in political behavior is (and is not) possible.[14] Political plasticity is limited by hardwiring both within and outside individuals.[15] Hardwiring within individuals and particularly in brains has been studied extensively, and is a major topic in the vast and fast-expanding research areas of neuroscience and cognitive neuroscience.[16] However, hardwiring outside people and its role in relation to political plasticity deserves far more research attention.[17] Hardwiring outside people includes the built environment, and everything we refer to as "culture," including the collectively constructed and collaboratively upheld narratives that we share.

The concept of political plasticity helps us to unravel the mystery at the heart of revolutions: why after revolutions on the surface so much seems to change, but at a deeper level, things seem to stay the same. Political plasticity points to the central role of hardwiring not only within but also outside individuals in limiting the speed and extent of behavioral changes. Insights from the application of political plasticity illuminate not only the processes before revolutions, but also during and after; not only collective action to bring about regime change, but also the coming to power of the new regime and its style of governance after the revolution.

Moreover, the concept of political plasticity helps us to develop a psychological account of revolutions that avoids the pitfall of psychological reductionism: the tendency to explain behavior by reference exclusively to the smallest units possible (such as parts of the brain, neural networks, and personality traits).[18] Only one kind of political plasticity is concerned with intrapersonal processes, and this is in many ways the least important kind of political plasticity as far as revolutions and revolutionary change is concerned. The larger and more important kind of political plasticity in this account of revolutions is concerned with hardwiring outside individuals, such as styles of leader–follower relations – with a focus on processes between rather than within individuals.[19]

In conclusion, then, the concept of political plasticity helps us to examine the highly complex topic of change in the post-revolution period. The available theories and empirical research in psychology have been applied most directly to the topic of collective action, and are specifically applicable to the processes leading to revolutions – but not what happens after revolutions. This is an important omission which I take steps to rectify in this book because, after all, the long-term success of a revolution depends on what happens *after* regime change has taken place. Of course, revolutionary action to bring about regime change is an essential first step, but an even more difficult challenge is to bring about behavioral changes in the post-revolution period. The examples of revolutions since the early twentieth century, from the 1917 Russian Revolution to the 1979 Iranian Revolution and the Arab Spring revolutions of the twenty-first century, suggest that bringing about regime change is in some respects more feasible than changing mass behavior in line with revolutionary goals after the revolution. For this reason, much of the focus of this book is on what happens after regime change has taken place.

Which Revolutions?

Written accounts of revolutions go back at least 4,000 years, so how should we limit the selection of revolutions in terms of time?[20] The number of revolutions around the world and across history could expand into the hundreds or even thousands, depending on our criteria for inclusion; for example, just modern Latin American revolutions could include Bolivia (1952–6), Cuba (1959–69), Nicaragua (1979–90), and Grenada (1979–83).[21] The Arab Spring revolutions (from 2011) could include Tunisia, Egypt, Bahrain, Libya, Yemen, and Syria.[22] The second-wave Arab Spring has involved major agitations in Algeria, Iraq, Lebanon, Morocco, Sudan, and Yemen.[23] Mark Beissinger, a scholar of revolutions, writes about a recent three-decade period in this way: "By my counting, from 1985 to 2014 there were approximately fifty-six revolutions worldwide involving mobilizations of at least a thousand civilian participants that successfully displaced incumbent rulers; there were also another sixty-seven attempted revolutions during this period that involved mobilizations of at least a thousand civilian participants but failed to gain power."[24] A number of other scholars of revolutions have provided similarly extensive lists, including mass rebellions in modern times.[25] While reviewing extensive lists of revolutions has some merit, particularly if a quantitative research approach is taken, my focus on examining the psychological processes underlying revolutions requires a different, narrower perspective, in order to delve deeper.

This study of the psychology of revolution narrows down in one critical way. My main focus is on what I interpret as (and on what are generally taken to be) the great revolutions in modern history, which include the French Revolution (1789), the Russian Revolution (1917), the Chinese Communist Revolution (1927–49), the Cuban Revolution (1953), and the Iranian Revolution (1978–9). I include the Iranian Revolution (1978–9) because of the monumental impact it has had on regional and global events.[26] I consider the American Revolution of 1789 as a special case because it had global influence (although its limitations are often overlooked).[27] However, I interpret it more as a war of independence against a foreign power (Great Britain), in the same way that I interpret the Algerian Revolution (1954–62), which involved a fight for independence from France. I also consider, but give less attention to, the seventeenth-century English Revolutions (in 1640 and 1688), the Irish Revolution (1916–23), the Mexican Revolution of 1910, the so-called Color Revolutions (involving mostly territories in the former Soviet Union, from the early twenty-first century), and the Nazi Revolution of the 1930s.[28]

In summary, then, there is one very important way in which this study of the psychology of revolutions is more expansive than traditional studies of revolutions: I include an examination of what happens *after* regime change, using the concept of *political plasticity* – in what ways, how much, and how fast political behavior does and does not change.[29] I address the following question: What are the psychological factors that limit change after regime change? If revolutions do follow a script as proposed by some researchers, an important component of the script is the failure of revolutions to reach their idealistic goals after regime change – a neglected topic, so far.[30]

Book Contents

Following Chapter 1, the other ten chapters (2–11) and the Afterword in this book are organized in four parts.

Part I: Getting to Revolutionary Collective Action

The two chapters in Part I critically discuss the psychological theories and research on collective action, and connect and apply this literature to revolution.[31] The theories and research are considered in two parts. First, theories that assume material factors and macro-structural conditions to be the main drivers of group and intergroup behavior are considered in Chapter 2. These include research in the traditions of realistic conflict theory,[32] resource mobilization theory,[33] the Five-Stage Model,[34] social dominance theory,[35] evolutionary psychology,[36] and system justification theory.[37] Second, theories that give priority to subjective factors as the main drivers of group and intergroup behavior are examined in Chapter 3. These include research in the traditions of social identity theory,[38] terror management theory,[39] relative deprivation theory,[40] equity and various other justice theories,[41] and psychodynamic theory.[42] The theories discussed in Chapters 2 and 3 all have implications for the conditions in which nonnormative collective action is more likely to take place, and when a collective rebellion against authority is more likely to happen. The discussions in these two chapters incorporate empirical research related to the major theories and the questions they raise, such as the issue of what happens when people taking collective action face difficulties and failures, as often occurs during the process of revolutionary movements.[43]

Collective action with the goal of revolution is often driven by particular ideologies, through which images of ideal societies are presented as alternatives to what currently exists. For example, Lenin and his associates active during the Russian Revolution (1917) were motivated and guided by communist ideology and the ideal of a classless society, just as Khomeini and his associates active during the Iranian Revolution (1979) were motivated and guided by their particular interpretation of Islamic ideology and the ideal Islamic society. Revolutionaries present and use the ideal society to motivate people to join the revolution against the rulers of the existing society. Social comparison processes, relative deprivation, and perceived justice are at the heart of how revolutionaries present their imagined ideal society and mobilize collective action against the ruling regime. These psychological processes and their association with revolutionary ideals and collective action are also discussed in Chapters 2 and 3.

Part II: Regime Change

The three chapters in Part II focus on psychological processes underlying different aspects of regime change. Chapter 4 examines power and authority in transition, and particularly when a tipping point is reached leading to regime collapse. Collective and individual psychological experiences involving confidence, trust, feelings of security, perceived threat, and risk-taking are centrally involved in regime collapse. Historical examples of regime collapse are referenced in examinations of these and related psychological processes, as well as the concept of a regime-collapse tipping point.

Regime change happens in different ways and over different time periods, with different psychological consequences for society; this is the topic of Chapter 5. For example, regime change can come about through a rapid *coup d'état*, involving a small number of army officers. An example of this is the coup that began on May 24, 2021, when the Malian military pushed aside President Bah N'daw. The Malian population was not involved in this regime change, and did not have an opportunity to become transformed through participation in collective action. I do not include such regime changes as examples of revolutions. In contrast, regime change can come about through a long process involving large sections of the population as participants in collective action. For example, the Iranian Revolution (1979) involved a longer process of collective action (about eighteen months) through increasingly large-scale public participation, at times with tens of millions of people involved. The Chinese Communist Revolution lasted decades, and was lengthened by the Great Leap Forward, the Culture Revolution, and other radical programs implemented by Mao Zedong (1893–1976).[44] I include the Chinese and Iranian examples in discussions of great revolutions.

Chapter 6 examines the psychological stepping stones people go through on their way to becoming full participants in revolutionary collective action. These stepping stones are derived from the theories and research discussed in Chapters 2 and 3, and begin with people becoming aware of an ideal alternative society – and the realization that we *can* do better with respect to the kind of society we live in. The psychological steps involve changes in cognition, including seeing the ruling regime as illegitimate and unstable and, finally, being willing (if necessary) to make huge sacrifices and take enormous risks in order to achieve regime change. However, a point I stress is that in some respects achieving regime change is easier than managing changes in the post-revolution period.

Part III: What Happens after Revolutionary Regime Change?

The three chapters in Part III explore what happens after regime change has taken place – a topic neglected by traditional research on revolutions. Chapter 7 examines the psychology of behavioral continuity and change in the post-revolution period, when policy changes in economic, political, social, and other arenas can take place very quickly. For example, a new constitution and new economic policies (e.g., collective ownership of resources) can be drawn up and ratified "on paper" relatively quickly by the new revolutionary government. However, the actual micro-level behavioral changes necessary to implement these new macro-level policies often take far longer to bring about, and sometimes the change is never successfully achieved. For example, on paper, farm ownership can be changed from "individual/private ownership" to "collective farming" overnight. However, the process of changing the actual behavior of farmers to perform effectively and happily as members of collective farms will take many years, if it is achieved at all. Indeed, the experiences of the Soviet Union, China, and some other societies could be cited as evidence to argue that such behavioral change is not possible in the relatively short term. If it is to become possible in the long term, then the conditions for this change must be identified and made ready – something not achieved in any large society so far. In Chapter 7, I examine this and other challenges related to behavioral change and continuity, in the context of revolutions and their ideological goals.

The puzzle of behavioral continuity after revolutions is the main topic of Chapter 8. I argue that even major revolutions only achieve within-system rather than between-system change: bringing about surface-level rather than deep-level system change. For example, one type of dictatorship is changed for another (e.g., communist dictatorship replaces the Tsar's dictatorship in Russia, or the mullahs' dictatorship instead of the Shah's dictatorship in Iran). I explain the puzzle of behavioral continuity through reference to *cultural carrier*, the means by which culture is propagated and extended, and the micro–macro rule of change, which proposes that the maximum speed of change is higher at the macro level than at the micro level. For example, a new revolutionary constitution can be ratified or new economic policies can be signed into law overnight by the revolutionary government, but micro-level behavioral changes among ordinary people to implement these new revolutionary constitutions and economic policies typically take far longer – if they happen at all.

Personality factors play a role in all stages of revolutions, but this role is probably most important in the post-revolution period, a topic discussed in Chapter 9. I refer to personality factors such as Machiavellianism, authoritarianism, openness to experience, extroversion, conscientiousness, narcissism, and aggression to assess the rise of particular individuals into leadership positions in the post-revolution period. References are made to important revolutionary leaders, including Stalin, Castro, and Khomeini, among others, in the discussion. One of the extremely difficult challenges in the post-revolution period is to avoid the coming to power of an authoritarian strongman, who invariably leads society to a dictatorship with a new facade.

Part IV: Reevaluating Revolutions

The two final chapters (10 and 11) and the Afterword in Part IV of the book present a psychological model of revolution, examine the relationship between human nature and revolution, and interpret revolutions as acts of collective creativity. All humans hold and are influenced by illusions in their everyday lives. The Illusion-Motivation Model of Revolution (Chapter 10) discusses the illusions that underlie each phase of revolution, and the motivations that arise from each particular illusion. I stress that the use of the term "illusion" in this context is not intended to have negative connotations. Illusions influence all humans, and in this chapter the focus is on illusions that are particularly influential during revolutions.

Chapter 11 directly addresses the following question: Are revolutions doomed to fail because of human nature? In addressing this question, I explore a number of psychological factors, including the personalities of the leaders who are more likely to rise to the top after revolutions, and areas of behavior with low political plasticity (such as in the area of work motivation, in relation to collectivization programs). The underlying theme of the chapter is limitations to the changes that can possibly be brought about by revolutions because of hard-to-change human psychological characteristics. In the Afterword, I interpret revolutions as acts of remarkable collective creativity, both on the part of those involved in revolutionary movements intended to achieve regime change, and those engaged in defending and upholding the ruling regime. Although the collective creativity demonstrated by both sides during revolutions is highly impressive, the outcome of these processes is seldom leading to open societies, in the short term at least.

PART I

Getting to Revolutionary Collective Action

A broad range of psychological theories are now available to explain how people come to take *revolutionary collective action*, meaning that they join movements with the explicit goal of overthrowing the ruling regime. Most of these theories have been developed since the 1970s, as part of a research movement in psychological science to give greater attention to group and intergroup relations. This research movement was highly influenced by Henri Tajfel (1919–82) and a number of other European researchers. The major theories of intergroup relations and the research traditions they established attempt to counteract the reductionism and individualism of mainstream psychology – the tendency to assume the causes of behavior to be internal to individuals and increasingly internal to the brain.

In the two chapters in Part I, I critically discuss this research movement focused on collective processes, with close attention to a variety of theories that assume material factors to be the main driving force for collective action (Chapter 2), and those that propose psychological factors as the main driving force (Chapter 3). Both sets of theories give close attention to material and psychological factors, but they differ in which set of factors they assume to be the main driver of collective action. The theories discussed include realistic conflict theory, resource mobilization theory, system justification theory, social dominance theory, relative deprivation theory, the Five-Stage Model, various justice theories (such as equity theory), evolutionary psychology, and social identity and self-categorization theories. These theories provide different explanations of why people contribute resources and invest in support of revolutions, including sacrificing their lives and becoming martyrs, taking part in pro-revolution protests, contributing money and material resources, and spreading information and news against the ruling regime. In a sense, these theories offer different perspectives on ideals and how they move people to action, or inaction. As Geoffroy de Lagasnerie has argued, "Some ideals encourage action, others prevent it." The challenge facing revolutionaries is to communicate an ideal to the population that will motivate a sufficient number of people with the necessary material and nonmaterial resources to join the revolution and bring about regime change.

Joining the revolution to overthrow the ruling regime involves huge risks and could result in death, imprisonment, property confiscation and loss of employment, or other severe punishments, not just for the individual rebel but also often for their family, friends, and associates. This harsh reality is being underlined by current events in Iran as I prepare the next draft of this section of the book. The mullahs who rule Iran have unleashed a string of vicious attacks on schoolgirls, including poisoning them, in retaliation for their participation in anti-regime demonstrations. Again and again, we are reminded that revolutions are dangerous for rebels and many attempts at regime change fail. Why should people take the risk of suffering the severe punishments that typically follow a failed revolution? The revolutionaries have to influence people to believe that regime change is possible, and that the rewards that regime change will bring to them personally and to their group are valuable enough to risk the costs of failure.

Irrespective of whether we assume material factors or psychological factors to drive revolutionary collective action, the processes of mobilizing people for collective action and the collective actions subsequently taken are characterized by some level of irrationality, meaning that people are often not aware of the factors that are shaping their behavior, and sometimes they are not even aware of how they are behaving. Irrationality can influence psychological processes involving social comparison, relative deprivation, and subjective justice, which underlie the shift from not participating to participating in revolutionary collective action. For example, revolutionaries influence people to feel comparatively deprived and treated unjustly in their present societies. Through social comparisons made with ideal societies, revolutionaries can lead people to feel a sense of deprivation and injustice, but these feelings are subjectively rather than objectively derived, driven by emotions, and at least to some extent arrived at irrationally.

CHAPTER 2

Psychological Theories and Revolution
Material Factors as Drivers

Economic conditions ... first transformed the mass into workers. The combination of capital has created for this mass a common situation, common interests. This mass is already a class as against capital, but not yet for itself. In the struggle ... this mass becomes united, and constitutes itself as a class for itself. The interests it defends become class interests.

Karl Marx (1847)[1]

Revolution, in the narrow sense of the term is an acute struggle, and only in the course of the struggle and in its outcome is the real strength of all the interests, aspirations and potentialities displayed and fully revealed.

Vladimir Lenin (1906)[2]

Materialist conditions shape the psychological characteristics and experiences of collectives and individuals – this claim presents a major challenge to psychological science because on the surface it seems to place psychology as dependent on, and shaped by, material factors. But an alternative assessment of this claim leads to a different perspective, one that gives central place to the psychological interpretation of the material world, to how the world is subjectively understood. For example, Jane and John have just got married, own a car, and together they earn $75,000 a year. From a psychological perspective, the key question is: How do Jane and John feel about their situation? Do they feel well off, or do they compare themselves to couples who earn $175,000 a year and feel relatively deprived? Thus, on the one hand we might focus on the subjective interpretations made by Jane and John, but on the other hand the materialist perspective could argue that how Jane and John feel about their situation will be highly influenced by those who control resources and shape the ideologies and belief systems dominant in society. The materialist claim is that, ultimately, how Jane and John feel about their situation will be shaped by material conditions. This is in line with interpretations of revolutions from economists and others, giving priority to macroeconomic features of revolutions.[3]

The materialist perspective in psychology that bears on revolutions, particularly as represented by realistic conflict theory, resource mobilization theory, the Five-Stage Model, and system justification theory, is directly or indirectly influenced by the Marxist tradition.[4] First, and most importantly, this tradition conceives of material conditions, and the struggles and conflicts people experience in their everyday lives, as eventually leading them to become conscious of different social classes, competing social class interests, and also of their own social class membership and identity. The recognition among workers that social classes exist and have competing interests, and that they themselves belong to a particular social class, eventually leads them to act as members of a class "for itself," in defense of their own social class interests.[5] In this way, the consciousness of workers, their understanding of the larger political world and their place within it, emerges through their practical everyday experiences within their material conditions.

It is through workers clashing with the capitalist class, the owners of the means of production, that they gradually become conscious of their collective interests as a distinct social class. Workers come to see themselves as having collective interests that are different from the collective interests of the capitalist class. Class consciousness emerges through repeated and increasingly serious clashes between social classes with competing interests, and in this way psychological experiences are shaped by material conditions.

Second, the Marxist tradition has influenced psychologists to give importance to, and to research, *false consciousness*, the lack of psychological awareness of one's own true social class membership and interests.[6] According to the Marxist tradition, the dominant ideology in society is shaped by the capitalist class. The explanations and justifications provided by all social classes, including the working class, stem from the ideology shaped by the capitalist class. The control of ideology by the capitalist class derives in large part from capitalist ownership of all major media and communications systems, including television, radio, electronic communications systems, newspapers, magazines, and film production, as well as social media, such as Twitter and Facebook. But this control also derives from the enormous influence of capitalists in the education system, for example through their influence on funding for training and research (the direction of twenty-first-century university research is shaped largely by research funding).[7]

The dominant ideology propagated by the capitalist class justifies the status quo, with its group-based inequalities, and it leads poor people (in particular) to ignore their own true social class membership and interests. In this way, the working class functions without experiencing and benefiting from class consciousness, and it acts in the interests of the capitalist class (the concept of false consciousness has also been used to explain the situation of women and other minorities, who can misperceive their own group membership and collective interests[8]). System justification theory and other theories in the materialist tradition are strongly influenced by these ideas.

The materialist perspective in psychology, particularly social dominance research and evolutionary psychology, is also strongly influenced by evolutionary theory (evolutionary psychology is the new term for sociobiology[9]). The focus in the social dominance theory approach is on surplus-producing societies and their group-based hierarchies, such as those based on (1) age, (2) sex, and (3) various constructed groups (such as ethnicity, social class, caste, and religion). The question is asked as to why these hierarchies are reproduced over time in different societies, so that consistently some groups enjoy greater status, power, and resources than other groups. However, proponents of social dominance theory take considerable pains to argue that they are not biological determinists, nor are they justifying group-based hierarchies as inevitable or natural. Social dominance theory is further discussed later in this chapter.

In the first section of this chapter, then, I further examine the perspective that psychological experiences arise out of material conditions. In the second section, I address the influence of evolutionary theory on materialist accounts of intergroup relations in psychological science. The common theme of all these perspectives is the proposition that material conditions shape psychological experiences.

Psychological Experiences Arise out of Material Conditions

The idea that material conditions shape psychological experiences might seem to pose a challenge to psychologists because at a superficial level this perspective seems to give a secondary role to psychological factors. However, as I explain in the following discussion, this perspective actually gives a central role to psychological factors and processes, but not as direct drivers of collective action.

We begin our discussion by assessing realistic conflict theory, which was largely developed by the highly innovative Turkish-American psychologist

Muzafer Sherif (1906–88).[10] Sherif's initial research[11] exploring this theory has inspired a solid body of scholarship by other researchers.[12] Sherif postulated that "functional relations between groups" determines intergroup relations,[13] including the psychological outlook of each group toward the other. Because people are motivated to maximize their rewards, they will cooperate with and be positively disposed toward outgroups who share their material interests, but will compete against and be negatively disposed toward outgroups who have opposing interests. The competitive or cooperative nature of relations between groups also has implications for the dynamics of behavior within groups, such as the kind of leadership that emerges within each group – a topic discussed further later in this chapter.

Sherif's conceptualization of intergroup relations has had far-reaching influence. For example, he conceived of intergroup relations as taking place when individuals who belong to one group individually or collectively interact with another group or its members *"in terms of their group identification."*[14] This emphasis on subjective identification with a group influenced social identity theory, which has become the most influential psychological theory of intergroup relations in the twenty-first century,[15] as we will explore in Chapter 3. This emphasis on subjective identification is also influenced by the Marxist concept of false consciousness: In some situations, group members do not identify with their "ingroup," even though on objective criteria they belong to that group. An example is working-class individuals who fail to recognize that they are members of this social class and act in ways that work against the interests of their own social class (e.g., when poor people vote for political parties and leaders that adopt tax policies against the interests of the working class and in favor of the rich). Thus, psychological identification is given the highest importance by Sherif, even though his explanation is functional.

The primary empirical support for Sherif's realistic conflict theory account of intergroup relations initially came from field research conducted in 1949, 1953, and 1954 by him and his associates in the context of summer camps for boys. Sherif and his associates played the role of summer camp personnel. The boys who were selected to serve as participants were healthy and well-adjusted, and they were all similar in terms of age (eleven or twelve years old), sex (male), ethnicity (white), and religion (Protestant). This ensured that naturally existing differences between the boys did not influence the study outcomes.

The development of groups at the summer camp evolved in four stages. The boys did not know one another before arrival at the camp. First, during the stage of *friendship formation*, they became acquainted. Sherif and his colleagues noted the friendship patterns that emerged between the boys. In the second stage of *group formation*, the boys were separated into two groups, with those who had made 'best friends' being placed into *different* groups. This was to ensure that friendship patterns would not explain the study outcomes (this was different in the 1954 "Robber's Cave" study, where the two groups of boys arrived at the summer camp in two separate buses and were kept apart, so they could first independently develop group culture before directly interacting with one another). Each group of boys carried out a series of activities, through which group norms, social roles, group leaders, nicknames, and the basics of a group culture and cohesion emerged. In the third stage of *intergroup competition*, the two groups were placed in direct competition with one another (by taking part in competitive games, such as tug-of-war and treasure hunt), in zero-sum situations where a victory for one group necessarily meant a loss for the other group. The groups were now competing for material rewards, as well as the prestige and status associated with winning group competitions.

Direct competition for scarce resources between the two groups of boys resulted in a number of psychological changes within each group. For example, attitudes toward the outgroup became highly negative and intergroup stereotypes hardened, so the outgroup were now accused of being "cheats" and "sneaks." This was despite former best friends being in the outgroup. Very importantly, the more aggressive boys rose in popularity and influence, so that a boy who had been labeled a "bully" before the intergroup conflict now gained a more positive status because his aggression was now seen as very useful against the outgroup. Less aggressive boys lost influence, as the main goal of each group became fighting against and defeating the outgroup. An attitude of "the ends justify the means" developed within each group, with the ends being victory against the outgroup.

Having created a context in which two groups engaged in direct and destructive intergroup conflict, the challenge for Sherif was to influence the two groups to once again become peaceful toward one another. He achieved this transformation by introducing *superordinate goals*, which are goals desired by both groups but not achievable by one group acting alone. A superordinate goal can only be achieved when both groups cooperate. For example, Sherif and his associates arranged for a truck bringing food to the summer camp to (supposedly) break down, so all the boys had to help pull the truck into the camp in order to gain access to food. In another situation, a water pipe (supposedly) broke, and the cooperation of all the boys was needed to restore the water supply. These cooperative activities resulted in the development of positive intergroup attitudes and friendships.

The concept of superordinate goals also suggests ways in which revolutions can be prevented. In order to mobilize the working class to act to overthrow the capitalist class, revolutionaries need to focus working-class minds on how their group interests conflict with that of the capitalist class. But authorities can also adopt an opposite policy, focusing on the common interests of different social classes – including the rulers and the groups representing them. For example, superordinate goals can be introduced to bring labor unions and business company management together. This conflict reduction approach to applying superordinate goals was adopted soon after Sherif introduced the concept and continues today.[16] In domains such as global warming, there is an urgent need for humanity to adopt superordinate goals and pull together toward the same unifying goals.

Resource Mobilization and Revolutions

In his summer camp field studies of intergroup relations, Sherif and his associates possessed the resources (such as expertise, power, knowledge, and so on) to shape the relationships between the groups of boys, moving them to experience friendship, then conflict, then cooperation, through to the introduction of superordinate goals. The possession of resources is the starting point for resource mobilization theory, which proposes that those who control the resources, as Sherif did in the setting of his field research, are able to mobilize people to take collective action, for example against the ruling regime.[17] Like realistic conflict theory, resource mobilization theory ascribes high importance to psychological experiences, but gives higher priority to how these experiences can be shaped by those who control resources. From this perspective, revolutionaries must make people feel deprived, angry, unjustly treated, and ready to take risks to overthrow governments – but all of these feelings can be brought about through the effective mobilization of resources (as Sherif mobilized resources in the context of his studies). The highest priority, then, is given to resources and the question of who controls resources.

The claim of resource mobilization researchers is that there is always present the *potential* for people to feel relatively deprived, angry, and unjustly treated. For example, there is always the potential for mine workers, factory workers, construction workers, or any other groups of workers, to feel underpaid and overworked. After all, the company management always receive larger salaries and better benefits. There is a strong potential for ordinary people to feel deprived and to be angry at the government. After all, government leaders invariably enjoy higher power, status, and material benefits than do ordinary people. Why is it that anti-government revolutions do not take place more often? What explains revolutions that do take place? According to resource mobilization theory, those who control resources are able to shape psychological feelings, such as relative deprivation, in order to manufacture and direct a social movement, involving a set of opinions and beliefs in a population "which represents preferences for changing some elements of the social structure and/or reward distribution of society."[18]

In order to better understand the resource mobilization perspective, it is useful to consider how resource mobilization functions in the domain of consumer products. For example, consider how we come to believe we have a need to purchase certain products, such as a deodorant. When I first conducted international research in the 1980s, I traveled to low-income countries where the vast majority of people did not purchase or use deodorants. This was not a readily available product in many low-income countries. How is it that forty years later, many middle-class people in those same non-Western countries now consider deodorants as essential? What led to this new perceived "need"? Resource mobilization researchers argue that this need was created through varieties of advertisements produced by people with resources in order to *create a market* for a product and make profits. In a similar way, needs, feelings and other psychological experiences, such as deprivation and perceived injustice, can be influenced through communications campaigns, with the potential result being seen in mass mobilization and revolution.

Consider the example of the women's liberation movement in the post–World War II era, particularly from the 1960s. Were women in Western societies treated worse in 1960 than they were in 1860 or 1760? Obviously not on the basis of objective criteria, such as women's legal, political, and financial status: Women were better off in 1960 than in 1860 and 1760. Then why did the women's liberation movement not mobilize in the 1860s or the 1760s? One answer is that it was in the 1960s that the elite with control over resources in Western societies saw it as beneficial to their own interests to have women work outside the home in large numbers. This was the time of the Cold War, and the Soviet Union and its communist allies had incorporated women into their economies. The capitalist West needed to harness the full power of women in the workforce in order to defeat the Soviet empire. Resources were mobilized to dramatically expand the participation of women in higher education and the larger workforce, with highly beneficial consequences for Western economies and the eventual economic defeat of the Soviet empire.

From a resource mobilization theory perspective, then, collective mobilization leading to revolution happens when resources are used to influence people to experience deprivation, injustice, and other psychological characteristics that lead to collective action. In the twenty-first-century context, new social media resources such as Twitter have become particularly important in mobilizing people to take collective action.[19] A study of digital activists and internet users leading up to the Tunisian Revolution in 2010–11 that toppled the dictator Ben Ali (1936–2019) showed the power of social media to achieve extensive mobilization among the mass population.[20] This study gave importance to "emotional mobilization" and the idea that people involved in social movements often are moved by emotions and irrational feelings. This is in contrast to researchers who adopt a purely rationalist interpretation of resource mobilization.[21]

Given that group-based inequalities and wealth concentration characterize major human societies,[22] and given the argument that it is through resource mobilization that collective movements come about, one conclusion is that revolutions only come about when they are backed by the small elite who own the major resources. But there are alternative interpretations because resources are conceived very broadly by resource mobilization researchers. In addition to material resources (e.g., financial and physical capital), there are human resources (e.g., leadership, expertise, skill sets, labor), moral resources (e.g., integrity and legitimacy, celebrity and sympathetic support), cultural resources (e.g., technical and tacit knowledge and skills about how to organize protests), and social-organizational resources (e.g., social networks and organizations, such as the Church and religious networks). Thus, even a group that is deprived of material resources and does not have the backing of the rich elite might be able to bring about mass mobilization against authorities by having access to other resources. For example, revolutionary movements in Poland in the 1980s and in Iran in the 1970s used the networks of the Catholic Church and Shi'a mosques, respectively, to mobilize the masses to overthrow the ruling regimes. In these cases, religious faith and religious networks represented valuable resources and played a central role in mass mobilization and revolution.

But if resources are of a wide variety and spread across groups, why are there so few revolutions? This question is taken up next, in a discussion of system justification theory.

System Justification and the Scarcity of Revolutions

Why are there so few revolutions against the ruling elite? Given that the modern era has been characterized by enormous group-based inequalities, and wealth is increasingly being concentrated in fewer and fewer hands,[23] why do the disadvantaged masses not revolt and overthrow governments more often? Indeed, why do the disadvantaged masses often endorse and support the status quo, which works against their own collective material interests? Why do the disadvantaged masses support politicians who lower taxes for the super-rich and for major corporations, but cut funds for programs that provide support for the poor? It is puzzling that the disadvantaged masses often show bias in favor of the outgroup (the rich) rather than the ingroup (the relatively poor); but why does this happen? What mechanisms explain why people support an outgroup that exploits them? The Marxist concept of false consciousness and the psychological theory of system justification which stems from the concept of false consciousness directly address this puzzle.[24]

In explaining "why so many members of disadvantaged groups reject egalitarian alternatives to the status quo,"[25] system justification theory builds on two highly influential psychological theories. The first is cognitive dissonance theory, which proposes that people are motivated to rationalize and justify their actions by resolving inconsistencies between their thoughts, feelings, and actions.[26] For example, Jane works extremely hard and for long hours, but her wages are tiny compared to the enormous salary and benefits of the CEO at the company where she works. How does she cope with the potential anxiety and unhappiness of working so hard, but having such a relatively very low income?[27] There are many different ways in which Jane could resolve this anxiety, but why is it that she resolves it in a way that leads her to accept her own situation? Why is it that Jane convinces herself that although her CEO is very rich, he has an unhappy family life, and that in comparison she is personally better off? Why does Jane *not deal* with her anxiety and dissatisfaction with her relatively tiny income by joining other employees in collective action against the company owners to force them to improve her salary and benefits? These questions are also at the heart of the *just-world hypothesis*, which proposes that people are motivated to see the world as just and fair (discussed further in Chapter 3).[28] But there are many different ways in which we could interpret the world as fair; why does this motivation to see the world as fair lead to the adoption of certain interpretations of events that favor the rich rather than the poor?

System justification theory argues that from among the many different ways Jane could interpret and explain her own situation, she is likely to be influenced by the ideologies that are dominant in her society. In capitalist societies, these ideologies are shaped by extremely wealthy people who influence the content of mass media, education, and the major forms of communications. The dominant ideologies result in interpretations of the world that tend to be victim-blaming rather than system-blaming – particularly when it comes to explaining the behavior of the poor and the disadvantaged. For example, if Mary and her husband David are both working very long hours, but still barely able to pay the rent and feed their three children, then explanations for this situation center on the characteristics of these two individuals (e.g., "Mary and David are low in skills, education, and talent") rather than the characteristics of the larger system (e.g., "The tax system and government policies should be used to make sure there is a far more financial support for people like Mary and David and their children, and a far smaller gap between the super-rich and the poor").

In response to the question, "Why are there so few revolutions?" system justification theory points to the power of the dominant legitimizing ideologies in society. On the one hand, these ideologies lead to victim-blaming in line with individualism and reductionism: Individuals are assumed to be the master of their own fate. In a self-help society, the rich deserve to be rich and the poor deserve to be poor. On the other hand, it is a just world, after all, because rewards are distributed in complex and balanced ways. The rich have more material resources, but the poor are happier.[29] There are all kinds of subtle ways that the poor are interpreted as being better off than the rich, and this is motivated by a need to justify the system and to "reduce any existential anxiety or fears about the dangers the world may hold for them."[30]

In addition to the motivation to justify the existing system, system justification theory proposes that people are motivated to justify their own personal thoughts and actions (ego justification) as well as the ingroup's ideas and actions (*group justification*). However, the dominant ideologies influence people to give priority to system justification, even when it is at the expense of ego justification and group justification. This perspective is very much in line with what I have described as looking at behavior "from societies to cells" (rather than "from cells to societies"), giving highest priority to macro rather than micro processes.[31] That is, the beliefs and actions of individuals are explained by looking "from societies to cells," from the legitimizing ideologies that justify the status quo to individual-level actions and processes.

Evolutionary Theory and Social Dominance Theory

Evolutionary approaches, including social dominance theory, have a special place in the materialist explanations of intergroup conflict and revolutions. These approaches are similar in that they are influenced by (their own interpretations of) Charles Darwin's (1809–82) theory of evolution.[32] However, they differ both in what they take to be the implications of Darwin's theory for human social behavior and in the extent to which they rely on genetic explanations of intergroup conflict and revolution. Even before the seminal genetics research of Gregor Mendel (1822–84) finally became known decades after his death, so-called social Darwinists, such as Herbert Spencer (1820–1903), were making claims about "racial differences" between human groups based on their interpretations of Darwinian evolution theory.[33] After the development of modern genetics research in the twentieth century, the field of sociobiology more directly took on the challenge of explaining human behavior through a genetic perspective.

The turn to the genetic level of explanation came through the influence of E. W. Wilson (1929–2021)[34] and Richard Dawkins,[35] but took a new twist in two ways. First, the focus turned to the reproductive consequences of social interactions.[36] Favoring and disfavoring others has implications for how genes spread, and individuals are motivated to spread their own genes – so they favor others who (they perceive to) have similar genes. Second, as a leading advocate of explaining social behavior through sociobiology argues, ethnic and racial sentiments are interpreted as "extensions of kinship sentiments. There exists a general behavioral predisposition, in our species as well as many others, to react favorably toward other organisms related to the actor. The closer the relationship is, the stronger the preferential behavior."[37]

This line of thinking led to the view that people are inclined to be more competitive, aggressive, and even destructive toward those who are genetically dissimilar to them, but more helpful and cooperative toward those who are genetically more similar to them. This is assumed to explain patterns of behavior in intergroup conflicts: that is, the tendency to maximize the spread of ingroup genes by killing men in the outgroup and stealing and/or raping outgroup women.[38] The implication is that revolutions will also be shaped by genetic similarity, so that both the rulers and those attempting to overthrow the government will become organized in such a way that those they are fighting alongside are genetically similar to them, and those they are fighting against are genetically dissimilar to them.

The genetic-based approach works best when tackling trends in revolutions that concern families and ethnic groups. That is, first when political leadership during and after the revolution is based on family ties and, second, when collective mobilization against a regime and governance after the revolution is in significant ways based on ethnic allegiances. There are some examples of the first of these phenomena, when power gained through revolution is kept and passed on within families. For example, Napoleon Bonaparte made his brothers Joseph, Jérôme, and Louis at different times kings of Spain, Westphalia, and Holland. There are many other examples of such nepotism in ruling families, but most examples do not qualify as involving revolutions – such as Saddam Hussein (1937–2006) and Muammar Gaddafi (1942–2011) governing Iraq and Libya through their families, giving enormous power to their own sons. Examples of rule through tribal allegiances are also numerous, such as the Ugandan dictator Idi Amin (1925–2003) and his loyalty to the Nubian tribe that helped him rule, and Bashar Assad ruling Syria through his reliance on the Shi'a minority (and Shi'a Iran, as a key external supporter). But, again, these cases do not qualify as involving revolutions – although the leaders in question have no hesitation in describing themselves as revolutionary.

On the surface, at least, examples of rule through tribal alliances do not work as well in the Western context because power is not tribal based in Western societies. However, in the sense that the American Revolution brought to power white males and excluded other ethnic groups (e.g., Black people, Chinese, and so on), the sociobiological perspective might be applied in the American case (but I do not include the American Revolution as one of the great revolutions, for reasons discussed in Chapter 1).

A shortcoming of the sociobiological and other genetic-based approaches to explaining revolutions is that certain assumptions are made concerning the relationship between phenotype and genotype. This is less relevant to family relationships because (very often, but not always) people with familial ties can correctly assume they have close genetic similarities. However, tribes and ethnic groups tend to number in the tens or even hundreds of thousands and millions, and it is impossible to personally know every other person in the tribe or ethnic group. In these cases, the assumption on the part of sociobiologists is that phenotype accurately reflects genotype: that someone who looks like a person in your tribe is genetically more similar to you than a person who looks like a member of another tribe. But the relationship between phenotype and genotype is more complex, and phenotype is not always a good indicator of genotype.[39]

Social Dominance and Group-Based Hierarchies

Although the particular interpretations that social dominance theorists make of Darwinian evolution theory lead them to highlight group-based hierarchies and group dominance,[40] they are at pains to argue that they are not endorsing oppression, but paving the way for "morally driven intervention."[41] But what leads to particularly heated criticisms of the social dominance theory approach is the apparent claim that group-based inequalities are inevitable and are "genetically mandated," as one set of critics argue.[42] To point out that group-based inequalities are universal, as others have done (a topic I discuss later in this section), is to highlight aspects of the world that many revolutions have attempted to change and improve upon, but to argue that there is a genetic mandate for group-based hierarchies is to wave a large red flag in front of the egalitarian bull.

The most ardent criticisms of social dominance research probably revolve around the issue of gender. Social dominance theory argues that there is a human predisposition to form group-based social hierarchies, and hierarchies based on sex and age are common to all societies (including those that do not produce a surplus). That is, in all human societies males and older people hold more power and resources. This arrangement arises in part from temperament, implying it is inbuilt. Moreover, social dominance theory claims that the roots of male–female differences in behavior are differences in the best possible strategies available to females and males to pass on their genes, stemming from biological differences between the sexes.

The point of departure for this explanation of human gender differences is the ability of males to have far higher numbers of offspring than females. According to social dominance theory, this results in differences in the best possible strategies for females and males to pass on their genes: Females are more conservative in selecting partners because they have to invest more highly in fewer offspring; males adopt a strategy of having as many partners as possible, but investing minimally or not at all in each offspring. Out of this biologically determined behavioral difference, there arises the female preference for males with high status and resources and the male motivation to acquire and monopolize status and resources, resulting in "exploitative social, economic, and political systems in which patriarchy and arbitrary-set stratification among males are assortative: adaptive for those who enjoy more social and economic resources and power, and maladaptive for those who do not."[43]

On the one hand, the social dominance theory position on sex differences can be severely criticized because it seems out of touch with twenty-first-century trends. Women now outperform men in many areas of higher education in most major societies, and have competitive earning power in the marketplace; they do not need to rely on males for resources.[44] Second, women and men use contraceptives to limit the number of their offspring, and cooperate to maximize the chance of their offspring becoming successful. Thus, parents now use bipartisan investment to maximize the success of a small number of children – a trend that contradicts the social dominance account. On the other hand, social dominance theory claims are in line with the continued dominance of men in leadership positions in business, politics, and other key areas related to power. For example, only about 5 percent of CEOs in Fortune 500 companies are women, and after close to three centuries a woman has yet to become US president – with important implications for policies.[45] Men still dominate political and economic leadership and material resources.

Thus, social dominance theory has correctly pointed to stable patterns of group-based inequalities across human societies, as well as individual differences in support for egalitarianism and group hierarchies.[46] This is the world of inequalities we inhabit. Revolutionaries and others can use this picture of the world characterized by inequalities as their point of departure, accepting the challenge to transform the world to achieve greater justice. However, critics do not accept the social dominance theory claim that these group-based inequalities, including those concerning females and males, are in part derived from temperament and inbuilt human characteristics. Skepticism toward such claims is in part based on a history of psychologists using so-called science to explain the status of females and males, including accounts of the supposed "lower intelligence of women" and their "inability to deal with the pressures of higher education." As the last half century has shown, after the contextual conditions were changed and women gained access to higher education, they excelled. It was not their supposed "lower intelligence" that held them back; it was the restrictions and hurdles places around them.[47]

Materialist Accounts and Linear versus Cyclical Models of Historical Change

The classic Marxist model of historical development assumes linear progression: Just as feudalism led to capitalism, capitalism will lead to socialism and, eventually, the dictatorship of the proletariat and the classless society. These changes will be punctuated by revolutions, such as the proletariat revolutions that (are assumed to) eventually bring an end to capitalism. However, an alternative materialist model of historical development assumes *cyclical* rather than linear changes. The most influential alternative cyclical model was developed by Vilfredo Pareto (1848–1923), who is well known as an economist, but has also contributed important ideas in social and political psychology.[48] The alternative cyclical model is reflected in some psychological accounts, the most prominent example being Donald Taylor's (1943–2021) Five-Stage Model of intergroup relations.[49]

Pareto adopts a psychological approach to explaining historical development as a series of cyclical changes. He begins by noting that humans have a range of talents in each domain of activity. For example, there are highly talented lawyers who should receive an evaluation of 10 out of 10, but there are also out-and-out idiot lawyers who should receive a zero.[50] He gives the term "elite" to those individuals who have the highest level of talent in each field of activity. The non-elite consists of everyone else. But elite individuals can have children who are of non-elite quality, and non-elite individuals can have children who are of elite quality. In a perfectly open meritocratic society, elite individuals born to non-elite parents would still rise to the top and join the ruling elite, just as non-elite individuals born to elite parents would be allowed to drop down to lower levels in society and become part of the non-elite. However, in practice societies are not perfectly open and meritocratic because the rulers set up all kinds of barriers to prevent the rise of talented individuals born to non-elite parents, and to help non-elite individuals born to elite parents (i.e., their own children) to remain in power as part of the privileged elite.

Because talented individuals born to non-elite parents are blocked from rising to join the elite, after some time they come to feel deprivation and injustice, and they organize as a counter-elite and take action in support of their own interests. Having failed to move up as individuals, they organize as a collective. But they are a small group and not able to overthrow the ruling elite by themselves. The counter-elite recognize that in order to succeed, they must mobilize the non-elite masses and lead them to overthrow the ruling elite. Thus, the revolution is led by the counter-elite, but the muscle and power driving the revolution is provided by the non-elite masses.

In order to harness the power of the non-elite masses in support of the revolution, the counter-elite and in particular its leader adopt a revolutionary rhetoric that is persuasive to the non-elite masses. Repeatedly in successful revolutionary movements, we find a special bond between a revolutionary leader and the non-elite masses. At the heart of this bond is the language used by the revolutionary leader, which is often ridiculed by the elite as simplistic, unsophisticated, and even crass, but is highly effective in communications with the common people. Napoleon Bonaparte was ridiculed by the French elite as a crude Corsican, but again and again he was able to persuade the common French foot soldiers to follow him, most miraculously after his escape from exile on the island of Elba in February 1815. Napoleon persuaded the French troops sent to capture him to follow him into battle once again. He managed to recapture Paris, but only for 100 days before a vast European army defeated him at the Battle of Waterloo (1815). I witnessed the same persuasive power wielded by Khomeini in Iran in 1979: the educated Iranian elite mocked Khomeini for his communication style, his simplistic language, and his common phrases, but lower-educated Iranians were moved by his speeches – enough to risk their lives in dangerous anti-Shah demonstrations.

But according to Pareto, revolutions involve cyclical rather than linear changes. After the counter-elite use the non-elite masses to overthrow the ruling elite, they simply take over as the governing elite and continue to rule and enjoy superior wealth and status. The result of revolutions, according to Pareto, is the replacement of one elite by another, without real change in the intergroup relationships and inequalities between the elite and non-elite.

As to when and how revolutions take place, the determining factor according to elite theory is circulation of talent. Pareto believed that all ruling elites make the same mistake of blocking circulation of talent, resulting in a lethal concentration of talented individuals among the non-elite and individuals with lack of talent among the ruling group. Because their path to individual mobility is blocked, talented potential-elite individuals come to see collective action as the only path open to them, and they lead the non-elite in a revolution (for a much earlier version of the essential role of circulation of talent in keeping society stable and free from revolution, see Plato's writings from 2,500 years ago[51]). Through this process, according to Pareto, history has become a "graveyard of the aristocracies,"[52] with one elite after another falling victim to revolutions led by counter-elites. As to why there are not more revolutions, elite theory explains it by pointing to the role of talent circulation in preventing revolutions.

The circulation of talent is also central to the Five-Stage Model, a recent social psychological account of intergroup relations which incorporates ideas from social comparison theory and social attribution theory. Like Pareto's elite theory, the Five-Stage Model proposes that when circulation of talent is thwarted, this leads to collective mobilization in support of a revolution to overthrow the ruling regime. Also similar to elite theory, the Five-Stage Model divides society into two groups, but uses the labels "advantaged" and "disadvantaged" (rather than elite and non-elite). In stage 1, groups are based on ascribed characteristics, such as sex and race. Groups are closed and there is no circulation between them. Group members make within-group (but not between-group) social comparisons. For example, consider a feudal system where there is a huge gulf between the aristocracy and the peasants, and the members of each group make social comparisons within, but not across, their ingroups. As a result of modernization and the growth of a middle class, in stage 2 group characteristics are assumed to be based on individual achievement and merit rather than group membership. In comparing themselves with others, individuals are influenced by legitimizing ideologies and come to believe that they are getting what they deserve. If they are in the advantaged group, they exaggerate their input and minimize their outcome, so the higher resources at their disposal become justified. Those in the disadvantaged group exaggerate their outcome and minimize their input, and this justifies their lower status (this interpretation is in line with system justification theory[53]).

The most talented members of the disadvantaged group attempt social mobility in stage 3. The Five-Stage Model assumes that individual mobility is preferred over collective action: Members of the disadvantaged group will first try to move up to the advantaged group on their own. This is consistent with the ideology of meritocracy and self-help individualism of Western capitalist societies, as well as evidence from experimental research in the Western context.[54] In stage 4, those few individuals who succeed in moving up to the advantaged group serve as tokens to endorse the legitimacy and openness of the social system. In addition, the talented individuals who move from the disadvantaged to the advantaged group become strong endorses of the system: "The fact that I made it shows the system is open and fair." But those talented individuals who fail to move up to the advantaged group make self-serving attributions and come to believe that their "failure" is because of their group membership and the structure of society rather than their personal shortcomings. Their explanatory framework moves from individual to group characteristics.

Those talented disadvantaged group members who are kept out of the advantaged group respond in a variety of ways, but the response that is most relevant to our discussion of revolutions is the attempt to instigate collective action. According to the Five-Stage Model, this path of collective action will only be taken after individualistic mobility has been blocked and talented individuals attribute this blocking tactic to group-based discrimination rather than their individual characteristics (such as lack of individual talent and hard work). The research evidence suggests that in the Western context, at least, as long as there is even a small chance of people moving up the status hierarchy by themselves individually, they will prefer this individualistic option over attempting collective action.[55]

The key role of circulation of talent, then, is agreed upon by thinkers from as far back as Plato 2,500 years ago to contemporary researchers such as Don Taylor in his Five-Stage Model. These thinkers all agree that the circulation of talent will work to prevent collective action and revolution. The underlying assumption is that people are naturally motivated to try to move up the status hierarchy on an individual basis. Only if their individual paths to upward mobility are blocked because of their group characteristics will they feel compelled to join collective movements to try to achieve regime change.

But why do people give priority to individual and not collective mobility? Rather than seeing this preference as inbuilt and part of human nature, Marx has influenced an interpretation through the concept of false consciousness: People give priority to individual mobility because this is part of the legitimizing ideology propagated by the rulers, and the result is false consciousness. People are influenced to misperceive their group membership and their true collective interests. This results in, for example, poor white men voting for right-wing politicians such as Donald Trump, who when they get into positions of political power lower taxes for the super-rich and weaken social support systems for the poor. For example, this alternative perspective is reflected in system justification theory.

The cyclical versus linear characteristic of social change is also interpreted differently by the above two traditions. One set of theories, in Pareto's elite theory tradition, propose that change is cyclical, and revolutions are part of a cycle ending in more group-based inequalities (but with a different set of slogans and revolutionary rhetoric). From this perspective, the most talented individuals will *always* lead revolutions that benefit themselves, using the non-elite masses as fodder to achieve regime change. But after coming to power, the new elite uses a new system justification ideology to continue to rule with the same group-based inequalities and injustices – until the next revolution. Alternatively, the Marxist tradition proposes that this cyclical pattern is a result of false consciousness, and *change will become linear* after the masses overcome legitimizing ideologies and come to accurately recognize their social class membership.

In essence, different explanations of a preference for the individualistic mobility option are at the heart of differences between capitalists and socialists, as well as between different groups of researchers. Underlying capitalism is the assumption that the preference for individual mobility is inborn and "natural" in humans. Underlying socialism is the assumption that the preference for individual mobility is a result of socialization and reflective of false consciousness, in conditions where individuals are taught to neglect their own social class memberships and interests. This account based on false consciousness has influenced system justification theorists, among other researchers. The elite theory account of cyclical evolution of intergroup relations, and the "inevitability" of elite rule and continued group-based inequalities, has influenced social dominance theorists, among other researchers.

Concluding Comment

The materialist perspectives we have considered in this chapter lead to the conclusion that the driving force in revolutions are material conditions, which shape psychological experiences. It is the functional relations between people, such as competition over resources, that lead to psychological experiences, such as relative deprivation, anger, and frustration. These psychological experiences move people to recognize an outgroup as the legitimate target of aggression. For example, in Sherif's summer camp studies, after the groups of boys entered competition for material resources, they developed hostile attitudes toward the outgroup and intergroup conflict arose. Competition for resources was the necessary precondition for intergroup conflict.

But careful analysis of Sherif's three summer camp studies reveals that in conditions where the groups of boys were not initially brought into direct contact with one another, as soon as they learned of the existence of a second group they became hostile toward them – without direct intergroup interactions taking place. Sherif notes that after the ingroup took shape, there was "a tendency to consider all others as out-group"[56] and to be antagonistic toward outgroups, even before intergroup competition for resources began.[57] This suggests that the mere categorization of people into an ingroup and an outgroup can result in intergroup biases, a possibility we examine in the next chapter. The broader focus of the next chapter is research that proposes psychological factors to be the primary driving force in intergroup relations and revolutions.

CHAPTER 3

Psychological Theories and Revolution
Subjective Factors as Drivers

What had been planned as an afternoon protest extended on into the night. People began to set up an impromptu encampment on Tahrir . . . Activists began planning for a "Day of Rage" on Friday, January 28. That was the day that Tagammu leftists, The Nasserists, and the Muslim Brotherhood decided to join the protests.

Amy Austin Holmes (2019)[1]

In describing the 2011 buildup to the revolution against the Hosni Mubarak (1928–2020) regime in Egypt, Amy Austin Holmes refers to the efforts by activists to channel the rage felt by many Egyptians in reaction to government mismanagement, repression, and corruption. Rational and deliberate planning, organization, and material and other types of resources are all highly important in revolutions (as discussed in Chapter 2), but at the heart of every revolutionary movement there must be the experience of rage! People must feel intense anger, hostility, hatred, deprivation, injustice, and rage against the regime in power. They must *feel so strongly* that they are willing to come face to face with tear gas, bullets, and even tanks; and be willing to risk their own lives and the lives of those most near and dear to them. This chapter is about theories and empirical research that propose the motor for revolutionary movements to be psychological experiences, such as the rage people feel, together with their perceptions, aspirations, motivations, and fears.

These psychological approaches to understanding revolutions, which include considering psychodynamics, social identity, terror management, and relative deprivation, as well as equity and various justice theories, do not deny the importance of material resources and material conditions. However, their claim is that what drives people to join (or not join) revolutions is first and foremost their subjective interpretations of material conditions, which can differ considerably from the actual material conditions. From this perspective, the same material conditions can lead to rage and revolution, but might also be tolerated with apathy and tranquility. On the other hand, rapidly improved material conditions might paradoxically lead to rising expectations and relative deprivation, resulting in mass rage. However, even when material conditions are impoverished or terrible for the masses, low expectations might lead to apathetic acceptance of the status quo. The most important factor, then, is how people subjectively feel about, interpret, and experience material conditions, rather than the actual or objective material conditions. Social comparison processes and subjective estimations of how one's group stands relative to other groups are central to these experiences, as we explore later in this chapter.[2]

Two themes are particularly important in discussing the psychological perspectives that are the focus of this chapter: identity and rationality. In general, by identity I mean the kind of people individuals perceive themselves to be, and the kinds of groups they view themselves as belonging to (I do not mean the horribly misunderstood and misused question, "Who am I?" – which can be answered simply by referring to one's driving license). However, in the present discussion we are more specifically concerned with the identification of individuals with groups; for example, do members of disadvantaged groups perceive their own group as having interests that differ from the interests of other groups, and do they identify strongly enough with their ingroups to join collective action, such as mass labor strikes, against the advantaged group? For example, Holmes describes how in the buildup to the anti-Mubarak revolution in Egypt, "in many ways the locus of the uprising shifted . . . from Tahrir to the workplaces . . . workers in textile factories, newspapers, government agencies, sanitation, and transportation all demanded economic concessions as well as the ousting of Mubarak. At the Suez Canal, up to 6,000 workers participated in a sit-in."[3] This mass identification with the collective anti-regime movement is a hallmark of the final stages of revolutions.

The second theme that is particularly important in discussing the psychological perspectives that are the focus of this chapter is *rationality*: the extent to which people are aware of the factors that shape their behavior and the even more basic question of the extent to which people are aware of how they are behaving. We have already explored in Chapter 2 the idea that irrationality plays a central role in *preventing* revolutions, particularly through the concept of false consciousness and its key role in psychological theories, such as system justification theory and social dominance theory. False consciousness suggests that the reason why revolutions rarely take place is because the disadvantaged group members are unaware that their behavior benefits the advantaged group rather than their own disadvantaged group. This lack of awareness, together with their inability to recognize their own group membership and distinct collective interests, means that they remain inactive in collective action to bring about regime change.

Our discussion of theories that assume psychological factors to be the motor for collective action and revolution begins with the psychodynamic view, which encompasses both the themes of identity and rationality.

The Psychodynamic View

Sigmund Freud (1856–1939) made monumental contributions to our understanding of intergroup conflict and collective action.[4] He spearheaded a perspective that depicts international wars as arising because of nations "satisfying their passions,"[5] but rationalizing their aggression on the basis of their (supposed) material interests. Human beings are extraordinarily good at providing rational explanations, but their rationalizing rhetoric often hides their irrational behaviors. For example, a study of explanations and justifications given by political leaders for taking their nations to war found a wide range of rationalizations along the lines of: we are going to war because we value and love peace.[6] Probably the most famous among these slogans that illustrate the rationalization of irrational behavior is the claim that this war is "the war to end all wars," first popularized during World War I (1914–18). Obviously, World War I did not end all wars, but this (misleading) slogan helped to popularize the war and persuade millions of young people to enthusiastically volunteer to fight, at least at the start of the war when it was assumed that victory would be swift.

Irrationality comes into effect through the functioning of what Freud calls libidinal ties, which are all the energies of those instincts which come under the term love. Broadly speaking, libidinal ties are emotional ties, and they involve both positive and negative feelings, both love and hate.[7] For example, consider a university soccer (football) team playing against teams representing other universities. Among the eleven team players on the field, there are some intense jealousies and rivalries. At times, some team members argue and even feel hatred toward other team members. However, once a soccer match is underway against a rival team, the team members all pull together and the team captain helps to channel their energies to try to defeat their rivals.

The team members are not necessarily aware that their negative energies are being channeled into competition against other teams, just as citizens of a nation are often unaware of how conflict with another nation is channeling their aggression outward onto an outgroup. For Freud, the redirection of negative feelings onto outgroups is closely associated with identity and identification with a group leader. Freud sees a primary group as individuals who have "put one and the same object in place of their ego ideal and have subsequently identified themselves with one another in their ego."[8] Perhaps the most important task of the leader is to redirect emotional energies within the group, so that negative energies are channeled outward against outgroups. But outgroups are not selected randomly to serve as targets. Freud was the first major psychologist to point out the role of similarity–dissimilarity in these processes: it is dissimilar outgroups who are the targets of the displacement of aggression, such as in the case of persecuted minorities, who are perceived as dissimilar to the majority group.[9]

Freud used the examples of the Catholic Church and the army to illustrate how leadership serves an essential function in binding group members together and redirecting negative affect. In both the Church and the army, group members hold the illusion that their leader, Jesus Christ or the commander-in-chief, equally loves all the individuals in the ingroup. The love that binds group members to the leader also sustains conformity and obedience within the group, leading individual members to behave correctly according to group norms and rules. All the brothers and sisters within the ingroup love one another through their identification with the leader, who helps redirect their negative feeling onto dissimilar outgroups. In this way, Freud explains, large numbers of people can feel bound together in love, "so long as there are other people left over to receive the manifestations of their aggressiveness."[10]

Freud was strongly influenced by the writings of the French researcher Gustav Le Bon (1841–1931) on crowd behavior in developing negative views of people in collectives.[11] Although efficient organization and effective leadership could help individuals in groups function at a high standard, in most cases joining a group results in lower standards involving a mixture of the "dwindling of the conscious individual personality, the focusing of thoughts and feelings into a common direction, the predominance of the affective side of the mind and of unconscious psychical states, the tendency to the immediate carrying out of intentions as they emerge."[12] This image of collectives as resulting in a lower standard of thinking has been shared by some revolutionaries, leading to a sense that people have to be strongly directed and shaped to reach revolutionary goals. This was particularly so during the years of Stalin's leadership in the Soviet Union, when Stalin waged what he saw as "a war against Russia's backwardness," according to Sheila Fitzpatrick.[13]

The redirecting of negative energies onto outgroups is evident in the major revolutions. For example, Castro and Khomeini focused almost exclusively on directing aggression (from Cuba and Iran, respectively) toward the United States and highlighting the threat of invasion from US-backed forces. The fact that the United States did attempt such invasions (as discussed in Chapter 9) made the task of displacing aggression onto the US government much easier – even though the attempted invasions were very poorly planned and executed. For example, I was working in Tehran in 1980 when the Carter administration attempted to send troops to rescue the US diplomats kidnapped and (at one time) held at the US Embassy in Tehran, which had been invaded and captured by Khomeini's extremist supporters. My childhood home was next to a sports stadium, across the road from the US Embassy. I was very familiar with that neighborhood and drove through it daily in 1980. The US plan was to land helicopters in the stadium, and then send troops across the road to free the US diplomats, take them back to the helicopters in the stadium, and fly them to safety outside Iran. This was a very poorly designed plan, and it inevitably failed. But the fact that the United States attempted a rescue of sorts gave Khomeini more ammunition in his redirecting of negative energies onto the United States, with a focus on a US intervention designed to bring about regime change (as the Central Intelligence Agency had done in 1953 to overthrow Mossadegh[14]).

Freud's perspective has five main implications for revolutionary movements. First, leadership is essential: Revolutionary movements can only succeed through effective leadership. Leaderless movements have very little chance of success. On the one hand, the French Revolution, Russian Revolution, Chinese Revolution, Cuban Revolution, and Iranian Revolution all support the idea that revolutions are led by strong leaders. On the other hand, the revolutionaries have to be careful because if revolutionary leaders are identified too early then they will be quickly eliminated by government security forces. An example is the case of Alexei Navalny, who has become a leader in the anti-Putin movement in contemporary Russia. Navalny was almost killed by Putin's agents and is now in jail in Russia. The democracy movement in Hong Kong was to some degree leaderless, but in as far as leaders emerged and were recognized, they were targeted, isolated, and severely punished by Chinese authorities.[15]

Second, individuals joining revolutionary movements experience lower objectivity and critical thinking, higher conformity and obedience, and are very susceptible to suggestions and directives from the leadership. These changes in individual psychological functioning explain the enormous risks and sacrifices taken by many ordinary people during the collective mobilization leading to regime change. Shopkeepers, butchers, teachers, dentists, road sweepers, engineers, cooks – ordinary people in all trades and professions – are swept along by the collective emotional power of the revolution. Ordinary people behave according to the new revolutionary norms, taking enormous risks they could not have imagined before the revolutionary movement began.

Third, dissimilar others (such as minorities who live in a country, as well as various outgroups) can serve as a target of displaced aggression and a distraction from problems and frustrations within the ingroup. The displacement of aggression onto dissimilar others is one of Freud's most powerful and influential insights. This type of displacement can be effective at different stages of revolutions. In the collective mobilization phase, it can help to mobilize people to join the revolutionary movement. For example, despite some efforts by the Bolsheviks to control antisemitism, they had to contend with antisemitism within their own ranks as well as the wider Russian society as they organized opposition to the Tsar's regime.[16] For some Russians, "putting the Jews in their place" was part of the overthrow of the Tsar. I witnessed the same attitude among some Iranians (particularly the extremist Islamists) in the 1970s, who blamed Bahais, Jews, Armenians, and all kinds of minorities for the problems in Iran. They saw the Shah as somehow being controlled by these minorities, and part of their motivation in joining the revolutionary movement was to "put these minorities in their places."

Fourth, individuals who become part of a revolutionary movement are not aware of the ways in which immersion in the collective changes them. During the lead-up to revolutions, the normative system is transformed and what is considered to be normal behavior changes. Many individuals adopt increasingly rebellious and radical attitudes, and even take greater risks in their actions. They come to see it as normal to not report for work, or to stay absent from school, and instead participate in protest marches and rallies. After a period of participating in collective anti-government activities, individuals become transformed in their self-presentation (including how they dress), as well as in their language and communication styles. However, this change often takes place with little conscious awareness on the part of the individuals involved. The invisible hand of collective influence changes individual behavior without individuals being conscious of the factors that changed their behavior.

Fifth, the process of identification and identity development play a central role in collective behavior generally and revolutionary movements specifically. Just as individuals who become part of a revolutionary movement are not fully aware of how their thoughts and actions have changed, they remain unaware of changes in their ideas about the kinds of people they are and the kinds of groups they belong to. In short, the process of *becoming a revolutionary* involves changes in both collective and individual identity, but mostly in subtle and implicit ways that remain outside of conscious attention.

In further developing the theme of identity, our discussion turns next to social identity theory, the most influential theory of intergroup relations and conflict in the history of psychology.

Identity and Identification

> *On 1 December 1960, the French government announced that a referendum on self-determination in Algeria would take place on 8 January 1961. Ten days later, on 11 December 1960, a huge wave of demonstrations began across Algeria in support of . . . independence . . . Men, women and children took to the streets, and notably took to the streets of "European areas" in the cities and towns of Algeria, waving the Algerian flag . . .*[17]

In her detailed account of the Algerian Revolution (1954–62), Natalya Vince presents a picture of the Algerian population gradually coming to identify themselves as "Algerians in a revolution" against France, which they came to see as a colonial power they had to expel from Algeria. Vince notes that "in Algeria, 'one and a half million martyrs' is the official number of Algerian combatants and civilians killed during the liberation struggle, and this figure has been central to the construction of Algerian national identity since 1962."[18] Algerian national identity was transformed through the harsh years of the revolution, with the image of "millions of martyrs" integral to that identity. On their part, the French refused to acknowledge that a revolution was taking place, insisting on referring merely to their "operations in Algeria," as they continued to depict Algeria as part of France. Their identity of France as a global power, an identity that was reconstructed after the Nazi occupation of most of France during World War II, included Algeria.

But despite facing death, torture, and extreme repression, the Algerian population came to passionately identify with the revolutionary movement and to act on the basis of this identity. Rage among Algerians led them to mobilize and eventually expel the French colonial power from their home-land. Central to the Algerian Revolution – and all other revolutions – is the psychological process of identification with a group and a cause, not just cognitively but also emotionally. Social identity theory directly engages with and provides invaluable insights into this identification process.[19]

Social identity theory was developed by Henri Tajfel (1919–82) and John Turner (1947–2011) in the context of a European social psychology move-ment that was critical of the reductionism of mainstream research, which they saw as dominated by American individualism. Social identity researchers aimed to give more importance to group and intergroup processes.[20] But at the same time as being focused on collective processes, social identity theory is firmly grounded on categorization at the individual level, a basic cognitive process which develops in the first few years of human life.[21] Social categorization emerged through evolutionary pro-cesses to play a foundational role in both human and animal behavior.[22]

Tajfel's early research on categorization used nonsocial stimuli; for example, he asked participants to judge lines with different lengths, placed either randomly or according to length size in groups labeled "A" and "B."[23] This research built on earlier studies suggesting that mere categor-ization has an impact on perceptions: for example, when four shorter lines were labeled "A" and four longer lines were labeled "B," this resulted in a tendency to exaggerate differences between the groups of lines (earlier research had also shown a tendency to minimize differences within groups following categorization).[24]

Evidence also accumulated from research on the categorization of social stimuli suggesting that how people categorize social phenomena is influ-enced by values and norms, while the mere presence of another group can trigger intergroup biases.[25] We recall that in Sherif's summer camp studies (discussed in Chapter 2), where the groups of boys were brought to the camp separately and initially kept physically apart, as soon as they learned of the presence of another group of boys at the camp, they expressed negative attitudes toward and became competitive with the other group. The accumulation of research findings over the 1950s and 1960s suggested certain continuities in the categorization of nonsocial and social stimuli: Categorization can lead to between-group differentiation, and when one is a member of one of the categories, then systematic ingroup favoritism can occur. Tajfel, Turner, and their associates developed the minimal group paradigm in order to experimentally test the impact of social categorization per se.[26]

The objective of the minimal group paradigm was to isolate the impact of social categorization on intergroup bias. In order to isolate social categorization as an independent variable, the following procedure was followed by Tajfel and colleagues. First, participants would carry out a trivial judgment task, such as estimating the number of dots on a screen. Next, participants were placed in groups "X" and "Y," (ostensibly) on the basis of how they responded in the trivial judgment task (e.g., on the basis of how many dots they estimated to be on the screen they were shown; in practice, participants were randomly assigned to groups "X" and "Y"). Participants were then asked to allocate points to the members of groups "X" and "Y." In the basic minimal paradigm procedure, the participants did not allocate rewards to themselves, only to others. Second, participants only knew the group identity of others (a member of group "X" or group "Y"), not their personal identities. Third, each person only received the amount of money others allocated to them.

The results of the minimal group paradigm studies demonstrated that individuals who were placed in groups "X" and "Y" on a trivial basis showed ingroup favoritism in allocating points, even though they did not know the identities of individuals in groups "X" and "Y," and the points they allocated would not benefit themselves personally. The initial research on social categorization expanded considerably since the 1970s, confirming the independent influence of social categorization on intergroup bias as far as it could be isolated.[27] Subsequent research also showed that in a context where there is only one basis for social categorization, this criterion is not necessarily trivial, despite being so in a comparative perspective outside the laboratory context.[28] For example, dot estimation is a trivial basis for creating groups in a real-world setting, but when it is the only criterion used for creating groups it necessarily becomes important and serves as a guide to action – because it is the only guide. This points to flexibility and possible manipulations in how different criteria can be constructed and reframed to serve as a basis for social categorization and collective mobilization in everyday life – and in the lead-up to revolutions.

There are many real-life examples of what objectively could be considered trivial differences between groups, which serve as a basis for loyalty to the ingroup and antagonism toward the outgroup. For example, consider the allegiance that soccer fans have to their teams, the way their identities become wrapped up with team identities, and how negative they become toward rival teams (I am a Tottenham Hotspur supporter and, of course, we are completely rational and unbiased in believing that our team is the best in the entire world! We have no idea why we have failed to win any trophies in recent years). There are also numerous examples of ethnic groups that are objectively very similar to one another, but have manufactured and exaggerated intergroup differences and engaged in bloody conflicts: a tragic example is the objectively very similar Tutsi and Hutu tribes in Rwanda, where about a million people are estimated to have died in Tutsi–Hutu intergroup fighting in 1994.[29]

An example from my own personal experiences concerns Shi'a and Sunni Muslims. As a child I played with other children in our neighborhood streets in Tehran, Iran, without taking notice of whether they were Shi'a children (like me) or Sunni – or Armenian, Jewish, or Bahai, or any other religious group. But since the 1970s, with the coming to power of Shi'a extremists in Iran and the growth of Islamic fundamentalism throughout the Near East and Middle East, differences between Shi'a and Sunni have been magnified and bloody conflicts between the two groups have become far more prevalent (Shi'a and Sunni Muslims have a long history of competition, but the level of violent conflict between them has fluctuated over time and has dramatically increased since the late twentieth century).[30] That is, in the new social context shaped by mutual radicalization and the emergence of extremist groups and extremist leaders (such as Khomeini), Shi'a and Sunni Muslims are positioned as being fundamentally different and as enemies to each other.[31]

Thus, perceived differences between groups are flexible – they can be minimized or exaggerated, manufactured or real, treated as trivial and ignored, or as vitally important and a highly salient basis for collective mobilization. In order for revolutionaries to mobilize people against the ruling regime, they must convince sufficient numbers to identify with and support the rebellious group, and to join in action against those in power. As indicated by the research using the minimal group paradigm, the basis for group formation need not be objectively important – it could be objectively trivial and still serve as a powerful basis for mobilization and action. System justification theory (discussed in Chapter 2) also suggests that the dominant ideology in society influences people's interpretations of how important or trivial a criterion is. The current dominant ideologies in Western societies and in many other parts of the world encourage individualistic rather than collective reactions to perceived injustice. Furthermore, they tend to shift attention away from social class as a basis for categorization and mobilization.[32] If collectives are given any attention at all, they tend to be based on ethnicity, gender, and sexual orientation. In the US context, a politician who prioritizes social class is likely to be labeled a socialist and dismissed as "too radical."

Social identity theory outlines a wide range of individualistic and collective strategies for action. The motivation for action is proposed to be the desire to achieve a positive and distinct social identity, which arises from the values and emotions attached to group membership in positive and negative terms. When individuals feel they have an adequate social identity, they attempt to maintain or even extend their comparative superiority. But when they feel they have an inadequate social identity, they are motivated to achieve change. These assessments of the adequacy of social identity are arrived at through social comparisons, which might lead people to feel relatively deprived. Individuals adopt individualistic or collective change-seeking strategies depending on whether they perceive cognitive alternatives to the current intergroup situation and whether they see the current power relations as legitimate. Do they recognize that the social structure of their society, with its power and resource allocations, could be different? Do they see the alternative possibilities as viable? Do they see the rulers as legitimate?

A major challenge for revolutionaries is to convince people that the current power relations are illegitimate and to educate the public about cognitive alternatives to the current political, economic, and cultural arrangements in their societies. If people become persuaded that society is unstable and illegitimate (rather than stable and legitimate), then one of the possible action paths is for collective mobilization and direct challenge to the ruling regime. This is the path that revolutionaries favor. However, research has shown that the path of direct challenge through collective action is probably the *last* option actually adopted by people, in the Western context at least.[33] The preferred options are individualistic, including *absorption*, such as minorities abandoning their heritage culture and language and completely adopting the culture and language of the host society; or *redefining ingroup characteristics*, as captured in the slogan "Black is beautiful"; or *creativity*, such as when people identify new dimensions on which they can compare their group with other groups and arrive at a positive outcome ("even though those other groups have better jobs and houses and more money than us, our group is happier than them. We are poor but happy.").[34]

One of the shortcomings of social identity theory as originally proposed is that despite setting out a wide range of possible actions people could take in response to perceived inadequate social identity, the theory did not specify what people would prioritize among the available options.[35] Given the individualism of Western societies, particularly the United States, and the priority given to individual action by the self-help American Dream ideology, it is not surprising that individual, rather than collective, action is the first priority of individuals experiencing inadequate social identity.[36] However, when individuals are persuaded to step into the network of collective action and become involved with groups in protest and rebellion, this involvement and their interactions with others on the same path transforms their identities.[37] They change and become embedded in the collective movement.

But the social identity account of collective action suggests that individuals might join revolutions and suffer enormous risks and hardships as a result, for reasons that are *not* purely or mainly material. This view is endorsed by studies of the motivations people have for joining collective action. For example, Elisabeth Wood describes in her examination of why rural people supported (or did not support) the FMNL (Farabundo Marti National Liberation Front) guerrillas in the Salvadorian Civil War (1979–92) that the most important motivators tended to be emotional ties and moral values.[38] The peasants did not expect material riches as a result of their risks and sacrifices in the face of extreme repression by government security forces. This kind of commitment to a collective cause, motivated by broad emotional, value-based, and moral concerns, better fits the social identity model than the materialist accounts (discussed in Chapter 2 of this text).

Building on social identity theory, researchers have attempted to identify specific factors that influence participation in collective action. The most advanced of these efforts has resulted in the Social Identity Model of Collective Action (SIMCA), which postulates three basic factors as influencing participation in collective action: *group identification*, the extent to which a person identifies with a group; *perceived group injustice*, the extent to which a person sees their group as being unjustly treated; and *group efficacy*, the extent to which a person believes their group is capable of achieving its goals through collective action.[39] Further research in both Western and non-Western contexts, including both disadvantaged and advantaged groups and with a focus on both short- and long-term processes, has shown solid support for the importance of group identification and perceived group injustice.[40] However, group efficacy receives less support.[41] This may be because group efficacy to some degree involves a rational calculation, estimating the probability of collective action success. But participation in collective action against authorities is often an irrational act. Government security forces have tanks, guns, and spies – surely any revolutionary movement has to rely on strong emotions and irrationality, and would falter if people stood back and made cold, calculated guesses about how likely they are to succeed. As I write this chapter, some people in Russia are demonstrating against Putin's war in Ukraine. The courage of ordinary people who stand up to dictatorial regimes is truly amazing. Such courage could only come from passionate beliefs and actions – not cold, calculated logic.

Assessing the adequacy of social identity emerges through social comparison processes and leads to a sense of justice or injustice – a topic I discuss next.

Justice and Revolutions

In order to succeed in making the transition from being the opposition (before the revolution) to being the people in power (after the revolution), revolutionaries have to bring about a number of changes in how people perceive and interpret justice in the world. For example, in the next section of this chapter I explain how after they come to power, revolutionaries try to influence people to switch from giving priority to their rights to giving priority to their duties. However, the broader switch revolutionaries must achieve after the revolution in how people perceive justice is even more dramatic. This is because revolutionaries must work against what Mel Lerner has termed the *justice motive*: the *need* for people to believe in a just world, where the self and others are believed to get what they deserve.[42]

The justice motive is at the heart of system justification theory (discussed in Chapter 2), whereby people psychologically interpret the state of the world and "the way things are" as just and "the way things ought to be." This motivation to interpret the "way things are" as just leads to the acceptance of all kinds of social relationships and group-based inequalities that objectively seem unjust. For example, even when a person is randomly placed in a situation where they receive electric shocks, they are devalued in ways that suggest they are somehow to blame for their treatment. In contrast, a person who receives rewards for carrying out a task is treated as if they deserve the positive outcome. If Jill but not Mary receives the reward, the interpretation is that Jill is in some way more deserving. Consequently, Lerner's research on the justice motive suggests that observers cognitively work backward to justify the outcome.[43]

An impressive research literature demonstrates the strength of a *blame the victim* tendency among people confronted with others who are disadvantaged or victimized.[44] For example, with respect to economic inequality, belief in a just world as an individual difference variable is associated with the tendency to see both rich and poor as deserving to be where they are.[45] When bad things happen to the self, there is also a tendency to justify the outcome, although there is some bias to make interpretations that are ego-defensive.[46]

The implication of the justice motive is that even what seem to be obviously unjust relationships tend to be interpreted by people as just. Consequently, people tend to justify the injustices of a system (this implication is fully developed in system justification theory, as discussed in Chapter 2). For example, if a small group of individuals owns most of the wealth of a nation, and tens of millions of people are living in poverty (as is presently the case in the United States and most other nations), this situation is interpreted as just because people are assumed to get what they deserve.[47] The billionaires are deserving because, for example, they are more talented and/or hardworking than everyone else, and those people living in poverty at the bottom of the status hierarchy deserve to be in that situation because they lack talent, hard work, and other individual merits. However, the world is fair because, for example, the billionaires tend to have unhappy family lives, and poor people have better personal relations and are actually happier.

More conservative and more religious people have a stronger tendency to interpret the world as just and to conclude that people get what they deserve and deserve what they get.[48] In the case of conservatives, this tendency is associated with an individualistic attributional style: "Joe and Jane are poor and unable to adequately feed and house their children because they do not work hard enough, they lack talent, and are not even self-motivated enough" – rather than, for example, "Joe and Jane are poor and unable to feed their children because although they each work fifty hours a week, their wages are too low and there is too little government support for their three young children in this gig economy." In the case of religious people, their interpretations of deservedness include the next world: the poor are suffering now, but they will get their rewards in the afterlife when they get to heaven.

The power and pervasiveness of the justice motive is an enormous challenge to revolutionaries because before the revolution they have to overcome the tendency for people to see the current situation as just and the self and others as "getting what they deserve." In essence, in order to mobilize the masses to overthrow the ruling regime, revolutionaries must temporarily negate the influence of the justice motive. They do this largely by manipulating social comparison targets (e.g., leading people to compare themselves with others who are better off, or with themselves as better off, as they should be), and in this way leading people to experience relative deprivation (a topic discussed in the next section). But after the old regime has been toppled and the revolutionaries have come to power, they attempt to once again reignite and revise the justice motive – so that people once again perceive the world as just.

Equity Theory, the Flexibility of Perceived Justice, and Revolutions

Revolutionaries must succeed in manipulating subjective justice before and after the revolution. This is to get people to believe the system is unjust and must be changed at the risk of their lives before the revolution, and that it is just and must be defended with their lives after the revolution. Consequently, the justice motive has to be overcome before the revolution and reignited after the revolution. This is a difficult feat to achieve, and the low political plasticity of the justice motive is one reason why there are so few revolutions that successfully bring about regime change. However, there are other aspects of subjective justice that are more easily manipulated. For example, social comparison targets and conceptions of rights and duties are relatively malleable and more easily manipulated. As I discuss later in the chapter, equity theory also points to other aspects of perceived justice that are also relatively more malleable and easily manipulated.

Although it has roots in classical philosophy, contemporary empirical-based equity theory took shape in the 1970s.[49] Equity theory research is mostly focused on individuals in relationships, but there have also been extensions and applications of the theory to the intergroup level.[50] Like Lerner's just-world theory, equity theory assumes that people are motivated to see the world as just, and they are distressed when they sense that it is unjust. This motivation is proposed as a major factor influencing people to interpret their relationships as just, even in conditions where objectively they appear to be obviously unjust. But equity theory provides insights not only into the plight of disadvantaged people (who are objectively worse off), but also into that of the advantaged (who are objectively better off), addressing how people react when they are getting less than they think they deserve, as well as when they are getting more. This is a strength of equity theory: it explains the cognitive manipulations experienced by the ruling elite as they justify their advantaged position in the fight against revolutionaries.

Equity theory proposes that people feel distress both when they are getting too much and when they are getting too little. Before revolutions, revolutionaries face the task of influencing disadvantaged people to feel that they are getting too little and advantaged people to feel that they are getting too much. After they come to power, revolutionaries must persuade both disadvantaged and advantaged people to feel they are getting what they deserve and that the power and resource arrangements are now equitable.

But how do people arrive at estimations of equity? According to equity theory, people perceive justice on the basis of estimations of inputs and their outcomes in a relationship. Inputs are contributions that people make, such as the hard work and the talent that they contribute, their connections and know-how, and their status and social assets (e.g., likability). Outcomes are the tangible and intangible rewards and punishments people get out of a relationship. Inputs and outcomes are subjectively estimated by people in relationships.

Equity theory postulates that justice is subjectively seen to exist when the ratio of inputs to outcomes for those in a relationship are perceived to be equal. Thus, the actual outcomes for those in a relationship need not be equal for the relationship to be seen as just. For example, Jane works as a mid-level manager in a large clothing company, where Clara is the chief executive officer (CEO). After the press publish statistics of employee salaries, Jane learns that Clara's annual salary is 200 times larger than her own. However, this does not cause Jane to complain because she concludes that the ratio of inputs and outcomes for herself and her CEO is equitable. Jane arrives at this conclusion because in her estimation, her input is 5 out of 10 ("I like my work, but I give priority to my family and personal life") and the CEO's input is 10 out of 10 ("My CEO only lives for the company – she has nothing else in her life. Her personal life is non-existent and her family life is miserable"). Jane estimates her outcome as 5 out of 10 ("My salary is so-so") and the CEO's outcome as 10 out of 10 ("The CEO has a great salary"). This results in the following:

$$\frac{\text{Inputs by Jane(employee): 5}}{\text{Outcomes for Jane(employee): 5}} = \frac{\text{Inputs by Clara(CEO): 10}}{\text{Outcomes for Clara(CEO): 10}}$$

Because the ratio of inputs to outcomes is estimated by Jane to be equal (1 to 1), Jane sees her relationship with the CEO to be equitable.

The power of equity theory is in part achieved through its analysis of what happens when the ratio of inputs to outcomes is perceived as being unequal.

In such situations, the restoration of equity can take place either through actual changes in inputs and outcomes, or through psychological changes in inputs and outcomes. For example, consider employees at a major corporation who go on strike for better pay and benefits. The employees point out that in the last five years, the average salary of top management in the company has increased by 135 percent and company shares have increased in value by 43 percent, while the average salary of regular company employees has increased only by 11 percent, but employee productivity has increased by 26 percent in the same five-year time period. In employee–management negotiations, the management argue that they have had to spend a lot of money to attract and keep top managers, and the 11 percent increase in employee salaries has kept up with inflation and is on top of additional benefits provided for employees. The additional benefits include job stability in an economy with a lot of uncertainties and a lot of stresses for company management. In the end, employees are persuaded to give a much higher value to their job stability and to give greater weight to the stress experienced by top management, so this increases the subjective estimation of their own outcomes, and there is a decrease in the subjective estimation of outcomes for management. The result is a restoration of a (subjectively arrived at) balance between input and outcomes for employees and management.

Before a revolution, revolutionaries give priority to the restoration of equity through actual changes in inputs and outcomes. That is, they argue that the actual inputs of people outside the ruling regime are far higher than their outcomes. Ordinary people deserve much higher actual outcomes. For example, their standard of living should be higher. But after they come to power, revolutionaries switch to a focus on psychological restoration of equity, emphasizing the victory of the revolution in terms of intangibles, such as the moral values in society. This switch from tangible to intangible criteria was obvious and stark in Iran. Before the revolution, Khomeini promised dramatic improvements in the standard of living of Iranians, but after the revolution he completely dismissed material criteria and switched to (supposed) benefits such as the banning of alcohol, the enforcement of the hijab for women, and other changes in line with Khomeini's extremist interpretation of Islamic values.

Relative Deprivation, Social Comparison, and the Cycle of Rights and Duties

Underlying the major psychological research approaches to explaining revolutions, including those based on materialism and identity, are the psychological processes of social comparison and relative deprivation. The experience of deprivation – relative to others or relative to what an individual imagines should be their own situation in a just world – is at the heart of mass revolutionary action. It is through making social comparisons that individuals come to perceive their identities and material conditions as being to various degrees adequate or inadequate, and in some cases come to experience *egoistical deprivation*, feeling deprived because of how they are being treated as an individual, and/or *fraternal deprivation*, feeling deprived because of how they are being treated as a member of a particular group (e.g., as poor or rich, government opponent or supporter, male or female, Black or White).[51] Before the revolution, the challenge for revolutionaries is to influence people to feel deprivation strongly enough so that they collectively mobilize against the ruling regime. This is achieved, as I discuss later in this section, in part through the manipulation of a cycle of *rights*, what we are owed, and *duties*, what we owe to others.[52]

In most cases rights and duties are replaceable; a right can be reinterpreted as a duty, and a duty can be reinterpreted as a right. For example, the "right to vote" can be reinterpreted as the "duty to vote." Similarly, the right to free speech can be reinterpreted as the duty to provide others with an opportunity to speak freely. The replaceability of rights and duties means that revolutionaries can shift from an emphasis on the rights of the people before the revolution to an emphasis on the duties of the people after the revolution (but there are instances where rights and duties are not replaceable, such as the "duty to obey the law," which loses meaning when we refer to the "right to obey the law").[53] By emphasizing the denied rights of the people before the revolution, revolutionaries influence people to compare themselves with what they should have ("We should have those rights!") and to feel deprivation because of a lack of rights, compared to the situation they should enjoy.

The idea that how people feel about their situation, specifically how much deprivation they experience, arises through comparisons (e.g., with others, or with themselves as they should be in a just world) has been discussed in various ways for centuries, at least.[54] For example, relative deprivation was discussed by Karl Marx (1818–83) as an explanation of social behavior,[55] and it was noted by Alexis de Tocqueville (1805–59) that rising expectations play a key role in anti-government movements and revolutions: when people expect better and better lives, but feel dissatisfied with what they have experienced as compared to what they expected to experience.[56] In contemporary research, the notion of rising expectations was invoked by Seamus Power to explain civil unrest in Ireland, which took place when the economy was improving (leading to even higher expectations) rather than when it was in recession (leading to lower expectations).[57] The analyses of Tocqueville and others point to variations in social comparisons: The outcomes of our comparisons depend in part on our social expectations, and rising expectations can lead to strong beliefs about the life we deserve to have in the future. We not only compare ourselves with others, but also with our perceptions of ourselves in the past (e.g., "I used to be much worse off"), the present (e.g., "I expected to be much better off than I am now"), and in the future (e.g., "I expect to be a lot better off by next year").

While over the centuries various researchers have noted the important role of social comparisons in feelings of relative deprivation, it was the US psychologist Leon Festinger (1919–89) who first put forward a formal theory of social comparison processes.[58] Festinger proposed that there is "in the human organism, a drive to evaluate" their own opinions and abilities,[59] and "to the extent that objective, non-social means are not available, people evaluate their opinions and abilities by comparison respectively with the opinions and abilities of others."[60] Festinger proposed that people tend to select similar others for comparisons, but in the case of abilities they tend to compare themselves with others who are slightly better: "There is a unidirectional drive upward in the case of abilities which is largely absent in opinions."[61]

Festinger's original proposition was that people are motivated to make social comparisons to achieve accuracy. However, subsequent research has shown that the motivations for making social comparisons are varied, as are the outcomes.[62] For example, in some situations people compare themselves with those who are worse off, so as to feel relatively good about their own situation. Making comparisons with others who are better off can be threatening, but it can also motivate people to feel fraternal relative deprivation and mobilize them for collective action against the ruling regime. Revolutionaries attempt to manipulate social comparison targets and to encourage people to focus on the rights that (according to the revolutionaries) they have been denied, in order to motivate anti-regime collective action. For example, prior to the American Revolution, a typical pamphlet was entitled "Parliament [meaning the British Parliament] is abusing the rights of Americans."[63] To counter this, those on the side of British authorities preached the virtues of duties, as did the Anglican minister Jonathan Boucher: "Obedience to government is every man's duty, because it is in every man's interest; but it is particularly incumbent on Christians. . .."[64]

In the buildup to the revolution, revolutionaries encourage people to make upward social comparisons – for example, comparing themselves with people who are better off in other countries or with images of how they themselves should be ("You deserve to have much better housing, health, and education; you deserve to enjoy freedoms and free speech. . ."). For example, before the 1979 revolution in Iran, I listened to tapes of numerous speeches by Khomeini (speaking from his temporary home in exile in Paris, France, and Najaf, Iraq, before that) telling the Iranian people that they deserve much better material conditions, that their rights have been trampled on, that the ruling regime is denying them their freedoms. But after coming to power, Khomeini ended even basic freedoms for Iranians, crushed civil liberties, and shifted to focus on social and moral issues (according to his interpretation of Islamic governance) rather than economic issues.[65] After coming to absolute power in 1980, he was no longer giving priority to rights, freedoms, and improvements in material life, but to duties and the importance of making sacrifices for Islam as interpreted by him.

The same shift in messaging is seen among other revolutionaries. Fidel Castro (1926–2016) gave priority to freedoms, democracy, and improved material conditions: "The people deserve more than freedom and democracy in abstract terms; every Cuban is entitled to a decent standard of living."[66] But after coming to absolute power, Castro and his brother Raúl (who became a dictator after him) completely squashed basic freedoms and did not move Cuba toward democracy. Marifeli Pérez-Stable points out that, once in power, the two Castro brothers never "brooked political opposition nor had anything but disdain for civil liberties."[67]

Thus, whereas before the revolution, revolutionaries give priority to the rights of the people, after they overthrow the old regime and ascend to power, revolutionaries typically shift to a focus on the duties of the people, and particularly the duty to be lawful and to obey new revolutionary authorities. This swing from rights to duties took a wild form in the aftermath of the 1789 French Revolution, when the celebration of free speech gave way to years of Terror, during which severe efforts were made to control the so-called excesses of free speech. This renewed focus on duties and the control of free speech during the Terror owed much to traditions in place *before* the revolution.[68] In this way, the control of free speech came full circle: the draconian repression of free speech before and after the revolution was interspersed by a several years of freedom, followed by the Terror years when thousands were imprisoned or killed because of (supposed) crimes involving the (supposed) misuse of free speech. Alongside this cycle of rights and duties that characterize changes before and after revolutions, there is a tendency for there to be a cycle of group-based inequalities, a topic I return to in Chapter 5 and in Part III of this book ("What Happens after Revolutionary Regime Change?").

Concluding Comment

The psychological perspective discussed in this chapter argues that revolutions are shaped by subjective interpretations of the material world rather than the actual material world as it objectively exists. After all, our assessments of how we are doing materially are arrived at through social comparisons with others and with ourselves as we (imagine we) were, are, and might become. Such social comparisons are continually shifting and can be manipulated to lead the same person in the same material conditions to feel they are doing extremely well rather than to feel extremely deprived. The other aspect of this psychological interpretation is the priority ascribed to emotions and irrationality. Given the enormously high risks involved with joining a rebellion against a ruling regime, an objective, calculated, rational cost–benefit analysis is far less likely to lead individuals to risk participating (typically unarmed) in anti-regime revolutions, standing up to bullets, tear gas, and government-endorsed violence.

The psychological perspective, then, highlights the role of passions and emotions in the mobilization of revolutionary collective action. The focus shifts to the subjective illusions people experience, communicate, and collaboratively share and uphold. These illusions are to some degree independent of actual material conditions, and are also independent of the actual material benefits that come to participants in revolutionary action. Later in this text (in Chapter 10), I present the Illusion-Motivation Model of Revolution, which derives from a psychological perspective we have explored in this chapter.

PART II

Regime Change

The three chapters in Part II explore the psychological processes underlying regime change. A point of departure for the discussion is the normalcy of life experienced by people in pre-revolutionary societies, even in conditions of the most extreme inequality and injustice. The current conditions of life and the norms that evolve are what people adapt to, and it seems hard for them to imagine the ruling regime collapsing. When it comes, the tipping point of regime collapse arrives suddenly and unexpectedly, an issue examined in Chapter 4. In many cases, revolutionary leaders scramble to position themselves at the head of the revolutionary movement, even though the collapse of the regime has caught them by surprise. The collapse of the regime is hastened when the ruling elite mistime their reforms, so the changes they make seem to signal weaknesses rather than genuine efforts at moving toward a more just society.

The focus of Chapter 5 is on the psychological changes experienced by the ruling elite and its revolutionary opponents. The model of mutual radicalization is used to structure the discussion, depicting the two opposing sides as experiencing, in turn, group mobilization, extreme ingroup cohesion, and antagonistic identity transformation. Throughout the process of mutual radicalization, the ruling elite and the revolutionary opposition move psychologically further and further apart from each other, and their communications and understanding of each other deteriorates. Their identities become transformed, so each side comes to define themselves in opposition to the other.

The psychological stepping stones to revolution are explored in Chapter 6. These stepping stones are based on the earlier discussions in Chapter 2 and 3 of this text, which examined the range of psychological theories of revolution, both those that give priority to material factors as drivers of behavior and those that prioritize psychological factors as drivers. The eight stepping stones that are examined all involve psychological changes that increase the probability of the individual participating in revolutionary action. Some of these stepping stones involve purely psychological changes, such as "become aware of an alternative ideal society," and some others are more closely linked to revolutionary action, such as "be prepared to risk making serious personal and collective sacrifices in the cause of progress toward the ideal society." These changes are strongly influenced by emotions and irrationality rather than rationality and logic. Also, they are shaped by collective processes, so that individuals are swept along by what they experience as enormous tsunamis beyond their control.

CHAPTER 4

The Tipping Point in Regime Collapse
Power and Authority in Transition

Dear Comrades ... the piratical imperialist war is the beginning of the civil war throughout Europe ... the hour is not far distant when ... the peoples will turn their arms against their own capitalist exploiters ... The worldwide socialist revolution has already dawned.

Vladimir Lenin (1917)[1]

The above words were spoken by Lenin on April 3, 1917, when he arrived back in Russia after almost seventeen years of exile abroad. The February 1917 revolution came as a surprise to Lenin. As I discuss in greater detail later in this chapter, Lenin had to rush back to Moscow from Zurich, Switzerland, in order to insert himself as a leader of the revolutionary movement in Russia. Historical cases show that the moment of regime collapse often comes about suddenly and unexpectedly. This is the same for more recent cases of regime collapse. For example, consider the collapse of the Afghan government in 2021, built up by the United States after US-led forces invaded Afghanistan in 2001 in response to the tragic 9/11 terrorist attacks.

Over a period of twenty years, US-led forces invested not only in infrastructure in Afghanistan, but also in developing and equipping a 300,000-strong Afghan military – at least hundreds of billions of dollars of US taxpayer money were spent on these efforts.[2] It was expected that this Afghan military would successfully defend the US-backed Afghan government, headed by President Ashraf Ghani, against Taliban forces. In the Washington DC area (where I have lived and worked since 1990), academic and government analysts generally agreed that the Afghan military was strong enough to ensure the continuation of the US-backed government for at least six months, and perhaps for years. However, as one group of critics put it, as soon as the Americans "decided to leave Afghanistan and packed up their bags, all that was built in twenty years, proved fragile and [was] gone in about twenty days."[3] President Ghani and other leading US-backed Afghan political leaders instantly fled abroad, abandoning their posts just as speedily as the 300,000-strong Afghan military melted into thin air. Clearly, this army only existed on paper.

Many Western experts were similarly bewildered by the sudden collapse of the Iraqi state after the 2003 invasion of US-led forces. A different type of occupation had been planned by the George W. Bush administration, as explained by Toby Dodge: "The collapse of the Iraqi state dramatically changed the nature of the USA's role in Iraq … The Iraqi state was to be seized by invading US troops who would use the indigenous institutions to rule the country. This would negate the need for a large number of foreign troops, the deployment of large-scale US resources or indeed an extended occupation."[4] But the rapid collapse of the Iraqi state left the United States with the task of creating a new state in Iraq, a task for which it was ill-equipped and unprepared. This created a power vacuum, which continues to be filled in large part by the mullahs governing Iran, intent on driving the United States out of the Middle East. This is a calamitous defeat for the United States in a war that has cost trillions of dollars.[5]

The same unpredictability has been expressed in assessments of the collapse of the Soviet Union in 1990–1, which (once again) had not been predicted by Western analysts. Remarking on the "latest Russian revolution," Leon Aron, an expert on Russia, argues: "Every revolution is a surprise. Still, the latest Russian revolution must be counted among the greatest of surprises."[6] The different post hoc assessments of the Soviet collapse have a common theme: The collapse was swift and unexpected.[7] Part of the surprise is the role played by government officials: low-ranked officials who refused to continue in their repressive roles played an important part in the collapse.[8]

My proposition is that in order to better understand the tipping point and the sudden unraveling of ruling regimes faced with serious revolutionary opposition, it is necessary that we first develop a comprehensive picture of factors leading to regime change. Without being equipped with this comprehensive picture, the "tipping point" resulting in (often very sudden) regime collapse is difficult to understand and explain, even by people directly involved in revolutionary movements – and especially by people within the ruling regime itself.[9] Next, I introduce the *three-factor account of the revolutionary tipping point*, which gives highest priority to the interaction between changes in context, changes in the ruling elite, and the timely presence of a persuasive revolutionary elite.

The Three-Factor Account of the Revolutionary Tipping Point

Imagine a dam, with water filling up behind it. The water is coming into the dam from many different sources, including rain, rivers and streams, as well as smaller overflowing reservoirs. As the water level behind the dam keeps rising, the pressure on the dam continually increases. At some point, the dam is completely filled. Cracks appear in the dam; then additional water acts as "the straw that broke the camel's back." The dam suddenly bursts. This image of a dam bursting is useful when we address the following question: How do societies reach a tipping point when a ruling regime collapses and revolutionaries come to power? The tipping point for regime collapse often comes suddenly and unexpectedly, like a dam that suddenly bursts – even though the pressure on the dam often builds up slowly and over a long time. After the dam bursts, the initial rush of water is powerful, uncontrollable, and a destroyer of anything that stands in its way – rather like the initial force of revolution when the tipping point is reached and a ruling regime crumbles and is swept aside. But what factors lead to the buildup of pressure toward revolution?

I answer this question from a psychological perspective, with a focus on three factors that each serve as different sources of the water pouring in and building up additional pressure on the dam. First, there are changes in society that prepare the ground for a revolution. Second, changes take place in the ruling elite that make the regime vulnerable to revolution. Third, there is the timely presence of an (often charismatic) revolutionary leader who helps to persuade both the opposition and key elements in the regime that the revolutionary tipping point has been reached and that disobedience and nonconformity, rather than obedience and conformity, to authorities is the correct way to behave. Because there are often multiple competing revolutionary leaders, each representing competing factions, it tends to be the most ruthless, Machiavellian, and tactically astute leaders who manage to position themselves at the very forefront of the revolutionary movement.

After the above-identified three factors take effect and the tipping point is reached, the leadership of the ruling regime abandon their positions and either escape or are captured, and revolutionaries seize power. But it is rare in history that these three sets of continually changing factors exactly intersect and take effect at the same time, resulting in a revolutionary tipping point. For example, changes in society, such as large numbers of people feeling a sense of relative deprivation, can prepare the ground for revolution, and a revolutionary leadership can claim that the revolutionary tipping point has been reached. However, if the ruling elite stands united and continues to use extreme repression with enough violent force, the opposition will be thwarted and the revolution will not succeed. An illustration of this is Iran in 2009, when Mahmoud Ahmadinejad was installed as president against the wishes of the majority of Iranian people. Despite widespread protests and international condemnation, the ruling regime remained united in using extreme repression and violence to crush the so-called Green Movement. A more recent example is Russia in 2020, when in many respects societal conditions were ready for revolution and the opposition leadership claimed that the tipping point for regime change had been reached. However, Putin and his regime used extreme repression to thwart the opposition – as shown by the treatment of the opposition leader Alexei Navalny, who was first poisoned and then jailed.

In the following sections, I examine the above-mentioned three factors and their role as prerequisites for revolution.

Changes in Society That Prepare the Ground for Revolution

As David Garrioch observes, "the Paris of 1789 was a very different city from the Paris of 1700."[10] In his meticulous analysis of changes in Paris in the decades before the French Revolution, Garrioch describes the numerous transformations that took place in the lives of Parisians, leading in many different ways to the ground being prepared for the French Revolution. These changes included the loss of influence of Church teaching (as reflected, for example, in rising illegitimacy rates[11]), the rise in popular interest in politics,[12] the increased perception of Parisian (and, by extension, French) authorities as despotic,[13] increasing geographical and social mobility,[14] and the "democratization and modification of elite culture" associated with the rising aspirations of a new middle class.[15] The result of these many different changes was that "late-eighteenth century Paris was moving out of a world structured by deference and hierarchy into one governed overwhelmingly by money and appearances."[16] When the defenders of "deference and hierarchy" refused to show sufficient flexibility and share enough power with the representatives of "money and appearances," the rising new bourgeoisie helped to bring about the French Revolution.

Of course, it was not only changes in Paris that prepared the ground for the French Revolution. As demonstrated by the scholarly tradition established by George Lefebvre (1874–1959), the preparatory stages of the revolution involved the aristocracy, followed by the bourgeoisie and the urban masses, rising up to pursue their particular goals and interests – but this was swiftly followed by the mobilization of the rural peasantry.[17] A multiplicity of social groups and classes mobilized in opposition to the monarchy in France; the entire national context changed in a way that made revolution more probable, if not inevitable.

Similarly, an examination of trends during the 1960s and 1970s shows how changes in Tehran, the Iranian capital city, and other major cities prepared the ground for revolution in 1979. The oil price increases of 1973 brought enormous additional wealth to Iran and helped to further accentuate social class differences in Iranian urban centers, particularly in Tehran.[18] During the 1970s I used to return from my studies in England to Iran each summer, and the opulent life of the rich elite in Tehran and other major cities was startling to witness – as was the dire poverty of the millions of people who had moved (often involuntarily) to the capital city from rural areas. The oil revenue was pouring into Iran, but inequality was also increasing, particularly in large urban centers.[19]

But inequality and wealth concentration are only a few of many factors that created a suitable context for the 1979 Iranian Revolution. Probably the most potent factor was the extensive support provided by Mohammad Reza Shah and his regime for the clergy and Islam in Iran, on the assumption that religion would provide protection against communism.[20] The Shah obviously believed in the Marxist adage that religion serves as the opium of the people. In his seminal study of the last Shah, Abbas Milani points out that the Shah made a number of moves to strengthen the clergy, including inviting back from exile a leading ayatollah and increasing the number of mosques, so that during his reign "the number of mosques increased to more than 55,000 (some say 75,000). The number of religious schools also witnessed a sharp rise, going from 154 to 214 in 1960. The rise in the second half of the Shah's rule was even greater."[21] Rising incomes and improved transportation systems meant there was a tenfold increase in pilgrimages to holy cities such as Mashad.[22] The Shah's regime also helped to spread the teachings of clerics such as Ayatollah Morteza Motahhari. As Afshin Matin-Asgari explains, "under the monarchy, his [Motahhari's] liberal-conservative reading of Shi'I Islam was allowed wide exposure, as it countered both Marxism and various forms of Islamic Marxism..."[23]

Thus, the last Shah invested heavily in building up mosques, religious schools, and Islamic networks. It was exactly this network of mosques and religious schools that Ayatollah Khomeini and other extremist clerics used to mobilize opposition to the Shah, thus helping to topple him.[24] Because the Shah's regime supported a more expansive role for religion in Iranian society, religious opposition to his regime could operate in relative safety. Jerrold Green argues that "it would be no exaggeration to argue that counter-mobilization rendered virtually all of the country's 180,000 mullahs agents of revolution."[25] Religious networks were used to spread anti-Shah communications. During my summer visits to Iran in the 1970s, I came across tapes of Khomeini's anti-Shah speeches, which were being duplicated and distributed through mosques and religious networks. In 1978, as the revolution was reaching a climax, mosques continued to serve as safe havens for anti-Shah activists, places where security forces would not attack revolutionaries. In the buildup to the revolution, when demonstrations against the Shah grew to include millions of protesters, marchers on religious days (such as *Tasuah* and *Ashura*) were not attacked by the security forces. Ironically, the Shah feared attack from communists, so he built up religion in Iran as a defense against communism – but it was religious extremists who opportunistically grabbed power after his regime collapsed.

Another important kind of change in societies that prepares the ground for revolution concerns images and symbols. Sarah Awad and Brady Wagoner argue that "revolution can ... be seen as a dramatized performance using powerful symbols to win over audiences that are both national and international."[26] Images and symbols played a highly important role in the Arab Spring societies. For example, the Arab Spring revolutions were sparked by the image of Mohammed Bouazizi, who set himself on fire in front of the municipal building of Sidi Bouzid, a small rural town in Tunisia, in protest against the corrupt dictatorship of Zine al-Abidine Ben Ali. The Tunisian dictator and his close associates attempted to manipulate the situation in favor of the regime by visiting Bouazizi in hospital and publicizing the regime's promises of help to his family, but it was too late (the Tunisian dictator was forced to flee to Saudi Arabia). The Tunisian Revolution and the Arab Spring had begun, leading to anti-regime movements across the Arab world and actual regime change in Libya, Tunisia, and Egypt.

Electronic communications have also helped to spread anti-regime images, symbols, and information, preparing the ground for collective anti-regime movements. The movement to topple the Hosni Mubarak regime in Egypt in 2011 has been referred to as the *Facebook Revolution*.[27] Of course, the regime in power can shut down electronic communications and prevent anti-regime activists from using Facebook and other modern media tools to spread their messages and organize activities. However, by making such a move, the ruling regime slows down the domestic economy and also signals to the world that it is facing serious opposition.

Changes in the Ruling Elite That Make the Regime Vulnerable to Revolution

Cohesion and unity in the ruling elite is absolutely essential for the continuation of dictatorships, but some level of disagreement and diversity strengthens democracies. The Achilles' heel of dictatorships is disunity and fragmentation in the ruling elite; the Achilles' heel of democracies is when there is too little disagreement and diversity in the ruling elite. In this section I discuss the kinds of changes in the ruling elite that make revolution more likely, particularly in dictatorships.

Dictatorial regimes are far more likely to collapse when the ruling elite splinters and there is no longer unity in using violence to crush dissent and prevent revolution.[28] This idea is shared by various thinkers, including communists. In the *Communist Manifesto*, Karl Marx (1818–83) and Frederich Engels (1820–95) highlighted the important role played by a part of the ruling class who break away to join and support the revolutionary class to bring about revolution.[29] In order for the dictatorial regime to survive, members of the ruling elite must in unity adopt and uphold the legitimizing ideology of the regime – whether it be communism, or Islam, or fascism, or monarchy, or some other ideology. We recognize the essential role of elite solidarity from the examples of the French Revolution (1789), the Russian Revolution (1917), the Cuban Revolution (1953), the Iranian Revolution (1979), and the Arab Spring revolutions (2011).[30] In each of these cases, there was serious disagreement among the ruling elite leading up to the revolution, creating weaknesses (the cracks in the dam) that were then exploited by the opposition groups mobilizing the masses against the regime.

Perhaps the clearest recent demonstration of how elite dissent can result in regime meltdown is provided by the dissolution of the Soviet Union (in 1991) and the so-called Gorbachev Revolution.[31] Lack of cohesion among the Soviet political elite resulted in a relatively rapid disintegration of the state apparatus. Within a few months, security forces went from seeming to stand firm to standing aside as mass disobedience occurred. To use Ellen Trimberger's phrase, this was another "revolution from above," with elite disunity opening the floodgates to mass mobilization and rebellion.[32]

Experimental demonstrations of this trend are also available. For example, in the seminal obedience to authority studies of Stanley

Milgram (1933–84), when the teachers (the only naive participants in the experiment) were faced with a single authority figure (a scientist in a white laboratory coat), their level of obedience to administer electric shocks to the learner (actually a confederate of the Experimenter, who acted his role and was not harmed) was between 40 and 90 percent (there was variation in levels of obedience across the United States and other countries).[33] This is a frighteningly high level of obedience by teachers to (ostensibly) give lethal levels of electric shocks to the learner. However, the level of obedience to authority in Milgram's experiments was lower when there was more than one scientist and these scientists disagreed with one another as to whether the electric shocks should continue. This finding has been replicated across cultures.[34] In the organizational setting, disagreements between leaders about the identity of an organization result in lower organizational performance, presumably in part because employees are following contradictory communications and signals from different leaders.[35]

The power of Milgram's obedience to authority study is in part his selection of ordinary people to serve as participants, and the demonstration that even individuals with normal personality characteristics can be pressured to seriously harm or kill others. This trend is repeatedly evident in dictatorships. For example, as I write these words there are widespread demonstrations against the dictatorship in Iran, and the security forces continue to follow orders from Ali Khamenei and other regime leaders to brutalize demonstrators. However, not all elite members agree that the killing and maiming of demonstrators should continue, and this can pave the way for leadership fragmentation and even regime change.

Another kind of change in the ruling elite that makes the regime vulnerable to revolution is the prevention of elite circulation, as proposed by Vilfredo Pareto (1848–1923), the founder of elite theory (discussed in Chapter 2). Pareto argues that all societies are governed by elites, but not all children born to elite parents have the necessary attributes for elite membership and government responsibilities. Also, some children born to non-elite parents do have superior intelligence and other elite characteristics. As long as there is elite circulation, the less talented individuals born to elite parents move down and join the non-elite, and the highly talented individuals born to non-elite parents rise up and join the elite. However, "if one of these movements comes to an end, or ... if they both come to an end, the governing class crashes to ruin ... Potent cause of disturbance in the equilibrium is the accumulation of superior elements in the lower classes and, conversely, of inferior elements in the higher classes."[36]

Unlike dictatorships, democracies have improved chances of survival when there is some level of disagreement among the ruling elite. The key question is, What is the optimal level of disagreement among the elite in democracies? Too little disagreement, and diversity in viewpoints among the ruling elite and society runs into a lack of elite circulation and eventual collapse, as outlined by Pareto. But too much diversity also results in dangers for democracy, particularly when one leader and/or a faction of elite political leadership does not accept the tacit and informal norms of democracy. As Steven Levitsky and Daniel Ziblatt argue, in addition to formal institutions and regulatory laws, democracies function through informal and tacit norms: "The genius of the first generation of America's political leaders was not that they created foolproof institutions, but that, in addition to designing very good institutions, they – gradually and with difficulty – established a set of shared beliefs and practices that helped make those institutions work."[37] These researchers add:

> When American democracy has worked, it has relied upon two norms that we often take for granted – mutual tolerance and institutional forbearance. Treating rivals as legitimate contenders for power and underutilizing one's institutional prerogatives in the spirit of fair play are not written into the American Constitution. Yet without them, our constitutional checks and balances will not operate as we expect them to.[38]

When an authoritarian political leader such as Donald Trump rejects established informal norms and tacit agreements, as is well documented,[39] democracy can face collapse. Trump meets at least some of the four key indicators of authoritarian behavior set out by Levitsky and Ziblatt: rejection of (or weak commitment to) democratic rules of the game; denial of legitimacy of political opponents; toleration and even encouragement of violence; and readiness to curtail civil liberties of opponents, including the media.[40] In earlier writings, I have also identified Trump as a potential dictator who has attempted to set up and use the springboard to dictatorship to grab power.[41]

Revolutionary Leadership Present at the Tipping Point

Both anti-dictatorship and anti-democracy revolutions are greatly helped by the timely presence of leaders who are either at the head of the revolutionary movement or manage to insert themselves at the head when the tipping point for revolution has been reached. But because the tipping point is so difficult to predict, revolutionary leaders are often caught off-guard by events and have to scramble to position themselves at the head of the revolutionary movement.

The February 1917 revolution in Russia caught Lenin by surprise and he had to make hasty arrangements to return to Russia from Zurich by train (other Bolshevik leaders were also away from Moscow at the time of the revolution: Trotsky was in the United States and Stalin was in Siberia). This proved to be extremely difficult to do because the train Lenin traveled on had to pass through Germany, and in 1917 Russia was still at war with Germany (these nations were on opposing sides in World War I, 1914–18). The outcome was that Lenin traveled across Germany on a sealed train, and rumors arose to the effect that he was a German agent, or at least that German agents had helped him return to Russia.[42] Because Lenin supported an end to the war, there is no doubt that the German government preferred to see him and the Bolsheviks, rather than the Tsar, lead Russia – and this soon came to be. However, Lenin eventually got to lead the Russian Revolution, more out of luck and the Tsar's mismanagement rather than his own planning. Just as Lenin was incorrect about the imminent dawning of the "worldwide socialist revolution,"[43] he had misjudged the timing of the 1917 Russian Revolution. Like many other Russian revolutionaries, Lenin was surprised by the swift collapse of the Tsarist regime.

Part of the reason that leaders, both in the ruling regime and in the opposition, are surprised by the collapse of a regime in the face of a revolutionary movement is what Mary Fulbrook describes as "the normality of every life," a strong sense of things being stable and rooted, that arises from existing arrangements in dictatorships such as East Germany, 1949–89.[44] This is particularly true in the case of societies ruled by long-standing regimes, in which what people have experienced throughout their lives seems routine, normal, and inevitable. In the case of the 1979 Iranian Revolution, every Iranian had only experienced Iranian society ruled by a shah (just as at the time of the French Revolution, French people had only experienced rule by monarchy). Iran without a shah seemed unthinkable, and this made the rulers overconfident. Charles Kurzman titled his book on the Iranian Revolution *The Unthinkable Revolution in Iran*,[45] and Michael Axworthy, writing about the 1979 Anti-Shah Revolution, notes that "paradoxically, the growth of the revolutionary movement was helped in the early stages by the regime's own self-belief; by the government's complacency. Initially, revolution was indeed unthinkable."[46]

Although the Iranian Revolution took about eighteen months to build up to maximum strength, with the water behind the dam rising and reaching sufficient pressure to burst the dam, the end of the Shah's regime came suddenly, when he finally made the decision to leave Iran in early January 1979. The dam burst when on January 16, 1979, the Shah and his family and entourage flew from Mehrabad Airport, Tehran, to Egypt. Khomeini returned to a triumphant reception in Tehran two weeks later, on February 1, 1979.

When he ended his long exile and reached Tehran, Khomeini was in important respects in a similar situation to Lenin when he returned from exile in Switzerland to arrive in Moscow in 1917. Khomeini had spent fourteen years in exile (in Turkey, Iraq, and France) and was now competing to position himself as the leader of the revolution. Like the Bolshevik followers of Lenin, the extremist followers of Khomeini were a numerical minority. Another important similarity was that the real views of Khomeini and Lenin were not widely known. In large part because of government censorship, very few Iranians had read Khomeini's writings (I found that his book *Hokumat-e Eslami; Islamic Republic* was not even well known among religious Iranians[47]), just as very few Russians had read Lenin's writings. However, Lenin was fairly frank in expressing his ideology after his return to Russia (his writings were obscure, so few people understood him anyway) because he felt Russia and the world constituted fertile ground for his ideas to spread. On the other hand, Khomeini was aware that he had to maneuver very carefully because many of the most important slogans of the revolution were the opposite of his views – particularly on the issues of women, freedom, and democracy.

It is common knowledge that Khomeini's expressed views in the year leading to the revolution in important ways contradicted what he said and did after the first year of revolution. This is particularly so after the end of the hostage-taking crisis and the start of the Iran–Iraq War, by which time he had killed, banished, or jailed all serious competitors for leadership in Iran.[48] This is another similarity he and his supporters had with Lenin and the Bolsheviks – the utter ruthlessness with which they dealt with competitors in the immediate post-revolution period. Both in Iran in 1979–80 and in Russia in 1917–18, there was a brief period when democracy had an opportunity to take root and grow.[49] But in both cases, the leaders who managed to position themselves at the front of the revolutionary movement and grab power, Lenin and Khomeini, were intent on preventing democracy.

Concluding Comment

Revolutions are rare in history. When they do happen, they are like a dam bursting, so that regime collapse comes suddenly, surprisingly in terms of timing, and typically with enormous destruction. Because of the unpredictability of when exactly the dam will break, it is not always possible for revolutionary leaders to be present at the right time and the right place at the forefront of the revolutionary movement. But in order to build up pressure and reach the tipping point of regime change, revolutionary leaders promise all kinds of rights, freedoms, and improvements before the dam finally breaks. After the chaos of regime change, and after the revolutionary leader comes to power, the rhetoric he uses (and invariably it has been a male) changes.

Following the tipping point of regime change, the rhetoric of revolutionary leaders shifts from giving priority to the rights and freedoms of the people to giving priority to duties, conformity, and obedience of the people to authorities. After the revolution, the right to rebellion becomes the duty to obey and defend the regime. Internal and external threats are highlighted and exaggerated. Dangers from real and imagined enemies are magnified, sometimes at local levels independent of national authorities.[50] In the name of defending the revolution, political competitors and rivals are isolated, jailed, or killed. Rival power centers are destroyed. The revolutionary leader is continuously conscious that the tipping point of regime change had been reached recently and that another explosive tipping point could arrive just as unexpectedly.

CHAPTER 5

Psychological Processes Underlying Revolutionary Regime Change

Poor naked wretches, wheresoe'er you are,
That bide the pelting of this pitiless storm,
How shall your houseless heads and unfed sides,
Your looped and windowed raggedness defend you
From seasons such as these?

King Lear (3.IV, 32–37)[1]

In Shakespeare's *King Lear*, a dramatic shift takes place in the behavior of Lear and his two oldest daughters, Goneril and Regan, after he has transferred his *authority*, his legal right to command, and *power*, his ability to exert influence, to them. When he becomes powerless, without influence, and completely dependent on his two oldest daughters, Lear comes to understand the world from the perspective of the downtrodden, the shunned, the poor. On the other hand, having become powerful and rich, Goneril and Regan shift from being submissive, meek, and outwardly kind to becoming authoritarian, aggressive, and savagely cruel. As suggested by historical examples and experimental research, absolute power absolutely corrupts Goneril and Regan.[2] Shakespeare's *King Lear* illustrates in a dramatic manner the socially constructed nature of authority and power, and how people can be transformed through the struggle for, and the transference of, authority and power.

Authority and power are embedded in social relationships and depend on mutual acceptance of the shared socially constructed world, such as relations between a teacher and students in a classroom.[3] As long as students accept the authority of the teacher, they follow instructions to carry out learning tasks. However, this power does not necessarily extend to outside school buildings and school hours. Nor is the teacher's authority unending – a retired teacher would not have the same authority, even in the classroom during the school day. After he announces his retirement and the transfer of his authority and power to his daughters ("and' tis our fast intent/ To shake all cares and business from our age/ Conferring them on younger strengths ...", 1.I. 40–42), Lear's relationship with his daughters, and many others, is transformed. Lear represents a regime fallen from power, whereas his two oldest daughters have gained power and become rulers. Both Lear and his daughters have been transformed.

In a similar way, the process leading to the tipping point of regime change and revolution transforms both the people defending and those attacking the ruling regime. This process can take many years and often involves what I have termed *mutual radicalization*, where two groups, such as a ruling regime and the revolutionary opposition, "take increasingly extreme positions opposing one another, reacting against real or imagined threats, moving further and further apart in points of view, mobilizing their resources to launch attacks, and finally attempting to weaken and destroy each other."[4] The process of mutual radicalization and the changes it leads to in the ruling regime and the revolutionary opposition can only come about through the relationships *between* two groups. The final result of mutual radicalization is often *pathological hatred*, where each side adopts a "your pain, my gain" attitude, believing that as long as the other side is damaged by attacks toward the ultimate destruction of the enemy, any and all pain and suffering experienced by the ingroup is justified.

Revolutionaries seldom are concerned with *how* they topple the ruling regime, believing that as long as they come to power, the ends justify the means. However, evidence shows that how revolutionaries come to power actually transforms them and shapes the new, revolutionary regime they construct. For example, in a study on the factors that result in certain dictatorships being resilient, Steven Levitsky and Lucan Way show that dictatorships are long-lasting and resilient when they have their origins in violent social and political revolutions, as did China, Cuba, Iran, the Soviet Union, and Vietnam.[5] This type of revolution results in counterrevolutionary reactions, which are also often violent. The outcome is that the revolutionary regimes which survive counterrevolutionary reactions build a highly cohesive elite, a strong and loyal army and security apparatus, and they also destroy independent power centers that could serve as their potential competitors. In other words, these regimes are highly undemocratic and use violence to maintain control.

With respect to these particular types of dictatorships, Levitsky and Way also report finding "little evidence that mass ideological commitments contributed to revolutionary regime durability."[6] This is in line with my argument in previous discussions of the psychology of dictatorship that in dictatorships, the masses are kept in line primarily through brute force rather than through ideology (in contrast, in democracies the masses adopt system justification ideologies, which legitimize the existing social and political order[7]). In dictatorships, in order for the regime to survive, the elite has to remain ideologically committed and cohesive.[8]

Using the framework derived from mutual radicalization research, I begin by discussing the psychological changes that are experienced by the ruling regime and the revolutionaries. I structure the discussion according to the main stages of mutual radicalization: group mobilization, extreme ingroup cohesion, and antagonistic identity transformation. Mutual radicalization is primarily a psychological process, involving changes in the perceptions, attitudes, attributions, motivations, and other psychological characteristics of both the ruling regime and the revolutionaries trying to topple the regime in order to climb to power. Moreover, mutual radicalization is a collective process characterized by irrationality. Within the mutual radicalization process, individuals can think though issues rationally and recognize that the collective is moving in the wrong direction, but in this context individuals are powerless to correct the actions of collectives. The general trend in this context is that most individuals end up conforming to incorrect norms and obeying incorrect commands, even when they recognize they are doing the wrong thing.[9]

Group Mobilization

The first major challenge for revolutionaries is to mobilize the population against the ruling regime. This mobilization is achieved by transforming the perceptions of the population, so that people come to see the ruling regime as: (1) distinct, different, and separate from the rest of society, including themselves; (2) illegitimate and immoral, so that rebellion against the regime is justified; (3) unstable, so that the regime can be toppled; and (4) an obstacle to a better future that is possible to achieve. That is, people have to be persuaded to believe that a better world is possible for them, but only if they topple the ruling regime. However, in order to achieve this change in perceptions, the revolutionaries have to overcome enormous challenges.

A first challenge is fear, and the general tendency of people under a dictatorship to learn to keep out of harm's way, to practice avoidance. This is how a doctor and rehabilitation specialist described her life in

Czechoslovakia, when it was a small dictatorship within the larger Soviet Union dictatorship:

> You had to learn avoidance. In fact, what would be the point in trying to stand up to the regime all by yourself? You would just hurt yourself and your family. So you just tried not to get involved in public life, keep away from activism of any kind, and if they forced you, you tried to wiggle out of it. And avoidance was possible. Sometimes with a bit of trouble like my husband: he was never promoted to an executive position because he had refused to join the Party. By then it was not so terrible that you couldn't survive. So we just lived. Being inconspicuous was a big advantage.[10]

I had to learn the same kind of avoidance when I lived under the mullahs' dictatorship in Iran in the early 1980s.

A second obstacle facing revolutionaries is that the main communications systems and propaganda machinery in their society are in the hands of the ruling regime, safeguarded by the regime's security apparatus. Consequently, in the period leading up to revolutions, revolutionaries are forced to create clandestine networks and use secret ways to communicate their messages. For example, the anti-communist revolution in Poland in the 1980s relied heavily on Catholic churches and networks to communicate anti-government messages. Similarly, the Anti-Shah Revolution in Iran relied heavily on mosques and religious networks to spread revolutionary messages in the 1970s. Of course, as is clear from the dictatorship of the mullahs in Iran, the complicity of the Church in the East German dictatorship (1949–89),[11] the support of the Russian Orthodox Church for Putin's dictatorship and the war in Ukraine, and many other examples, religion is often used in support of, rather than against, dictatorship – and in support of the authorities in their repression of revolutionary movements.[12]

Both revolutionaries and ruling regimes adapt to changing technologies. For example, activists working to overthrow the mullahs' dictatorship in the twenty-first century have come to rely on electronic communications, which results in the regime shutting down the Internet whenever there is unrest (as there was most seriously in 2009 and 2022–). Electronic communications enable people outside dictatorships to try to help democratic groups under dictatorships, just as dictatorial governments (particularly Russia) have interfered in democracies and weakened them.[13]

The security apparatus of the ruling regime invests heavily to develop a range of strategies to prevent revolutionaries from spreading their messages and mobilizing support. At the extreme, living under a dictatorship means not even being able to trust close family members because your uncle and aunt, your children, and even your husband or wife could report on you to the authorities. Orlando Figes describes private life in Stalin's Russia in this way: "The idea of mutual surveillance was fundamental to the Soviet system. In a country that was too big to police, the Bolshevik regime (not unlike the tsarist one before it) relied on the self-policing of the population."[14] This self-policing was facilitated by the communal living policy of the Bolsheviks, which forced families and individuals to share cramped living spaces. "Eavesdropping, spying, and informing" became rampant, as there was nowhere to hide in cramped living spaces.[15] In this situation, privacy and private space became suspect and almost obsolete among ordinary people.

Despite the pervasive and powerful surveillance apparatus of the state and the "normalcy" of life under surveillance dictatorships, in some rare instances revolutionaries do manage to mobilize enough of the population to topple the ruling regime. Group mobilization first requires a cognitive shift, so that enough people come to perceive the ruling regime as a distinct and different group from the rest of society, with interests that contradict their ingroup interests. A shift also takes place in perceptions of the moral attributes of the ruling regime, so they come to be seen as unjust and immoral. This often involves the immorality of particular individuals in the ruling elite, such as rumors about illicit affairs between the Tsarina and Rasputin in the years leading to the 1917 Russian Revolution, and the thousands of pairs of shoes and extravagant jewelry bought by First Lady Imelda Marcos of the Philippines in the revolutionary years leading to the overthrowing of her husband's dictatorship (1965–86).

Moral outrage is used by revolutionaries to create a greater distance between "them," the evil ruling regime, and "us," the people whose rights have unjustly been deprived. During this collective mobilization phase, the revolutionary leaders give priority to the rights of the people that have been trampled on by the ruling regime. They also encourage people to make upward social comparisons to real or imagined others who are better off than themselves: "Think of the much better life you could have had if this evil regime had not unjustly deprived you of your rights and wealth," and "look at all those other people who are enjoying the good life that you deserve to have and will have after we get rid of this regime." Such upward social comparisons are intended to make people feel deprived relative to their own situation as it could be, or the situation of others as it is at present.

Thus, in the first phase of mutual radicalization, revolutionaries have to bring about cognitive shifts in enough of the population so they come to see the ruling regime as separate, illegitimate, unstable, and as an obstacle to the much better life they could have. Collective mobilization is driven not only by a hatred of the ruling elite, but also by the vision of the collective better life that is seen as possible only after regime change.

Extreme Ingroup Cohesion

The second major stage of mutual radicalization leading to revolution involves the two opposing sides developing extreme ingroup cohesion in opposition to one another. During this stage, both leadership and follow-ership in the two opposing sides become more aggressive. Second, conformity increases within each opposing side, so that people on the two sides get pushed to adopt, and conform to, more extreme positions. Third, the people on each opposing side converge around a cohesive ideology that further differentiates and distances one side from the other.

The ingroup cohesion achieved during the second stage reflects the triumph of collective processes, which during this stage can become destructive and irrational, over individual-level processes, which during this stage have a greater potential to be constructive and rational. However, although individuals on each side can recognize that they are moving toward destructive conflict, they often find themselves in situations where the pressure to conform to destructive group norms and obey an aggressive leadership is unavoidable – as are the conflicts ahead. This is particularly true on the side of the regime and its supporters, where leadership and hierarchy are much clearer delineated relative to the revolutionary side, where there are often multiple competing leaders and factions.

To some degree, the changes that take place within the regime and its supporters differ from changes taking place among the revolutionaries and the anti-government movement. As the regime comes under increasingly serious attacks, there is pressure for greater conformity and obedience within the ruling elite; this is in line with experimental evidence as well as the classic field studies of Muzafer Sherif.[16] The more moderate elements that attempt to build bridges and work with the opposition run the risk of being treated as traitors by the regime and as spies and tricksters by the opposition. These same processes are evident within the ruling regimes facing revolutionary forces in great revolutions, such as in eighteenth-century France, as well in modern revolutions, such as in twentieth-century Iran and twenty-first-century Arab Spring countries.

Faced with growing opposition, the ruling regime must decide on an effective strategy to stay in power. Part of this strategy is to maintain the support of key groups. In the case of King Louis XVI of France (1754–93), his closest allies were the French nobility who turned against him in part because of the reforms he advocated (such as the abolishment of serfdom). The king's support for the successful American Revolution could have won him middle-class support in the longer term, as commercial opportunities expanded in the United States. But in the short term the French government incurred enormous debts because of the costs of supporting the American Revolution. France supported this war because it was seen as a war of independence from Great Britain, a fierce rival to France. But the resulting financial crisis in France brought further unpopularity for the French monarchy, particularly among middle- and lower-class people. The king became indecisive and seems to have suffered depression from around 1787, pushing his Austrian-born wife Marie Antoinette (1755–93) into the center of the political stage – a role for which she was ill-equipped, and which made her and the monarchy ever more unpopular.[17]

A similar formula, involving an indecisive male leader withdrawing to leave decision-making to his unprepared and unpopular wife, characterized the lead-up to the Russian Revolution of 1917. Tsar Nicholas II (1868–1918), like Louis XVI of France, was determined to cling to absolute rule, but he was indecisive, and when he did make decisions during the crisis years, they were invariably the wrong ones. He led Russia into two extremely costly and unpopular wars, the first one with Japan (1904–5) and the second one with Germany (1914–18). Russia was completely unprepared for both of these wars, which created enormous suffering among the general population and paved the way for revolutions. Nicholas II barely survived the 1905 revolution, but the 1917 revolution came in the midst of World War I, when Nicholas was away from St. Petersburg acting as Supreme Commander of the military. This left his extremely unpopular wife the empress, and her hated spiritual advisor Gregor Rasputin (1869–1916) in charge of the government (Nicholas had taken command of the armed forces and moved to the Russian military headquarters at Mogilev, almost 800 kilometers away from St. Petersburg, in August 1915).[18]

The weak leadership of Louis XVI in France and Tsar Nicholas II in Russia is associated with a decline in the coercive power of the state, which has also been noted as an important factor in the lead-up to other revolutions (such as the Chinese Revolution[19]). Similarly, in the mid-1970s the Shah of Iran became inconsistent in his crackdowns on dissent, possibly because he had begun to receive medical treatment for the cancer that would end his life in 1980. When the Shah did go on the offensive, as with the attack against Khomeini published in the mass circulation newspaper *Etela'at* on January 7, 1978, the attacks were ill-timed, misjudged, and they invariably backfired. In different ways, particularly by financially supporting the expansion of mosques and religious centers and networks, and by making ill-timed direct public attacks on Khomeini, the Shah helped to position Khomeini rather than one of his secular rivals as the leader of the Anti-Shah Revolution.

As the intensity of revolutionary attacks on the ruling regime increases, pressure on the ruling elite to conform and obey also intensifies. The ruling regime itself embarks on a purification process, so that those members of the elite who are deemed to be less pure are peeled away, banished, jailed, and/or killed. But this process is only successful in upholding the ruling regime if the leader remains single-minded and consistent in words and actions. When both purification of the ruling elite takes place, so that some members are expelled, and the ruler is inconsistent in their actions, then the regime weakens and falls. For example, in his last year in power the Shah of Iran ordered the imprisonment of a number of the ruling elite, including his longtime prime minister Abbas Hoveyda (1919–79), in an attempt to purify the regime and appease the opposition.[20] In the case of Tsar Nicholas II of Russia, he had become so incapable of taking action that some other members of his ruling elite took the lead in attempting purification: The hated "holy man" Rasputin was murdered and plans were made to replace Nicholas II with his son and his younger brother Grand Duke Michael Alexandrovich (1878–1918). But the 1917 revolution derailed these plans.

The pressure for conformity is less severe among the anti-regime forces because they are made up of a number of different groups, hold different ideologies, and follow different leaders. What unites them at this stage is the goal of toppling the ruling regime. Repeatedly, we see the most ruthless of the opposition groups, the one that takes an extreme "whatever it takes" approach to grab and monopolize power, come to dominate center stage in the final phase of the revolution (as well as after the moderates have been driven out in the post-revolution period). This monopolization of power is greatly helped through war with internal and/or external enemies. For example, the almost continuous wars between 1792 and 1815 positioned France against a series of other nations who (purportedly) posed threats to France, with Emperor Napoleon as the French leader who French nationalists were obligated to support. The Napoleonic Wars coupled the fate of

France with that of Napoleon, so that support for the Emperor was synonymous with support for revolutionary France and the exporting of the revolution. The 1980–88 Iran–Iraq War came to play a similar role for Khomeini, as he positioned the interests of his regime with that of the Iranian nation. Khomeini decimated opposition to his regime during the eight-year Iran–Iraq War, using the excuse that opponents were traitors to the Iranian nation. By the end of the war, the opposition to Khomeini had been wiped out within Iran. In a similar way, following the 1917 revolution, the Bolsheviks used the civil war in Russia (roughly 1917–23) to gain absolute control, as Tony Brenton explains: "One of the by-products of the Civil War was 'War Communism' – a brutal imposition by the Bolsheviks of total control over the Russian economy and population, enforced by mass killings and arrests, which in many ways pre-figured Stalinism."[21]

After a ruling regime has been toppled, the revolutionary opposition often replaces the fight against the ruling regime with a fight against internal and external enemies, including foreign forces and their internal agents who are accused of planning to invade and overthrow the revolutionary government. In this way, the revolutionaries and the revolution are continuously confronted by real or imagined threatening powerful external enemies, and this also requires that so-called enemies within should be identified and eliminated. This theme of foreign threats is reflected in the rhetoric of leadership in Cuba, Venezuela, Iran, and a number of other countries that have experienced revolutions, with the United States being the nation most often identified as the external enemy threatening invasion. Indeed, anti-Americanism has become a master framework for revolutionaries around the world.[22]

The highlighting of external and internal threats, real or imagined, enables the ruling regime to put pressure on the population to conform and obey. Those who step out of line and attempt to rebel against the regime are branded as traitors and blamed for setbacks. For example, during the anti-government demonstrations in Iran, on October 26, 2022, about fifteen people were killed in attacks at the Shah Cheragh mausoleum, in the historic city of Shiraz. The government immediately blamed the attack on Sunni extremists, claiming that they were encouraged to use violence by the anti-government movement (the opposition blame the attacks on government forces, who are accused of attempting to deflect attention away from the government's unpopularity by fermenting Sunni–Shi'a conflicts). Of course, dictatorships have a long history of opportunistically using crisis incidents to strengthen their control of society and enforce conformity and obedience. Examples of such crisis incidents are Adolf Hitler's use of the fire on February 27, 1933, at the Reichstag Building, Berlin, to bring an end to civil liberties in Germany, and Khomeini's use of the 1979–80 hostage-taking crisis at the US Embassy in Tehran to persecute his opponents as traitors working for the United States.[23]

In summary, enormous pressures build up in the ruling regime to rigidly enforce conformity and obedience within its own elite ranks. But on the revolutionary side, the main focus of conformity and obedience is anti-regime rhetoric and actions. The different factions of the opposition are tolerated as long as they support efforts to overthrow the regime and do not attempt deal-making and compromise. Both sides use varieties of internal and external threats, real or fabricated, to enforce conformity and obedience.

Antagonistic Identity Transformation

During the Velvet Revolution, the movement against the communist dictatorship in Czechoslovakia underwent identity transformation, the third stage of mutual radicalization that characterizes relations between a revolutionary movement and the ruling regime they are trying to topple. As Miroslav Vanek and Pavel Mücke note: "Inspired by the rallying cry of Václav Havel during the demonstration on Wenceslas Square on November 22, 1989, Czechoslovakians across the land took up the shout 'We're not like them! We're not like them!'"[24] The chant "We're not like them!" was used by the Czechoslovakian anti-communist revolutionary movement to distance themselves from the ruling regime. This process of between-group distancing and within-group identity transformation is evident in the lead-up to all the major revolutions. This is a process of collective *becoming*, as the identity of the revolution takes shape and transforms and sweeps individuals along in a collective movement. As a military officer commented during the Terror of the French Revolution: "A man does not begin as a revolutionary; he becomes one."[25]

In the period leading up to the tipping point of regime change, the main unifying identity of anti-regime groups is constructed in opposition to the regime in power: "We're not like them!" Within this wide umbrella of anti-regime identity, a number of sub-identities associated with different anti-regime groups develop and compete for space. But after the tipping point is reached and the ruling regime collapses, open hostility and sometimes violent conflict breaks out between the competing revolutionary groups, as they each attempt to establish their group identity as *the one* that should dominate the new revolutionary government. For example, prior to the French Revolution, at different times the French nobility, the French bourgeoisie, and the French peasantry all acted against Louis XVI to bring about his downfall. However, after the execution of the king, it was the French bourgeoisie who more than other groups shaped the identity of revolutionary France, through Napoleon Bonaparte. In the lead-up to the 1917 Russian Revolution, the Bolsheviks were a relatively small group in the anti-Tsar movement. As Alan Bullock notes, "the Bolsheviks were the smallest of the Russian socialist parties, with no more than 25,000 members at the beginning of 1917."[26] However, after the abdication of Nicholas II in March 1917, there was chaos and a power vacuum in government, and Lenin persuaded the Bolsheviks to launch a coup. The revolution took on a Bolshevik identity, and this identity became dominant after the defeat of the White Army in November 1920. Similarly, during the 1977–8 buildup to the revolution in Iran, different secular and religious anti-Shah groups were actively working side-by-side to bring down the Shah. But after the fall of the Shah, it was the extremist followers of Khomeini who were the most ruthless and effective in the competition for power, and they stamped their identity on the revolution most decisively – eliminating a number of other secular and religious groups from the competition to eventually define the identity of the Iranian Revolution. They claimed it as a Khomeini-led Islamic revolution. In this way, numerous groups that had been active in the movement against the Shah, including pro-democracy women and men, were eliminated from the political arena in post-revolution Iran.

The process of antagonistic identity transformation involves the ruling regime and the revolutionaries moving further apart, developing identities in opposition to one another, and taking increasingly extreme positions. But this process of identity transformation is dynamic and the revolutionary identity that emerges is continually changing. This is in large part because revolutionary leaders have a tradition of transforming into dictators, with the habit of revisiting and reconstructing the past identity of the revolution to present themselves in a more positive light. For example, Joseph Stalin (1878–1953) failed to play a leading role in the 1917 revolution; Leon Trotsky (1879–1940) played a far more important role. However, as soon as Stalin became absolute dictator (from around 1929) he acted decisively to rewrite the history of the Russian Revolution, making his personal role central, next to Lenin's. Alan Bullock gives the example of when the Bolshevik leaders went to join Lenin on his train, who was returning to Russia (in 1917) after his long exile abroad. Stalin was not present at this event, but in his official biography published in 1940, it was reported that it was Stalin who went to meet Lenin:

> It was with great joy that the two leaders of the revolution, the two leaders of Bolshevism, met after their long separation. They were both about to launch into the struggle for the dictatorship of the working class to lead the struggle of the revolutionary people of Russia. During the journey to Petrograd Stalin informed Lenin of the state of affairs in the party and of the progress of the revolution.[27]

This fabrication typifies how the role of revolutionary leaders is revised after moderates are pushed aside and power monopoly is achieved by extremists following the early phase of the revolution.

The tradition of leaders reconstructing their own and the revolution's identity in retrospect was very much evident in the case of Napoleon and the French Revolution. Napoleon took pains to dress and present himself in line with the symbols and values of the revolution. As David Jordan describes, Napoleon:

> made a point of wearing the green uniform of an Imperial Guard . . . a gray redingote that became ratty with the years, and a cocked hat, an affectation he declined to alter. He liked the contrast of his own simplicity and even shabbiness amid the dazzling dress of his army. He made himself unique by dressing below his deeds and power. The conqueror presented himself as a soldier of the Revolution.[28]

But the story Napoleon wanted to tell the world about the revolution was reconstructed in his image; for example, he used major paintings of himself to present an identity that manufactured and altered reality, such as the painting *Napoleon Crossing the Great Saint Bernard Pass* (painted by Jacques-Louis David). David Jordan has noted that "as the portrait of the young hero the painting is unsurpassed"; however, "virtually everything about the painting is legendary . . ."[29] Napoleon had at least four copies of this painting made and the fictional image it presents became part of the legend of the revolution and its hero.

The reconstruction of the past to shape the identity of the revolution takes place in a way that further distances the post-revolutionary regime and society from everything that existed before the revolution. The revolutionaries attempt to transform the identity of the new regime and the new society to be in line with the goals of the revolution as espoused by them, and any links with the past that do not agree with their interpretation are depicted as regressive, backward, and dangerous. This goes hand in hand with the complete rejection of those with ties to the old regime, as well as those actually or apparently trying to take society back to what it was prior to the revolution. After each revolution, the new revolutionary identity is fiercely protected – and distanced from all that is positioned as anti-revolutionary. This positioning and repositioning, to arrive at a pure, revolutionary identity, is accompanied with many casualties. As Jacques Mallet du Pan (1749–1800) famously noted, revolutions devour their own children.

The identity purification process of revolutions intensifies after regime change, and there is a predictable culling of moderates, further radicalization, bloodletting, and coming to power (for a while) of the most ruthless and extreme factions and leaders. To some extent, the ruthlessness of the revolutionaries when they come to power is a continuation of the ruthlessness that existed in the pre-revolution period. The security apparatus that operated before the revolution continues more or less intact after the revolution (in Iran, after a brief interval, most of the Shah's security agents were rehired by the mullahs). But there is a new zeal and even greater ruthlessness that comes after the revolution, and the source of this is worth pondering. This is how Charles Walton raises the question in relation to the Terror in the French Revolution:

> If the legacy of the Old Regime policing goes a long way in accounting for the Revolution's policing of public opinion, it does not explain the Terror's lethal brutality. It is one thing to monitor and manipulate opinions, quite another to send individuals to the scaffold for them. What, then, drove revolutionaries to kill each other for speech and opinions?[30]

This is a question I asked myself in Iran in 1979 and 1980, as the extremist followers of Khomeini ruthlessly wiped out all their relatively moderate secular and Islamic rivals. One by one, the relatively moderate leaders and their followers were eliminated – Karim Sanjabi (1905–95), Mehdi Bazargan (1907–95), Sadegh Ghotbzadeh (1936–82), Abolhassan Banisadr (1933–2021), and many others were either killed or forced to escape and go into hiding outside Iran. The Tudeh Party, the Soviet-backed communists in Iran, attempted to survive by backing everything that the Khomeini extremists undertook. However, in 1982–3 there was a severe crackdown on the Tudeh Party, and soon after I witnessed Tudeh Party leaders appear on Iranian television to confess to their alleged treasonous behavior. A number of Tudeh Party leaders were killed during interrogations involving torture.[31] In answering Charles Walton's question (posed above), "What, then, drove revolutionaries to kill each other for speech and opinions?" I argue that in their drive to monopolize power and resources, the pro-Khomeini extremists recognized the effectiveness of purifying the identity of the revolution to make sure it emerges as Islamic in the image of Khomeini. This same trend characterizes the move to extremism and the elimination of moderates during the post–regime-change period in other revolutions.

Concluding Comment

Through the process of mutual radicalization, the ruling regime and the revolutionary opposition move further apart, purifying their collective identities in opposition to one another. The ruling regime enforces conformity and obedience, so that all elites are forced to either strictly adhere to the ideology of the regime or suffer being banished and eliminated in one way or another. The revolutionary opposition groups go through two phases of identity development. During the first phase, which lasts until regime change, the global identity of opposition groups is anti-regime. With some exceptions, the different opposition groups are relatively tolerant toward one another and all operate under the broad umbrella of being anti-regime. But after regime change and an initial phase during which different radical and moderate groups share power, all moderates are swept aside and the most ruthless and determined extremist group and their leader comes to power, defining the identity of the revolution. The identity of the revolution is purified and the history of the revolution is revised, so that the extremists in power are positioned as the only true revolutionaries.

CHAPTER 6

Psychological Stepping Stones to Revolution

Although the tipping point of regime collapse often arrives suddenly and is not predicted even by those leading the revolution, the sequence of psychological changes that lead to revolution is patterned, predictable, and relatively slow in some domains of behavior (e.g., leader–follower relations are very often slow to change). These psychological changes can be envisaged as stepping stones, each step sequentially preparing the ground for the next step. What changes from step to step is the psychological experiences of people moving along this path, including their perceptions of and willingness to take risks, together with their estimations of the likelihood of achieving regime change. All along this revolutionary path, the driver of behavior is psychological factors, including feelings of relative deprivation, perceptions of risk, and the estimated likelihood of regime change.

But we should not limit our attention to individuals moving independently along the sequence of steps because in the lead-up to revolution group-level processes are far more powerful and consequential than individual-level processes. Indeed, group-level processes shape individual-level processes, with the direction being from societies to cells rather than cells to societies.[1] For example, it is through social interactions and shared narratives in communities that individuals arrive at basic beliefs about how fairly they are being treated in society; how just, legitimate, and stable the ruling regime is; and what possibilities are available for change toward a better society. Beliefs in these domains are collaboratively constructed and collectively upheld, particularly through shared narratives as part of daily social life. Beliefs do not just develop in isolation within independent individuals.

Thus, a continuous theme in this discussion is the dominance of collective over individual processes and often also the dominance of irrational over rational processes. Just as I emphasized in our discussion of mutual radicalization in the last chapter, in the processes leading to revolution individuals are pushed along as part of collectives and they are moved by strong feelings to take risks and put themselves in harm's way. As part of a revolutionary movement, individuals conform and practice obedience in their behavior; these behaviors would be less likely if they were given the opportunity to act as rational, independent individuals who could make objective cost–benefit analyses.

Assessing and Facing Risks

> Marie Jeanne Trumeau, *wife of Bertin, fish merchant, was condemned to hang for inciting arson and looting while crying "Long live the Third Estate" during the riot against the manufacturer Réveillon on 28 April 1789 . . ..* Marie Charpentier, wife of Haucourt, *washerwoman from Faubourg Saint-Marcel, the only woman among the official "Conquerors of the Bastille," was crippled during the siege of the fortress.*[2]

Revolutions bring enormous risks and dangers to the individuals and groups who challenge the ruling regime. During the French Revolution, the two cases cited above by Dominique Godineau reflect the experiences of the many brave women who risked life and limb in support of the Third Estate (consisting of the commoners, the other two estates being the clergy and the aristocracy). As I write this chapter, thousands of courageous women – many of them teenagers – are challenging the Mullah's dictatorship in Iran and attempting to mobilize a revolution. Some of these women have been beaten, raped, and killed by the Mullah's thugs. Despite the severe dangers faced by women confronting unjust regimes, from the French Revolution to today, some women continue on this path. Like all revolutionaries, they are inspired by ideals and visions of a far superior alternative world that they believe is possible.

The most important component of any revolutionary movement is faith in revolutionary ideals and an image of an alternative society that is *imagined* to be better and possible. The most important contribution of Lenin, Mao, Castro, Khomeini, and other revolutionary leaders has been to persuade enough people to have faith in revolutionary ideals and the possibility of a better society, so they become willing to take greater risks and make more serious sacrifices for the revolution. In order to be persuasive, such revolutionary leaders make promises that portray an ideal society where people enjoy freedom, equality, and material benefits – promises they invariably do not keep after they come to power (either because they do not want to or because sometimes they are not able to).

In the last chapter I outlined the process of mutual radicalization through which the ruling regime and the revolutionary opposition become increasingly radicalized against one another, taking on ever more purified oppositional collective identities, so that compromise becomes impossible. In this chapter, I further clarify the central role of revolutionary ideals in mobilizing the anti-regime forces, as well as the basic psychological stepping stones for collective mobilization and sacrifice to bring down the regime. These psychological stepping stones are derived from the theories discussed in Chapters 2 and 3, and particularly the preconditions identified as leading to feelings of fraternal relative deprivation (discussed in Chapter 3).[3]

These stepping stones can be envisaged as developmental stages on the road to fully participating in revolution, leading people to:

1. become aware of an alternative ideal society
2. feel deeply dissatisfied with their lives in the present society
3. see their dissatisfaction as not being their own fault
4. interpret the ruling regime as being responsible for their dissatisfaction
5. believe that the ruling regime is illegitimate
6. conceive that it is possible to overthrow the ruling regime
7. have faith that the fall of the ruling regime will be followed by progress toward an ideal society
8. be prepared to risk making serious personal and collective sacrifices in the cause of progress toward the ideal society

The above eight steps prepare the ground for people to become part of a collective mobilization toward revolution and regime change. All of the steps are based on emotion-driven subjective assessments and experiences, often influenced by factors that remain implicit rather than explicit for the individuals involved. That is, these processes are often characterized by irrationality rather than rationality.

Step 1: People Become Aware of an Alternative Ideal Society

The history of the Quotations from Chairman Mao Tse-tung is probably the most astounding publishing tale ever. The estimated number of official volumes printed between 1966 and 1969 ranges just over a billion, second only to the Holy Bible in terms of circulation numbers and this figure even excludes local prints, foreign language editions, internal army volumes, and innumerable mimeographed or handwritten collections … During the Decade of Cultural Revolution, all in all some 10.8 billion Mao texts or posters were printed by the state, making Mao the best-selling author ever . . .[4]

In order to gain a large following, revolutionary leaders do not have to portray the ideal society in detail, nor do they need to demonstrate the ideal society as being workable or feasible. Rather, like the ideals presented by the Holy Bible (mentioned in the above quotation by Daniel Leese), the Torah, the Koran, and other religious texts, descriptions of the ideal society put forward by revolutionary leaders have to inspire followers to have faith in an ideal future society that can be achieved through revolution, motivating them to make sacrifices toward achieving that society. In this very important sense, the task of revolutionaries is similar to that of religious prophets and missionaries – to emotionally move people, to sweep them along, to capture them as part of the collective transformation toward an imagined ideal society (or heaven, in an imagined afterlife).

The process of persuasion in both religious and revolutionary movements – as well as marketing in twenty-first-century economies – predominantly relies on the *peripheral route*. This means that it focuses more on how the message makes people feel rather than relying on the *central route*, which emphasizes the content of the message, its logical arguments, and factual details.[5] Being persuaded by revolutionary leaders to join a revolutionary movement, with all the risks and dangers involved, is more a matter of being carried along by emotions and *feelings* of injustice rather than by objective rationality and cold, calculated facts and logic.[6] After all, if each individual actually weighs up the costs and benefits of participating in the revolution in a rational way, the most cost-effective strategy might well be to step aside and let others take the risk of facing the bullets and truncheons of the security forces – and then step forward to reap any benefits that become available if the revolution actually succeeds (and very few of them do achieve regime change). But revolutions come about when people who join the collective opposition do not use rational cost–benefit analysis, instead allowing their feelings to move and guide them as part of the larger anti-government movement. In the major revolutions, persuasion through the peripheral route led enormous numbers of people to be moved by emotions to take to the streets and march in support of regime change. In order for this to happen, these people have to become convinced that there really are alternative possibilities, imagined other worlds that are better than their present one.

It is the imagined nature of other possible worlds that gives a central place to psychology, and more specifically to irrational processes and emotions. In this way, "selling a revolution" becomes similar to selling a car or other similar products. The typical television advertisement used to sell a car shows a group of happy young people or a fun-loving family driving along a beach or up an open mountain road (never in a traffic jam, which would be more realistic). The television advertisement does not give any technical specifics about the car and its engine, but it does lead us to associate the car with positive emotions and experiences. We come to *feel* good about the car without actually knowing anything about its performance and engineering details. We feel that the car being advertised represents a positive improvement for us. Similarly, revolutionary leaders advertising the ideal society do not need to provide practical details; all they need to do is communicate an appealing image of an alternative society that they convince us is within reach.

Step 2: People Feel Deeply Dissatisfied with Their Lives in the Present Society

As William Panning points out, "encouraging social comparisons of income or wealth is a tactic frequently used by political movements to arouse opposition to the existing institutions or policies of a society."[7] As I have discussed in Chapter 3 of this text, influencing social comparison processes is a tactic routinely used by those interested in changing how people feel about the present economic, cultural, and political arrangements. Extensive research literature shows that social comparison processes are a ubiquitous characteristic of human behavior.[8] The style of social comparisons undertaken is strongly influenced by culture, and by norms more specifically.[9] Leaders can influence the norms regulating social comparison styles, so that, for example, people make social comparisons with targets who are much better off than themselves, or with themselves as they could have been in a more ideal world.

Making social comparisons with targets who are much better off is associated with rising expectations, feelings of relative deprivation, and actual rebellion.[10] That is, people who experience rising expectations are likely to feel relatively deprived because they are comparing themselves with social comparison targets who are better off than they are in the present. For example, they compare their actual living conditions with the much better living conditions they expected to have, resulting in them feeling relative deprivation and joining social movements to remedy the situation. There is evidence that the urban social disorders of the 1960s stemmed from rising expectations and feelings of relative deprivation.[11]

The central role of social comparisons in the process of collective mobilization underscores the important role of psychology in revolutions. From the motivation to make social comparisons with others or with the self as one might have been, to whether upward or downward social comparisons are made, to how the results of social comparisons are interpreted – all the key elements of social comparisons are shaped by subjective rather than objective criteria. Changing any of the elements of social comparison, such as whether to make upward or downward comparisons, can change the outcome. However, the lack of objective criteria does not mean that only intra-individual factors shape social comparisons. Far from it: the collective culture dominant in the larger society strongly influences the social comparisons we make.[12]

In the lead-up to revolutions, changes in the collective culture influence people to make social comparisons that result in them feeling fraternal deprivation. These cultural changes can be brought about through revolutionary leadership. For example, revolutionary leaders before the French, Russian, Chinese, Cuban, and Iranian revolutions all encouraged upward social comparisons, resulting in feelings of fraternal deprivation. But in order for fraternal deprivation to result in nonconformist collective action, individuals must interpret their unsatisfactory situation as not being their own fault.

Step 3: People See Their Dissatisfaction as Not Being Their Own Fault

"Why am I poor? Why are some people in my society so enormously rich compared to me?" *Attributional style* refers to how people explain the circumstances in their lives, such as their levels of poverty and wealth. There are differences across individuals and groups in attributional styles. For example, some individuals are more likely to interpret their conditions, such as poverty, as the result of factors that are internal to themselves (e.g., "I am poor because I lack talent and valued skills") and stable and constant across time (e.g., "I was born with my lack of talent; it is fixed and not something I can change"). Attributional style is related to motivation and action, in the sense that how individuals interpret the causes of events in their lives will influence the kinds of actions they take.[13] For example, if Jack feels that he is poor because he lacks talent, and lack of talent will keep him poor in the future, then he is less likely to join collective action to change a political system that discriminates against people like him (who are poor and low in education) and prevents them from improving their lives. After all, Jack believes that it is his fault he is poor.

Individuals are not born with particular attributional styles that are already developed. Rather, attributional styles are in large part learned through socialization processes and vary across cultures and groups.[14] For example, right-wing political orientation and higher income is associated with attributing the causes of poverty to factors internal to individuals (e.g., "Those people are poor because they do not try hard enough and, besides, they lack talent").[15] Certain ideologies dominant in society serve to nurture particular attributional styles. For example, the American Dream ideology, the idea that the United States is an open meritocracy and anyone can make it in America, is in line with self-help and individual responsibility; it nurtures an attributional style that interprets the causes of poverty and related outcomes to factors internal to individuals. However, more liberal and politically left-wing individuals adopt attributional styles that assume the causes of circumstances such as poverty and unemployment as being more external to individuals (e.g., poverty could be solved by appropriate government policies and progressive economic programs) than internal to individuals (e.g., laziness, lack of skills and motivation).

Step 4: People Interpret the Ruling Regime as Being Responsible for Their Dissatisfaction

Revolutionaries face the challenge of persuading people to attribute the causes of poverty, unemployment, poor education opportunities, inequality, lack of employment opportunities, nepotism, corruption, and other related problems to the ruling regime, and not to other sources such as human nature in general or their own individual characteristics specifically. Thus, before the revolution, revolutionaries must nurture external and stable attributions – the ruling regime is to blame for our problems; as long as this regime is in power our problems will continue, and life will only improve toward the revolutionary ideal after regime change.

The ruling regime must be seen by ordinary people as being the stable cause of their societal and personal shortcomings. This perceived stability shuts the door to the possibility of reform being the solution to the problems confronting people. Moderate elements in the anti-regime movement are often satisfied with bringing about reforms rather than a complete regime collapse – which tends to be destructive, chaotic, and unpredictable in outcome, often leading to extremists (at least temporarily) coming to power. For example, in the lead-up to the French and Russian revolutions, the aristocracy were critical of the king/tsar and wanted changes, but they did not seek the downfall of the hereditary monarchy. Similarly, in the

1970s moderates in Iran wanted to establish constitutional monarchy, not to bring down the Shah and destroy the monarchy altogether. In the Cuban post-revolution context, there were possibilities for a more moderate rather than revolutionary outcome to regime change.[16] But by interpreting the ruling regime as a stable and unchanging source of problems, extremists in revolutionary movements reject the idea that the regime can be reformed and, instead, give priority to regime change. This justification for regime change is partly based on assessments of the legitimacy of the ruling regime.

Step 5: People Believe that the Ruling Regime Is Illegitimate

An essential precondition for individuals to support and join revolutionary movements is the perception that the ruling regime is illegitimate, meaning that it is seen as morally invalid.[17] David Beetham argues that there are three main dimensions to perceived legitimacy, and these can be labeled as legal, cultural, and consensual: Did the regime come to power by following the rules? Are the rules accepted by both the rulers and the people? Do the people consent to the existing power relations and rulers?[18] When individuals make personal material gains, this increases the probability that authorities are evaluated positively.[19] But it is not just *distributive justice*, the distribution of rewards, that determines evaluations of authorities; *procedural justice*, the perceived fairness of the procedures used to distribute rewards, also has been found to influence these evaluations.[20] Thus, perceptions of both procedural and distributive justice influence the perceived legitimacy of a ruling regime.

The task of revolutionaries is to persuade people that the ruling regime is illegitimate, and that they have both the right and the duty to force regime change. Because people have a tendency to interpret the world as just, a place where good things happen to good people and bad things happen to bad people, their tendency is to interpret the ruling regime as legitimate rather than illegitimate (this relates to our earlier discussion of the justice motive in Chapter 3). Consequently, revolutionaries are to some extent working against the normative tendencies of people to interpret the ruling regime as legitimate rather than illegitimate.

In order to influence people to see the ruling regime as illegitimate, revolutionaries must also overcome the tendency for people to be conformist and obedient in interactions with authorities. Early research showed that even a person in a guard uniform will be more likely to be obeyed by strangers asked to carry out small tasks (e.g., to move away from a bus stop) in a field setting than a person dressed as a milkman or a civilian.[21] Part of the power of authorities, including those in government bureaucracies, is the protections they get from one another against any criticisms and attacks on their legitimacy from outsiders (such as ordinary citizens).[22] Thus, revolutionaries must work against the self-protective characteristic of government authorities, so that at least some of those working for the government join the revolution. This transformation did come about in the French, Russian, Chinese, Cuban, and Iranian revolutions, so that the ruling regimes were gutted by rebellion from within as government employees joined the revolution.

Step 6: People Conceive It Is Possible to Overthrow the Ruling Regime

Revolutionaries face the task of not only convincing people that the ruling regime is illegitimate, but also that it can and should be overthrown. This is an extremely difficult task to achieve because people tend to see the existing living arrangements as normal and "the way things should be." We are socialized to live according to the normative system and rhythms of our own societies. In the process of socialization, we enter society and learn to become social beings, just as society and its normative system becomes a part of us and regulates our behavior.[23] This two-way integration leads us to experience the way things are in our society as natural and the way things should be. This experience is enhanced when the pace of change is slow in systems of government.

Often the existing governance arrangements have been stable for very long periods of time and are the only arrangements that people have known for all of their lives. For example, before the revolutions in America, France, Russia, China, and Iran, the only system of government that most people had known was hereditary monarchy. Because of legitimizing ideologies such as the "divine right of kings," for many people in these societies, it seemed inconceivable that the ruling monarch (emperor) could be overthrown. After all, this system of government seemed natural and inevitable, and many people believed it was put into place by God. This is partly why revolutionaries very seldom manage to persuade people that the ruling regime can and must be overthrown.

Another factor that helps to strengthen continuity and stability, and work against disruption and change, is our behavioral inclination toward conformity and obedience. Psychological research supports the view that people are for the most part conformists to local norms and obedient to established authorities.[24] Through socialization processes, individuals come to adopt as their guide to behavior the culture of their own society, with values, norms, and rules for the generally accepted "correct way to behave." In this way, different practices are followed by people in different societies, with each group believing and insisting that their way of doing things is the correct one. This is the universal tendency toward ethnocentrism, particularly well documented in cross-cultural and anthropological research.[25] For example, in Shi'a Islam a man can have four permanent and numerous temporary wives (a temporary marriage could be for varying lengths of time, from minutes to decades).[26] On the other hand, some groups in Kinnaur, Western Himalaya, practice *fraternal polyandry*, where one woman marries one or more brothers (i.e., all the brothers marry the same woman).[27] Each group sees their marriage practices as correct. This tendency to perceive one's own cultural practices as the correct ones includes historical practices and beliefs concerning governance, together with the relationship between the rulers and ordinary citizens. The ruling regime is seen to be part of the natural and inevitable world order both by the elite rulers themselves and by ordinary citizens.

Our tendency to directly or indirectly support continuity in systems of government runs parallel to continuity in habits in everyday life. *Habitual behavior*, actions performed daily in stable contexts, helps us to weave through our daily activities without necessarily attending to the details of what we are doing.[28] Consequently, we are able to invest cognitively in new tasks and challenges that are more demanding of our attention, as well as to make progress in new projects. Habitual behavior is also associated with our (typically stable) employment, family, and social roles, all of which support certain role-associated patterned behaviors. For example, consider the case of Jean, who is a middle-school teacher and a mother of six-year-old twin boys. Continuities across time and context in Jean's role as middle-school teacher, mother, PTA member, and other related roles also support certain of Jean's habitual behaviors, such as cycling in the neighborhood with her twin children and other children and their parents, as well as participating in clean-up projects around the local canal.

Thus, the regularity and continuity of certain patterns in our society, in those around us, in our social roles, and in our own behavior leads us to experience our current world – together with its government – to a large degree as natural and the way things should be. For many people, the downfall of the present political system and the rulers seems inconceivable. But even if such drastic changes were possible, would they lead to improvements for society and the self?

Step 7: People Have Faith That the Fall of the Ruling Regime Will Be Followed by Progress Toward an Ideal Society

As activists in Iran attempted to overthrow the Shah's dictatorship in Iran in the 1970s, I heard a lot of discussion around the question, "What if the Shah's regime is replaced by an even harsher dictatorship?" All revolutionaries confront this question about the possibility of the next regime being even worse than the regime they are trying to overthrow. Indeed, for most Iranians the mullahs' dictatorship has proven to be even worse than the Shah's regime. The suffering of some groups, such as educated women, at the hands of the mullahs is particularly cruel. Similarly, for many French people after the Great French Revolution, the Terror and what followed was even worse than rule by King Louis XVI. And for those sent to Siberia by Stalin, and those suffering through the Cultural Revolutions in China (in the 1960s), the new revolutionary regime seemed far worse than the former regime. Consequently, revolutionaries face the challenge of presenting an ideal that inspires people to action and sacrifice, while reassuring them that their lives will be improved after regime change – even though history provides many examples where this is not the case for everyone, or even for most people.

A close examination of promises made before revolutions and the actions taken by revolutionaries after regime change shows that revolutionaries are not careful in promising ideal societies that they can actually deliver. This is because before regime change, revolutionaries are tempted to make any and every promise in order to mobilize people to join the anti-regime movement. But after regime change, when revolutionaries come to power, they are confronted with practical resource limitations and often find that what they had promised is impossible or inexpedient to deliver. In the domain of freedoms, they now find that what they had promised allows their political competitors to criticize and weaken them. As a result, their promises tend to be erased and they use their power to force the rewriting of history.

There are numerous examples of revolutionaries going back on, and even rewriting, their promises after coming to power; indeed, this is the rule rather than the exception. Joseph Stalin's falsifications of what happened leading up to and during the 1917 Russian Revolution has been much discussed by Leon Trotsky and others.[29] The process of rewriting Soviet history continued after Stalin as well.[30] The Chinese Revolution and important events that followed, such as the Cultural Revolution, have been rewritten a number of times with dramatic twists and turns depending on the factions in and out of power in China.[31] In Cambodia, the Pol Pot regime tortured and killed people who remembered a different history of the Cambodian Communist Party and the revolution than the one they wanted to tell.[32] The story of the Cuban Revolution and Fidel Castro has involved a great deal of rewriting and myth making, so that it became difficult to differentiate between actual and imagined history.[33] In the case of Iran, I witnessed how after Khomeini and his extremist followers took full control around 1980, they systematically censored Khomeini's speeches and all the promises made before the revolution.

Given that revolutions do not lead to the realization of all the promises made by revolutionary leaders, are they still worth going through? Another way of addressing this question is to consider the changes that would have been made in France, Russia, China, Cuba, and Iran without revolutions, and assess whether more progress would have been made through peaceful incremental reforms rather than giant disruptions resulting from revolutions. Greg Berman and Aubrey Fox are among those who have argued for the benefits of incremental rather than radical change, and I am very sympathetic to this view.[34] But unfortunately, we will never know if "a little change in a time of change" would have led to better outcomes than revolutions because the leadership of King Louis XVI of France, Tzar Nicholas II of Russia, Emperor Ching Hsuan-Tung of China (who was a child during his reign), President Fulgencio Batista of Cuba, and Shah Mohammad Reza Pahlavi did not provide a path to meaningful reform in their countries. These leaders were part of the reason why there was explosive and often destructive revolution rather than steady reform, and why many ordinary people felt compelled to take enormous risks and to make life-and-death sacrifices.

Step 8: People Are Prepared to Risk Making Serious Sacrifices in the Cause of Progress Toward the Ideal Society

Revolutionaries have the task of persuading people to face bullets and bayonets, with no guarantee that they will succeed in overthrowing the ruling regime or that they will make any real progress toward the ideal revolutionary society. This raises the following question: Under what conditions will people make personal sacrifices for the collective revolutionary cause? Different explanatory traditions can be identified, each with supporting evidence.[35] One of these is a rationalist-materialist tradition, arguing that people will take part in collective action when they think it will succeed and bring them resource benefits (discussed in Chapter 2).

Another is an identity-based approach, which sees people participating in collective action when they self-categorize with the group that is committed to take collective action – even though the individuals involved might be skeptical of the likelihood of reaching their idealistic goal (discussed in Chapter 3). This identity tradition is also in line with evidence that individuals will join collective movements and make sacrifices when their participation results in them feeling a sense of personal significance.[36]

In addition to the rationalist-materialist and identity approaches to explaining why some people take such enormous risks during the fight to bring about regime change, we should also consider an irrationalist-normative perspective. The two components of this perspective are, first, that during the collective mobilization against the ruling regime, there are gradual changes in the normative systems (including norms, rules, values, and beliefs) that regulate behavior and influence people about what is the "right thing to do" in any given situation. During the collective mobilization that takes place before major revolutions, influenced particularly by revolutionary leadership, these normative systems lead people to adopt nonnormative, anti-government behavior as correct. In essence, the right thing to do becomes to join the revolution, with strong passions and emotions driving and shaping the conviction that "we must bring down the government."

But people are not necessarily aware of such changes in normative systems or of the influence these changes have on their behavior. In this sense, the influence of these changes is irrational and particularly driven by emotions (such as anger, and even hatred), rather than being rational and driven by objective cost–benefit analyses. This involves people throwing themselves into the revolutionary movement with passion – to stand barehanded in front of helmeted troops and bayonets, throw stones and Molotov cocktails at armored cars and tanks, and risk life and limb for the revolution and the great leader (or the "Great Helmsman" as Mao Zedong came to be known).

Concluding Comment

The psychological stepping stones to participation in revolutionary movements involve cognitive, emotional, and behavioral changes in collectives and individuals. This is very much an irrational and passion-driven process, in the sense that individuals are often unaware of the factors influencing their actions, and they are driven by strong feelings. Second, in these changes, the collective is supreme, and the direction of influence is very much from societies to cells rather than from cells to societies. There is a change in what is accepted as correct behavior, so that it becomes normative to disobey and become nonconformist in relation to authorities.

While the sequence of stepping stones I have outlined, from becoming aware of an alternative ideal society to being prepared to risk making serious personal and collective sacrifices in the cause of progress toward the ideal society, is fairly predictable, this does not translate to predictability in either the timing or the actuality of regime collapse. There are many cases where large numbers of people in a society, even the majority, progress through the psychological stepping stones I have outlined and make enormous sacrifices to overthrow the ruling elite, but regime collapse and regime change does not happen. Recent examples include the movements to overthrow the Assad regime in Syria, Putin in Russia, and the mullahs in Iran – all three movements *could* have ended in regime change, but so far have not.

PART III

What Happens after Revolutionary Regime Change?

How do revolutions happen? This is the main question psychological researchers and also lay people have asked about revolutions. The society we live in seems so natural, stable, and difficult to transform or even alter in small ways – as many of us have said when we try to bring about change. The way things are appears normal. How is it that suddenly under some circumstances the world turns upside down, to borrow a phrase from the historian Christopher Hill in his writings about the English Revolution? What turns the world upside down? The intense focus on this question seems natural. But there is an even more profound question about revolutions, one that has seldom been addressed, and almost never by psychologists: What happens after revolutions?

From a psychological perspective, the most important aspect of what happens after revolutions is *continuity* – rather than change – in certain styles of behavior. The three chapters in Part III explore this theme of behavioral continuity in collective and individual behavior. Continuity in behavior is seen by revolutionaries as a stumbling block, preventing them from reaching the ideal revolutionary society. For this reason, some revolutionaries have followed Mao Zedong's example of trying to achieve perpetual revolution (discussed in Chapter 7), where revolutionary change is continuously a priority. Perpetual revolution is an attempt to overcome the influence of cultural carriers that support continuities in behavioral style (discussed in Chapter 8).

Much of our focus in this exploration of the psychology of revolution is framed from a "societies to cells" perspective, with considerable emphasis on macro processes. However, personality factors also have an important role in revolutions. Of particular importance are the personality characteristics of extremists (including the extremist revolutionary leader) and moderates in the revolutionary movement. Of course, I am using the term "moderates" in relative terms; many of those labeled "moderates" in this discussion of revolutions would be labeled "extremists" in other contexts. They are only

99

characterized as "moderates" relative to the extremists; for example, the Iranian prime minister Mehdi Bazargan is labeled "moderate" in relation to extremists such as Khomeini and his supporters, just as relative to the Jacobin Club and Maximillian Robespierre (1758–94), most of the aristocratic critics of XVI were moderate. Certain personality differences were associated with the different tactics of the extremists and the moderates for getting to, and remaining in, power. The ruthlessness of extremists and their "ends justify the means" approach in large part explains why they come to achieve power dominance (for a while) after numerous revolutions.

CHAPTER 7

Behavioral Continuity and Attempts at Perpetual Revolution

I regret the fact that this [behavior] has taken such deep root in people. I'd almost say in our genes, because it's been twenty years since we got rid of Communism, but people still act as if nothing had changed. They steal away merrily, and they think they are stealing from the state, from someone who is extorting ungodly taxes from them, and I don't know what else. Which is also true, but they steal from private companies too, and they somehow can't stop doing it. They just keep on stealing.

A technical college teacher explaining the continuation of behavior (stealing) before and after the anti-communist revolution (1989) in Czech society[1]

Revolution changes the ruling regime, the political leaders of society. However, both the new leaders in power and the masses they govern were socialized in the society that existed before the revolution. They acquired their styles of thinking and acting, problem-solving, habits, motivations, values, social skills, trust in and honesty toward others, ways of relating to authority and leadership, and all their other psychological characteristics in the context of the *ancien regime*. The revolution wrestles power from one group and hands it to another, but this does not change the cognition and actions of the new group in power, or the behavior of followers, or relationships between leaders and followers, or between different groups of followers themselves. On the contrary, there is a strong tendency for both leaders and followers to continue, or to return to if they were temporarily abandoned, their former styles of behaviors. Continuity in behavioral style is so strong after regime change that we are tempted to agree with the technical college teacher quoted at the beginning of this chapter that behavioral style continues because it is in our genes. However, such an interpretation is overly simplistic and misleading, although the environmental factors that shape continuity are in some respects just as rigid and low in plasticity and challenging to change as are genetic factors.

In this chapter I discuss behavioral continuity after revolutions, as well as attempts by revolutionaries to manage and in some domains to end behavioral continuity, so as to maneuver society toward their revolutionary ideals. All major revolutions, irrespective of their avowed Marxist, nationalist, fascist, Islamic, or other ideologies, have faced the same challenge of trying to control or even end behavioral continuity, and their programs for dealing with behavioral continuity have evolved to be in some important respects very similar. All of these different programs are designed to try to achieve perpetual, permanent, or continuous revolution – the idea being that the revolution should not happen at one point in time and then stop, but should develop as a continuous process without necessarily having an end. The perpetual revolution is seen to be needed by (at least some) revolutionaries because there is no guarantee that people, including the revolutionaries themselves, will continue to change in the direction of the goals of the revolution, if they change at all. Indeed, both revolutionaries and the masses often change (or do not change) in ways that contradict the goals of the revolution. At no stage does the struggle to reach revolutionary goals end because at all times there exists the possibility of backward movement to the situation before the revolution.

This chapter is in three main parts. In the first part, I discuss the challenge of behavioral continuity after revolutions, when regime change has taken place but most people continue to behave as they did before the revolution. In the second part, I examine the idea of continuous revolution, put forward as a broad solution to what, from the revolutionary perspective, is stagnation after revolutions. In the third part, I examine more specific programs used by revolutionaries to try to manage and prevent behavioral continuity after revolutions.

It is not always clear the extent to which revolutionaries are explicitly influenced by one another in the programs they adopt, but there is no doubt that there are similarities in their programs. For example, the Cultural Revolution launched by Khomeini in Iran in 1980[2] was in many important respects similar to that launched by Mao in China in the mid-1960s.[3] In both China and Iran, the Cultural Revolution was a disaster for the country and national interests (and probably resulted in anti-regime attitudes[4]), but it was a means through which the grip of the extremist revolutionary leader (Mao and Khomeini) could be tightened and the revolutionary movement could be maintained in the image of the leader.[5] However, rather than Khomeini copying Mao, this might be a case of the same solution being adopted by two similarly old and extremist revolutionary leaders, Khomeini on the extreme political right and Mao on the extreme political left, faced with very similar challenges in the post-revolutionary period.

Behavioral Continuity and Political Plasticity after Revolutions

I began teaching at universities in Tehran, the capital city of Iran, in the so-called Spring of Revolution, in 1979. The Shah had escaped and no one political group had managed to gain power dominance immediately after the revolution. The atmosphere on university campuses was exhilarating and liberating. Students were using their newfound freedoms to express themselves in pamphlets, debates, poetry competitions, theatrical dramas, political rallies, and in just about every other way imaginable. There were scores of newspapers and hundreds of pamphlets, representing so many different political viewpoints. Female faculty and female students participated relatively freely in the political and cultural activities; they were not forced to wear the Islamic hijab. People felt liberated.

A visitor who knew what universities in Iran were like before the revolution might well witness this post-revolution scene in 1979 and imagine that the revolution had changed everything. Whereas before the revolution, faculty and students were afraid to openly speak out about politics and to be critical of political leaders, now they felt free to express their views and frankly raise criticisms. We had very lively, uninhibited debates in my classes, with students expressing a wide range of opinions. It seemed that we had left behind dictatorship, censorship, and the closed society. The Spring of Revolution brought great hope. The government was headed by Prime Minister Mehdi Bazargan (1907–95), a moderate Islamic politician. Barzargan was married to a distant relative of mine, and even before the revolution he insisted that his wife wear the Islamic hijab. But he was seen as mild-mannered and moderate – not at all radical or dangerous. Bazargan received graduate education in France and seemed conventional in his views about education.

Unlike moderates such as Bazargan, the radical followers of Khomeini were very unhappy with the reopening of society and the resumption of everyday life after the revolution. Khomeini's extremist followers were particularly unhappy with the reopening of universities, and there were two main reasons for this.

The first reason why Khomeini's radical followers were dissatisfied with the state of universities in 1979 is that a wide range of secular and religious groups now enjoyed freedom on university campuses. These groups included a variety of atheists, Marxists, feminists, as well as left-wing and liberal Islamists who opposed Khomeini's interpretations of Islam – which happened to endorse an Islamic dictatorship, through the idea that governance must be through a Muslim cleric who is the ultimate decider on all matters (*velayat-e faghih*). Khomeini's followers wanted *only* their group, and no other group, to be free to engage in political activities. Consequently, the first goal of Khomeini's followers was to end political freedoms on university campuses. But this was a relatively straightforward goal, which involved getting university campuses back to what they were like before the revolution during the Shah's regime – a place where students and faculty were not free to be critical of the ruling regime or to engage in political activities. In essence, Khomeini's followers wanted to achieve the same dominant role that the monarchists enjoyed before the revolution, with no individual or group having the right to question them.

But there was a second, more profound reason why Khomeini's extremist followers were dissatisfied with universities in 1979, and this had to do with everything the modern Iranian university was and stood for – the architectural design of the campus; the system of university education being put into practice; the contents and nature of courses; the characteristics of the faculty teaching the courses (the vast majority of the faculty with advanced degrees were trained in the universities of Western societies); the wholesale importation of the Iranian university system from the United States and other Western countries; and just about everything else about universities. Moreover, the modern universities were associated with the monarchy; the first and most important university, Tehran University, was established in 1934 by Reza Shah (1878–1944), the founder of the Pahlavi dynasty. Thus, there were many reasons why Khomeini and his extremist followers were very unhappy with the state of Iranian universities after the 1979 revolution.

During that first term of teaching after the 1979 revolution, among my students there were a number of dedicated Khomeini supporters, part of the "students in the line of the Imam" who later invaded the US Embassy in Iran. I got to know them very quickly because immediately after the first class they came to me to complain about some of the female students in my class: "You have to stop them coming to class in skirts and sleeveless blouses," these extremist students demanded, "you have to do your duty!" At that time, the Islamic extremists did not have the power to force women, or men, to conform to their ideas about correct dress, but it was already clear what their intentions were if they came to power. When I got to know them better, I learned that they saw a lot more wrong with universities than the way women and men dressed. The entire modern university system was against their ideology. They were particularly incensed by the freedoms female faculty and students enjoyed on university campuses.

Traditional Islamic learning is through study at single-sex schools, with advanced education at seminaries (*hawza*) attended only by males. Education at traditional seminaries prepares men for different types of religious professions, such as being a mullah who regularly leads prayers at a neighborhood mosque. In 1979, the curriculum at the seminaries was steeped in traditional philosophy, including logic (*mantiq*), jurisprudence (*fiqh*), Koranic interpretation (*tafsir*), and Islamic traditions (*hadith*).[6] Over the next few decades, seminary education would be reshaped by extremist Khomeini-inspired Islamic ideology,[7] and there would also be greater efforts to also make Iran's modern universities more Islamic. But in the immediate post-revolution period, the seminaries and the universities remained even further apart than they are today. The universities served as a bastion of science, knowledge, and skills – as well as values, attitudes, gender roles, and many other cultural characteristics – all imported from the West.

The dilemma faced by the "students in the line of the Imam" and other extremist pro-Khomeini groups was that they wanted the advanced scientific and professional training, particularly in domains such as medicine and engineering, but that training came with the cultural baggage of the Western-style universities. Just being on a modern university campus was anathema for the pro-Khomeini students because they saw everything around them as shaping behavior in un-Islamic ways. Speaking with these extremist pro-Khomeini students reminded me of the Khmer Rouge, who took control of Cambodia in 1975 and were in power until 1979.[8] The Khmer Rouge saw urban centers as hostile to their radical communist goals. From the Khmer Rouge perspective, by their very nature, the purpose, design, and construction of modern cities had evolved to support capitalism. Since cities could not be reconstructed quickly to align with communist goals, the Khmer Rouge forcibly evacuated the cities and sent most people into the countryside (I discuss these tactics in greater detail later in this chapter). Similarly, the pro-Khomeini students and their supporters saw the modern universities in Iran as inherently against what they stood for because these universities supported behaviors that continued trends from before the revolution. These universities were seen as inherently counterrevolutionary. The dilemma was what to do about the modern universities (an issue I discuss in greater detail in the last section of this chapter). The larger question confronting the pro-Khomeini extremists was what to do with the tens of millions of people who had supported the revolution, but now continued to behave as they had before the revolution.

The dilemma faced by the pro-Khomeini forces confronts all extremist revolutionaries after regime change. In order to topple the ruling regime, extremist revolutionaries typically require the collaboration and support of a wide range of political groups, including many moderates. For example, in the great French and Russian revolutions, the aristocracy, the middle class, and the peasants all contributed at different times and in different ways to bringing down the ruling monarchist/Tsarist regimes. But after regime change, the extremists in France and Russia faced the challenge of how to sideline the other groups and achieve power monopoly. In both cases, the extremists forced their way to power through a period of widespread violence, which in France was initially led by Maximilien Robespierre and resulted in the Terror (a period of extreme violence, during which there was an obsession with conspiracies against the revolution[9]), and in Russia involved an enormously destructive civil war. In Iran, the pro-Khomeini extremists achieved a similar power monopoly through large-scale executions and the persecution of their rivals, made possible in an atmosphere of crisis. Specifically, there was the US Embassy hostage-taking crisis (1979–80) and a long and tortuous war (the 1980–8 Iran–Iraq War) that was allowed by the extremists to continue longer than necessary so that they could use the pressures of war to more fully control Iranian society.

A similar process took place in China. First, a broad coalition helped the communists to spearhead a revolution. This is how Mao urged a broad coalition of groups to band together to defeat the Chinese nationalists in the civil war in China that followed World War II (1939–45): "Unite workers, peasants, soldiers, intellectuals and business men, all oppressed classes, all people's organizations, democratic parties, minority national- ities, overseas Chinese and other patriots; form a national united front; overthrow the dictatorial Chiang Kai-Shek."[10] But not long after gaining power monopoly, Mao turned against a number of his former allies, such as the intellectuals and business people who earlier were part of the broad revolutionary coalition, but were viciously attacked during the Cultural Revolution of the 1960s.

In each case, extremists seek power monopoly after revolutions in order to implement their programs, intending to change the behavior of the population toward the ideal society they envisage. But the extremists first have to exclude rival groups and achieve power monopoly, and then they have to bring about the behavioral changes they see as necessary to arrive at their revolutionary society. Extremists have found it far easier to achieve power monopoly after revolutions than they have to change actual behaviors among the masses in the direction they desire after regime change. This is in part because the behavior of the extremists themselves needs to change in line with the ideals of the revolution, and this has proven to be an extraordinarily difficult goal to achieve. For example, Mao and his communist supporters found it easier to defeat the nationalist forces led by Chiang Kai-shek than to bring about the communist society they had in mind – a goal that continues to elude Chinese communists in the twenty-first century, China having evolved into a government-controlled capitalist economy.[11]

Revolutionary extremists, such as the pro-Khomeini students in the line of the Imam, the Bolsheviks in post-revolution Russia, and Robespierre and his supporters after the French Revolution, can master the rhetoric of revolution and idealistic goals, but this does not mean that they have changed *their own behavior* to be in line with these goals (a reminder of the ancient phrase "Who will guard the guards themselves?" "*Quis custodiet ipsos custodes?*"[12]). Like everyone else in their societies, extremist revolutionaries have acquired their ways of thinking and doing over a lifetime and are enmeshed in networks of social relationships that began and took shape before the revolution. There tends to be continuity after the revolution in both their styles of behavior and styles of social relationships. This continuity is perpetuated in part because after they gain absolute power, people dare not challenge or question behavioral continuity among the radical revolutionaries; they are the ones with the guns and they are the ultimate deciders on life and death.

Conceptualizing the Perpetual Revolution

The idea of perpetual revolution has been discussed directly and indirectly by thinkers committed to a wide range of ideologies and interests. These include hardline Marxists, as well as Trotsky and his followers, but also English Romantic poets and, in the twentieth and twenty-first centuries, Mao Zedong and his followers, extremist revolutionaries such as the Khmer Rouge in Cambodia and the Shining Path in Peru, as well as some groups of extremist Muslims[13] (also, the playwright Tom Stoppard has written a trilogy of plays that reflect some of the themes of perpetual revolution[14]). All of these different groups have explored the idea of perpetual revolution because of their interest in better understanding and bringing about radical change that is sustained, and their realization that revolution – even the most violent and extreme – does not guarantee that the behavior of people will change in a sustained way in line with espoused revolutionary goals.

Trotsky is one of the revolutionaries who has delved deeply into the nature of perpetual revolution.[15] In his investigation, Trotsky points to three factors that he sees to be integral to the perpetual revolution. The first two are more political in nature: first, the overthrowing of capitalism through the leadership of the proletariat; second, (what Trotsky sees as) the necessarily international nature of the fight to defeat capitalism. But far more interesting from a psychological perspective is the third factor: the continuous struggle and conflict *after the defeat of capitalism*, which would gradually result in behavioral changes and arrive at socialism and eventually the classless society. Revolution and power dominance would not mean that the proletariat had reached its goals; that is just the beginning of the behavioral changes needed. But bringing about these behavioral changes would be an enormous challenge, not guaranteed to be successful even after the defeat of capitalism.

Trotsky used Marx as a point of departure to develop his ideas about perpetual revolution. Writing about the revolutionary movements across Europe in the mid-nineteenth century, culminating in the 1848 mass uprisings, Marx and Engels wrote: "While the democratic petty bourgeois want to bring the revolution to an end as quickly as possible ... it is our interest and our task to make the revolution permanent ..."[16] The permanent or perpetual revolution would mean continual transformation of behavior in line with the goals of the revolution, rather than regression to behaviors (such as the motivation for individual profit and wealth) that were normative before the revolution.

Counterrevolution is one way in which regression could take place, with a return to behaviors that were normative before the revolution. For example, the civil war that followed the 1917 Russian Revolution involved counterrevolutionary forces, with the help of foreign governments, attempting to overthrow the Bolshevik government. The governing elites of Britain and other European nations feared that the Russian Revolution would spill over the borders of Russia and spread to other countries. The civil war that raged in Russia until 1923 was savage and brought a huge loss of life; the population within the Soviet territory fell by 12.7 million in the period from 1917 to 1922.[17] The civil war that followed World War II in China (1945–9) also involved counterrevolutionaries (led by Chiang Kai-shek, 1887–1975) attempting to overthrow the revolutionary communist government led by Mao Zedong, with enormous human and material costs.[18] But counterrevolutionary forces are in some respects relatively simple to identify and plan for; far more infused in everyday life and difficult to change are cultural factors that are more effective at resisting revolutionary change and could shift behavior back to what it was like before the revolution. For example, consider the continuous influence of literature and architecture on behavior and the larger society.

I consider here the relationship between literature and revolution, to which Trotsky gave great importance.[19] Literature is central to culture, and (from the perspective of revolutionaries) culture needs to be in line with the goals of the revolution – not just communist revolutionaries, but just about all revolutionaries, would endorse this idea. However, complexities arise, in part because literature is from the past, and the classic or "great" literature of major societies took shape over hundreds and sometimes thousands of years prior to the revolution. Moreover, this classic literature was produced by creative individuals who tend not to be from the proletariat or the revolutionary vanguard. Much of this classic literature seems to be counter-revolutionary. For example, after the 1917 Russian Revolution the Bolsheviks put into place a massive program of collectivization, through which private property was abolished and people were supposed to work for collective and not individual profit. But the classic literary heritage of Russia – including novels, poetry, plays, nursery rhymes, myths, and children's stories – does not extol these collectivist ideals. This seems to call for a new revolutionary literature and permanent revolution in culture. But does such a permanent revolution mean that all the past literary heritage of Russia should be forbidden in the post-revolution era?[20]

I encountered a similar dilemma with respect to classic literature in post-revolution Iran. The mullahs attempted to "purify" contemporary Iranian culture and eradicate everything they considered un-Islamic, and to reflect Western values. But more than this, the mullahs attempted to push into the background the classical Farsi literature that they saw as going against their extremist interpretations of Islam. For example, this included shunting aside the *Book of Kings* (*Shahnameh*) of Abolqasem Ferdowsi (940–1020 CE).[21] Ferdowsi's *Book of Kings* was deemed to be counterrevolutionary in a number of ways. First, it recounts Persian history by focusing on kings and heroes, who extol values and virtues that are in some respects universal and in some respects nationalistic, but not distinctly Islamic or even broadly speaking religious. Second, in writing the *Shahnameh*, Ferdowsi incorporated Farsi vocabulary and excluded the Arabic vocabulary brought into Iran after the Arab invasion (which also brought Islam to Iran – some

Iranian nationalists regard the invasion of Iran and the importation of Islam as the greatest tragedy that has befallen their nation). For these and other reasons, Ferdowsi is lauded by Iranian nationalists, and shunned by the mullahs. However, despite (or perhaps because of) the anti-Ferdowsi bias of the mullahs' dictatorships, Ferdowsi remains highly popular among many Iranians in post-revolution Iran.

Of course, the mullahs have attempted to ban public readings of what they consider to be counterrevolutionary (i.e., anti-Islamic) poetry, but this could result in the banning of a great deal of classical Persian literature. Is this even possible?

An even more formidable task faced by revolutionaries is how to deal with the impact on behavior of the *built environment*, the surroundings for human activity that have been built or changed by humans (this includes architecture, city planning, and landscaping). The built environment includes heritage buildings, such as cathedrals and mosques, palaces, historic structures, sports stadiums, and major government buildings. But the built environment also includes numerous historic villages and large cities, with their thousands of roads, parks, zoos, and millions of houses and apartment complexes that serve as homes for ordinary people.

A first characteristic of the built environment is that it is already present when we arrive in this world, and substantial parts of it remain the same during our lifetimes and after we leave.[22] A second characteristic is that we are not able to speedily change the built environment; some aspects of it continue more or less the same over our lifetimes, and often far longer. Consequently, the same built environment can continue to shape behavior in similar or the same ways in a society over very long-term periods, sometimes centuries and even longer. Generation after generation of families are influenced by the same city and building design, which helps sustain similar patterns of behavior across different generations. In the next section, I discuss this continuity in greater detail, as part of a broader discussion on behavioral continuity.

Programs Used by Revolutionaries to Try to Increase Political Plasticity and Prevent Behavioral Continuity

So far in this chapter we have reviewed how after helping to topple the ruling regime, defeating their rivals, and gaining power monopoly, radical revolutionaries are faced with the challenge of ending behavioral continuity and changing the behavior of both the elites and the masses toward their revolutionary ideals. I have also proposed that the radicals find it easier to push aside their political rivals and achieve power monopoly after revolutions than they do to change behaviors toward their revolutionary ideals. This is because the ideals put forward by revolutionaries typically require considerable behavioral changes at both the collective and individual levels, including in domains where political plasticity is very low (such as moral purity, collectivization, and leader–follower relations).

Before coming to power, many revolutionaries put forward ideals of egalitarianism, moral purity, and even classless societies. Terms such as equality and purity become highly popular as part of revolutionary rhetoric before revolutions, with the understanding that large economic inequalities, corruption, and wealth concentration must be ended. These kinds of ideals were commonly discussed in the media and were even part of everyday rhetoric both during the buildup to the revolution and in the immediate post-revolution period in Iran. Of course, it was promised that in the Islamic society being built under the leadership of Imam Khomeini, all forms of graft, bribery, and corruption, as well as enormous wealth inequalities would end. However, these are all domains with low political plasticity – meaning that in these domains behavioral change is slow and behavioral continuity is normative. For example, there is a tendency for group-based inequalities to reemerge after revolutions (even in the large communist societies of the Soviet Union and China), as there is a reversion to how things were prior to regime change. As a solution to such dangers, revolutionaries have put into place programs to bring about the kinds of behavioral changes their ideals require. The most far-reaching and expansive program was attempted by Mao Zedong (1893–1976), who proposed a "perpetual revolution."[23]

Mao believed a perpetual revolution was needed because there is a danger that even after revolutions that topple capitalist regimes, society will return to the pre-revolution patterns of behavior. As Susan Shirk notes: "In the mid-1960s Mao Zedong diagnosed the most serious ills of Chinese society fifteen years after Liberation: the growth of bureaucratic elitism and class privilege, the persistence of bourgeois intellectual, artistic, and social values, and the degeneration of revolutionary elan into privatism and opportunistic competition."[24] Mao's conclusion was that in post-revolution China, there was a tendency to return to individual rights and individual competitiveness, linked to an individualistic reward system.

One view is that a perpetual revolution is needed because the natural inclination of humans is individualism, and the natural priority of people is to seek personal profit. This view is supported by psychological research on *social loafing*, showing that individuals work less hard when they compete as part of a group and their win or loss is based on group effort.[25] But there is also a research literature that supports *social laboring*, when working in a group leads individuals to become *more* hard working and productive.[26] Social laboring suggests that human motivation is plastic and can change with changing conditions. This suggests that behaviors that were dominant prior to the revolution will gradually disappear when societal conditions no longer encourage them. Consequently, the revolution will have an end point – for example, when the classless society is achieved. As part of the perpetual revolution, radical revolutionaries have attempted a number of more specific programs to bring about behavioral change toward their revolutionary goals.

Emptying the Counterrevolutionary Vessels

After coming to power, some groups of radical revolutionaries put into practice the idea that the pre-revolution context in which people continue to live is counterrevolutionary, and so the people must be moved to a new context – the counterrevolution vessels in which people exist must be emptied. This broad tactic targets everyone living in the counterrevolution context, and not just a minority of people. The most radical example of this tactic being put into practice in the modern era is by the Khmer Rouge in Cambodia.

The Khmer Rouge, led by Pol Pot (1925–98), regarded cities as breeding grounds for counterrevolutionary and pro-capitalist sentiments. They saw city dwellers as unproductive and cities as inherently places where inequalities thrive and exploitation takes place. As they captured major cities, the Khmer Rouge emptied them. Soon after capturing the capital city of Phnom Pehn, the entire city population was forced to move to the countryside. This was part of a Khmer Rouge plan to transform Cambodia into a revolutionary society at the forefront of a world revolution. Not surprisingly, the millions of people who had grown up as city dwellers and who were forcibly moved to the countryside found it extremely difficult to adapt to an agricultural life. Many of them starved and about a fifth of the total Cambodian population perished.[27] This extreme approach was in line with Khmer Rouge ideology, as Lek Hor Tan explains: "According to Khmer Rouge documents, their revolutionary vision of man asserts that when a man has been spoiled by a corrupt regime, he cannot be reformed. He must be physically eliminated …"[28] This thinking is in line with the radical purges that took place during the Terror of the French Revolution.[29]

By emptying the cities and moving the Cambodian population to the countryside, the Khmer Rouge (whose forces numbered 70,000–100,000) planned to better control the roughly ten million people of Cambodia. Moreover, by changing the context of behavior from city to countryside, the Khmer Rouge believed the Cambodian population would become more pliable and change more quickly to become the revolutionary citizens they aspired to create. Such citizens would become egalitarian and motivated to work their best as part of collectives, rather than as individuals working for personal profit.

Another context that radical revolutionaries saw as counterrevolutionary is the modern university. Both in communist China ruled by Mao Zedong and in Iran ruled by Khomeini, universities came to be seen by radical revolutionaries as obstacles to reaching the goals of the revolution, as counterrevolutionary vessels that had to be emptied. This emptying took place as part of the cultural revolutions in these two countries, a topic discussed next.

Cultural Revolution

Mao Zedong justified the perpetual revolution by pointing to the continued influence of what he viewed as counterrevolutionary forces, who were thriving even after the revolution:[30] "The representatives of the bourgeoisie have sneaked into the party, the government, the army, and the cultural sectors. They are a bunch of counter-revolutionary revisionists."[31] To combat this regressive tendency, Mao launched the Cultural Revolution in the late 1960s, as part of an effort to prevent the growth of new forms of elitism and group-based inequalities. For about a decade, from the start of the Cultural Revolution to the demise of the so-called Gang of Four (radicals who attempted to keep Mao's revolutionary vision alive after his death), programs were put into place to try to sustain Mao's vision of an egalitarian society.

Mao identified the enemy as the "four olds": old thoughts, old culture, old customs, old habits. In launching the Cultural Revolution in the mid-1960s to fight these four "olds," Mao relied heavily on youth, and his vanguard groups of youth came to be known as the Red Guards. They dressed in military-style uniforms, wore red armbands, and slavishly did Mao's bidding. These young people were irreplaceable instruments for Mao because of their idealism, naivety, propensity for aggression and risk-taking, and their absolute loyalty to "the Great Helmsman" above everything else.[32] They were sent into schools and universities to attack their teachers and professors, and into offices and organizations to attack office workers of all kinds, particularly the managers and technical experts. Mao had taught them that chaos was good and rebellion a virtue, and their task was to ensure the vitality of the perpetual revolution.

Mao's first massive national attempt to push China forward had been the Great Leap Forward, launched in 1958. The goal was to transform China from an agrarian to an industrial society. Collectivization of farms and factories was implemented and ordinary people engaged in steel production in their backyards. It was proclaimed that China would surpass Great Britain in industrial production in fifteen years and the United States in twenty to thirty years. The Great Leap Forward was announced as the second five-year plan of communist China, but it was abandoned after the third year because it proved to be a disaster and brought starvation to tens of millions of people.[33] The Cultural Revolution was different from the Great Leap Forward because it was (ostensibly) launched not to achieve material progress but as necessary to safeguard the revolution and the continued dominance of the proletariat against revisionist backsliding. The Cultural Revolution was about the upholding of revolutionary values.

As a symbol of Mao's close links with the people, in July 1966 the Chinese media showed images of the seventy-three-year-old Mao swimming in the Yangzi River at Wuhan, the site of a 1911 uprising that overthrew the Qing dynasty. Mao was accompanied on this swim by groups of supporters. This was part of Mao's flamboyant launch of the Cultural Revolution, and in the following years the Red Guards would repeatedly attack professionals, intellectuals, managers, scientists, and just about everyone with advanced training and expertise. Teachers and professors were primary targets. Schools and universities were emptied and formal educational programs came to a stop for several years.

Before proceeding further with a discussion of the Cultural Revolution in China in the late 1960s, it is useful to include a discussion of the Cultural Revolution in Iran in the early 1980s. There are remarkable similarities across the two cultural revolutions. They were both initiated and pushed forward by politically extremist old men (when they launched the cultural revolutions in China and Iran, Mao was in his mid-seventies and Khomeini had turned eighty) and implemented by their fanatical young followers. In both cases, young fanatics were encouraged to attack their teachers and professors, and universities were emptied and educational programs were halted for several years. In both the contexts of China and Iran, there ensued debates about the value of advanced training by itself, independent of ideological purity, and the need for ideological commitment to the revolution rather than having mere technical expertise. In both cases, the Cultural Revolution resulted in a huge loss of trained personnel – and in the case of Iran a vast brain drain that continues to this day.[34]

At the core of the Cultural Revolution in both China and Iran was the attempt to transform universities to fall in line with the goals of the revolution, as defined by Mao in China and Khomeini in Iran. But in both cases the attempt failed because of the contradiction between the goals of higher education and the system of dictatorship followed by both Mao and Khomeini. University education is designed to not only teach students new information and technical skills, but also to train them in critical thinking broadly. This includes critical thinking about government policies and leadership, including the leadership of Mao and Khomeini. But this raises a dilemma: On the one hand, Mao and Khomeini served as absolute dictators with the power to have the last word on everything (as did Napoleon, Lenin, and Castro); on the other hand, universities are supposed to nurture critical thinking and objective assessment, including of government decision-making. Extremists resolve this dilemma through violence.

I was present when in 1980 groups of Khomeini's extremist supporters, armed with chains, knives, clubs, and other such weapons, attacked Tehran University and expelled faculty and students from campus. As far as Khomeini was concerned, the universities had become centers of counter-revolutionary activity, and they had to be shut down and rebuilt. But the dilemma that confronted the pro-Khomeini radicals is still facing Islamic radicals in Iran today, decades after Khomeini's death: How to allow centers of advanced learning and research to remain open, but ensure that they do not question the "revolutionary" government. A tactic used by some radical revolutionaries involves forcing people to conform with revolutionary values by continually reprogramming their behavior, discussed in the next section.

Self-Criticism and the Continual Reprogramming of Behavior

Yet for the majority of villagers living under Shining Path control, the materialist programme to replace human affection with "class consciousness" simply revealed the Sendero's perverse insensitivity to their actual needs as human beings. At Sendero "base camp" their children were forced to undergo military and ideological training from the age of eight or nine years. The guerrillas sought to mould the children into fighters who would kill and die without question, who did not know the meaning of pity and who retained no sentimental family ties. Terms like mama, papa, and señora were prohibited and replaced by the nomenclature of compañero and camarada, though the older terms of affection kept re-emerging in the children's vocabulary.[35]

Ronald Osborn's description of tactics used by the Shining Path insurgency in Peru shows the radical measures taken by some extremist revolutionaries to reprogram behavior in a population. The basic assumption underlying these reprogramming efforts is that behavior can be molded in line with the goals of the revolution. The human being is assumed to be a blank slate (*tabu rasa*), in line with Lockian and behaviorist propositions. The characteristics of humans can be shaped to be in line with the requirements of the revolutionary society, and to ensure that people do not return to their style of behavior before the revolution.

Criticism and self-criticism are also used by some extremist revolutionaries to try to achieve continual change and to try to prevent regression to pre-revolution behavior. Criticism and self-criticism were repeatedly used during the Cultural Revolution in China.[36] The processes typically involved one person (and then another) being singled out for criticism. The alienated individual would be criticized by others, but would also be pressured to engage in serious self-criticism. Such self-criticism actions were often painful for the targeted individual, and were a way in which loyalty to the Chinese communist leadership (and Mao specifically) was demonstrated.

After the revolution in Iran, the radical revolutionaries did not engage in such criticism and self-criticism practices among themselves. Rather, the radicals focused their efforts to achieve "purification" and the exclusion from power of all those they considered not to be in the line of the Imam (Khomeini). Anyone who in any way directly or indirectly questioned Khomeini's decisions was excluded from power, and then persecuted. This included nonconforming mullahs such as the Grand Ayatollah Hussein-Ali Montazari, who was demoted to mere "Mr." after daring to criticize torture and illegal imprisonment carried out by Khomeini's extremist followers and the Republican Guards.

Concluding Comment

Revolutions change the people in power, but they do not necessarily change how people behave. Indeed, a great deal about the context of behavior, what I have termed hard wiring outside individuals, continues as it did before the revolution, and this continuity in context also influences continuity in behavior.[37] To counter this tendency for behavioral continuity, extremist revolutionaries have attempted to achieve perpetual revolution. Indeed, why should the revolution come to a halt? Why should it not continue forever? Drastic tactics have been tried, such as moving people from cities to the countryside, emptying universities and schools, reeducating people en masse, banning private property, and reorganizing everyone in collectives and communes. But all of these tactics face two main obstacles: first, the challenge of changing behavior fast enough to meet revolutionary goals; second, the challenge of changing the context that supports behavioral continuity. This second challenge is the most foundational, and it is the focus of the next chapter.

CHAPTER 8

Cultural Carriers and the Failure of Revolutionaries to Reshape Behavior

Following the French Revolution, Robespierre and other extremists unleashed a bloody reign of terror that deeply scarred French society, but failed to reshape the behavior of French people in the way the extremist revolutionaries had intended. After the 1917 revolution in Russia, the Bolsheviks gradually gained power monopoly and mobilized a widespread campaign of collectivization, which Stalin tried to enforce through severe brutality, killing tens of millions of people in order to force behavioral change in the direction he wanted. After the revolution in China, Mao waged an at times savage campaign of perpetual revolution, punctuated by fever-pitch mass programs such as the Great Leap Forward of the late 1950s and the Cultural Revolution of the late 1960s – all intended to remold the behavior of Chinese people and to create a revolutionary society based on collective ownership and work motivated by collective rewards. Having established himself as the absolute dictator in Iran after the Anti-Shah Revolution, Khomeini ferociously attacked his political competitors, killing or imprisoning hundreds of thousands of Iranians, forcing millions to take refuge abroad, and implementing oppressive policies particularly targeting women to try to change the behavior of the Iranian people in accordance with his repressive interpretations of Islam.

Extremist revolutionaries have repeatedly used mass killings, torture, and imprisonment, among other deadly tactics, to try to bring about the behavioral changes they see as necessary to arrive at their ideal revolutionary societies. But they have invariably failed. The French Revolution, despite the Terror and decades of devastating war, ended with the return of monarchy to France. Collectivization and perpetual revolution proved to be failures in the Soviet Union and China; in both countries the drive for private property and personal profit continues to strongly influence the behavior of both the masses and the elites in the twenty-first century. Billionaires now thrive in both Russia and China. Far from becoming an Islamic paradise, Iran is now a highly corrupt dictatorship dominated by greed for money and power, with young people especially turning against religion and the governing mullahs, and the majority of the population preferring the separation of religion and politics.[1]

Earlier attempts at radical revolutionary change were also of limited success. For example, after the execution of Charles I (1600–49), king of England, Scotland, and Ireland, a republic was declared with Oliver Cromwell (1599–1658) serving as Lord Protector (with powers similar to that of a monarch, although Cromwell refused the crown when parliament offered it to him).[2] But shortly after Cromwell's death, the monarchy was restored through King Charles II. The resurrected monarchy was different, in that the monarch now governed through the consent of parliament. However, other major political changes in England took place very slowly over the next few centuries, despite the so-called *Glorious Revolution* of 1688 – which helped prepare the ground for industrialization in England, but through changes that were gradual, long term, and institutional rather than swift and radical.[3] We could add many other examples of failures by radical revolutionaries trying to bring about behavioral change, such as the Khmer Rouge, who killed about 20 percent of the Cambodian population in their disastrous programs that collapsed in only the fourth year of their rule. Why is it so difficult, then, for extremist revolutionaries to speedily bring about the behavioral changes they seek, even when they have absolute power monopoly and use deadly violence, torture, mass imprisonments, and killings to try to mold how people behave?

In this chapter, I build on the discussion of behavioral continuity in the previous chapters by exploring in greater detail the role of *cultural carriers*, the means by which styles of thinking and doing, as well as important cultural characteristics, are perpetuated and extended across societies and generations.[4] I argue that the influence of cultural carriers has meant that almost all revolutions, even the so-called great ones, bring about only within-system change, but they fail to achieve between-system change. That is, in the short term of decades or even a century, revolutions bring about surface-level changes, particularly in rhetoric (the language used, the explanations given, the titles and names of people and places, and so on) and symbols (such as flags and clothing), but they do not bring about a change of political system and political behavior at a deeper level. Most importantly, the style of leadership and followership remains the same. For example, the French Revolution, the Russian Revolution, the Chinese Revolution, the Cuban Revolution, and the Iranian Revolution all brought about within-system change and perpetuated the same leadership–followership style. After these revolutions, Napoleon was dictator in France, Stalin was dictator in Russia,

Mao was dictator in China, Castro was dictator in Cuba, and Khomeini was dictator in Iran. In each of these societies, the rhetoric of revolution created a surface appearance of change, but at a deeper level the system of dictatorship remained, with an authoritarian male dictator dominating the rest of society and pulverizing all political opposition individuals and groups.

This surface-level change after revolutions, accompanied by deep-level continuity, was highly painful for me to experience after the 1979 revolution in Iran. Before the revolution, whatever the Shah said was treated as sacred, as law, as unquestionable – and after the revolution, whatever Khomeini said was treated as sacred, as law, as unquestionable. Both the Shah and Khomeini claimed to have been placed in their leadership positions by God. Questioning whatever the Shah/Khomeini said was considered as heretical as questioning the commands of God (just as today, questioning whatever Khamenei, the latest dictator in Iran, says is treated as blasphemy).

We have already touched on (in Chapter 7) the role of two important cultural carriers, the built environment and literature, in perpetuating behavioral continuity. In this chapter, I begin by discussing what I call the micro–macro rule of change, which concerns the maximum speed of change that can be achieved at micro-psychological and macro-societal levels. Related to this is the distinction between two types of behavior, concerning *performance capacity*, how well human beings can do things (e.g., whether or not a person is able to hear a poem being recited in the next room), and *performance style*, how behavior is carried out and the meaning it is given (e.g., the style in which a person recites a poem and the meaning the poem has for her).

The Micro–Macro Rule of Change

In discussing regime change (Chapter 4 and 5), we reviewed how in the lead-up to revolution the final regime collapse typically happens suddenly and unexpectedly. Regime change is an example of the way in which macro-level changes can take place very quickly. For example, a ruling regime can collapse and the new government can in a matter of days pass a law that prohibits private property and collectivizes all ownership and work arrangements. Following a revolution, radically new revolutionary constitutions and economic policies can be ratified (on paper) overnight. The name of a political system can be changed instantly, from monarchy to republic, or dictatorship to democracy. The title of the national leader can be changed from "king" to "supreme leader" or "chairman," or even "president" or some other democratic-sounding title. The name of the entire nation can be changed. These kinds of macro-level changes can be brought about relatively quickly.

In contrast, micro-level psychological changes involving styles of thinking and doing are relatively slow to change. For example, a law can be passed prohibiting private property and placing people in collective farms and publicly owned factories and organizations, where individuals have to work for collective (and not personal) profit. This change took place after revolutions in the Soviet Union, Cuba, and China. But in order for this new collectivization program to be efficiently implemented, people have to change how they think and act, how they are motivated; they have to become motivated to work harder or just as hard for collective rewards as they did for individual rewards. The small business owner, the factory worker, the lawyer, the farmer, the researcher, the medical doctor, the manager – everyone who used to work for personal rewards would now have to be motivated to work as part of a collective, to receive rewards based on group effort. The historic experiences of the Soviet Union, Cuba, and China demonstrate that this type of behavioral change is extraordinarily difficult to achieve, and comes about extremely slowly, if it is possible to achieve at all.

Research on social laboring (discussed in Chapter 7) suggests that under certain conditions, it is possible to organize individuals into groups so they are motivated to work harder for collective rewards.[5] For example, consider how the different research teams of a pharmaceutical company compete to develop different drugs to reach the marketplace and consumers, and team members individually excel as part of their team efforts for collective rewards. But creating the conditions to achieve social laboring on a massive societal scale proved to be impossible for the Soviet Union and China. I would add that from my experiences of travel in, and study of, Eastern European countries during their communist days (before 1991), as well as more recently in Cuba, smaller communist countries have also found it extremely difficult, if not impossible, to create the conditions necessary to achieve social laboring. In Cuba, the government has had to take at least small steps toward individual incentives and move away from collective farms in order to try to improve productivity.[6]

Leader–follower relations is another domain in which macro-level change can be fast, but micro-level change is relatively slow. This is most obvious after anti-dictator revolutions, when the old dictator is overthrown (typically killed or forced into exile), a new constitution is put into place, and a new dictator comes to power using a new title and a revolutionary and/or democratic front. In practice, the new dictator can be even more ruthless and deadly than the overthrown dictator, but now he justifies his mass killings and arrests using revolutionary rhetoric. For example, in leading the charge to force collectivization of farming, Stalin had identified the *kulaks*, entrepreneurial farmers who owned a farm and typically hired labor, as an enemy. In implementing *Dekulakization*, Stalin explained in 1929: "We have gone over from a policy of limiting the exploiting tendencies of the kulak to a policy of liquidating the kulak as a class. To take the offensive against the kulaks means to deal the kulak class such a blow that it will no longer rise to its feet. That's what we Bolsheviks call an offensive."[7] In the name of the Marxist revolution, Stalin acted as a dictator in a way that was as ruthless as any previous tsar; just as in Iran I witnessed Khomeini in the name of Islamic revolution implementing mass killings and arrests that were as ruthless as those of any shah who had ruled Iran before the 1979 Iranian Revolution. In essence, the behavior of the post-revolution leader can be essentially the same as, or even harsher than, the pre-revolution leader, but using revolutionary rhetoric that camouflages the continuity.

Continuity in the behavior of the post-revolution leader is not only a result of the leader's characteristics; it also arises from continuity in the characteristics of followers and that of the context. To begin with the characteristics of the followers, the style of behavior of followers was learned over their lifetimes before the revolution, and it does not instantly come to an end with the revolution and regime change. The people living under a dictatorship have only had experience with dictatorial leadership; they grew up learning to show absolute obedience to the dictator. The first place of learning how to be a follower, and how to relate to the leader, is in the family.

From research on the authoritarian personality and authoritarianism in the family, we know that family dynamics in dictatorships tend to also mirror dictatorial relationships at the level of the state, with the children and the mother expected to be obedient to the father, who acts as a mini-dictator in the family.[8] I witnessed a prime example of this after the revolution in Iran, where Khomeini and his followers pushed hard to reestablish traditional authoritarian relationships in families.[9] Of course, the basic laws emanating from Islam as it is actually practiced in post-revolution Iran, such as the rights of men to have multiple "regular" and also infinite temporary wives, the relative ease with which men can divorce their wives, the rights of husbands to keep children in the case of divorce, and the low labor-force participation rate of women (translating into their lack of financial independence), contribute to the dominance and superior power of husbands relative to their wife(s).

The second major socialization unit that teaches children how they should behave in relation to authority and leadership is the school. It is generally assumed that increases in education among a population result in more democratic politics.[10] However, more years of education do not necessarily result in more democracy because a lot depends on the *kinds of education* being implemented. In dictatorships, obedience to the teacher (and school authorities generally) mirrors obedience to the dictator and government authorities. The school implements the policies of the state, and in dictatorships children are encouraged to practice obedience, but not critical thinking – either in relation to the teacher or the dictator. For example, in the Soviet Union the main function of schools was to make children into good communists.[11] In post-revolution Iran, schools are supposed to make children into good Muslims (as interpreted by Khomeini), part of which is to be obedient to the Supreme Leader and report on anti-revolutionary behavior in their families (the collective movements in 2022, led mostly by young women, against the dictatorship of the mullahs shows that despite the authoritarian nature of schools in Iran, achieving control of young minds is extremely challenging[12]).

A serious problem dictatorships run up against is the difference between young people being able to pass ideological tests and actually being committed to the ideologies they are tested on. For example, students could achieve high marks in tests assessing knowledge of communism, or "Islam according to Khomeini," or fascism, or any other ideology, without believing in and being committed to act according to such ideologies. Indeed, families can train the young to show two faces to the world: a public face that is in line with regime ideology and a private face that is critical of the regime. I witnessed families in Iran transition smoothly from the dictatorship of the Shah to the dictatorship of Khomeini, maintaining the public/private distinction seamlessly by remaining publicly obedient to the dictator Shah/Khomeini, but privately criticizing the dictator and his regime as corrupt.

Thus, continuity in parenting style and education style in schools is another factor leading to low political plasticity across revolutions. Parents and teachers functioning in dictatorships develop certain styles of socializing the young. These socialization styles are shaped by the context of dictatorship and for the most part meet the demands of the larger dictatorial society. Children are taught to at least outwardly be obedient and uncritical toward authority, and to jump through the various hoops the regime has set in front of them. For example, in order to gain entrance to higher education, students have to pass ideological litmus tests. Parents and teachers adopt teaching styles to get children through these tests. The socialization styles that parents and teachers learn over a lifetime living under a dictatorship cannot be instantly transformed after revolution to a socialization style fit for democracy. The dictator can be overthrown and a new regime (supposedly) "representative of the people" can come into place relatively quickly, but the micro-level changes involving how parents and teachers should behave in a democracy take far longer to come about – particularly if they are to learn the skills needed to socialize children to become democratic citizens, capable of being active in and supportive of a democracy.

The objection could be raised that in dictatorships, many people privately refuse to conform and obey, and therefore this hidden disobedience and nonconformity could open a path to open resistance, and eventually democracy. Speaking about the communist dictatorships before the collapse of the Soviet Union, Robert Sharlet explains how "the individual is forced to live a double existence. By day one conforms to the image of a public person nominally committed to the party's goals, while by night one plays the role of private citizen actively pursuing one's own projects in the 'antiworld' immanent within the official reality."[13] I witnessed and experienced this double existence in the mullahs' dictatorship in Iran, where tens of millions of people were forced by guns, jails, and torture to publicly go along with a corrupt religious system, but in private they abhorred and rejected the regime. But while this double existence and hatred of the regime can provide motivation and energy for the next anti-dictator revolution, it is not sufficient to ensure that people have the psychological characteristics needed to serve as democratic citizens, capable of participating in and sustaining a democracy.

An unfortunate consequence of this double existence is that it normalizes high levels of corruption.[14] Children in dictatorships such as China, Russia, Iran, Cuba, and North Korea learn from a young age that one publicly conforms and obeys, one bows to the dictator, but this is only a deception that needs to be maintained in front of outsiders. One studies for the ideological test to get into a school or university, or to get a job, but within the ingroup the ideology is ignored or even dismissed and laughed at. The most important characteristic of the ingroup is that its members steal *together*. They are the civil servants who steal from the ministry budget; they are the factory engineers and managers who steal the factory products to sell on the black market; they are the officials in the mayor's office who profit from manipulating the price of land and buildings ... they are the endless numbers of people who publicly praise the regime, but privately steal from, or rather with, the regime. They can do this because they have been socialized to live a double existence, and because in dictatorships anyone who criticizes their actions will be identified and punished as a critic of the regime and the supreme dictator. The lack of transparency and opportunities for people to criticize authorities means that dictatorships end up experiencing high levels of corruption.[15]

Change and Two Types of Behavior: Performance Capacity and Performance Style

So far in this section, we have discussed how change is possible at a far faster pace at the macro level (e.g., of government policy) than at the micro level of psychological processes. At this stage, it is also necessary to distinguish between two types of behavior: *performance capacity*, how well humans can perform certain activities, and *performance style*, the meaning that certain actions have. Performance capacity is causally determined and accurately described using the terminology of efficient causation. That is, the cause precedes the effect it causes – the tree branch falls on Jack's head and causes him to suffer brain injury and memory loss. To take another example, the music teacher very softly plays a note on the piano and asks his student, "Can you hear that note?" In this case, the piano teacher is testing the auditory capacity of the music student: How well can you hear?

Performance style is about meaning and how people make sense of the world; it is not correctly described using causal language. For example, the music teacher plays a few notes on the piano and asks the student, "What does that sound mean to you? How do those notes make you feel?" The student might respond: "That music brings to my mind images of a festival; I feel happy hearing that music." Another student adds: "Yes, the sound of those notes makes me feel like I am at a wedding celebration."

For the most part, after revolutions the struggle of revolutionaries is to change performance style – how people make sense of the world and the meaning systems that regulate their behavior. For example, consider the question: What is the relationship between women and men in society? In most democracies, women have made tremendous advances and are in terms of formal law equal to men. There are still areas where women lag behind, such as at the highest echelons of business and politics, but in many other domains women have caught up or are very close to catching up with men. However, we need to keep in mind that change in perform-ance style is not necessarily only in one direction; women can be pushed backward, as has happened through the influence of the mullahs in Iran and the Taliban in Afghanistan. Women in Iran have lost basic human rights and freedoms they enjoyed before the 1979 revolution, and women in Afghanistan have similarly lost rights and freedoms they had before the return of the Taliban in 2021. In assessing, then, why it is so difficult to achieve change in performance style, we must keep in mind that change is not only in one (progressive) direction. Cultural carriers can be influential in resisting progressive change and dragging behavior style to earlier primitive times.

Cultural Carriers, Context, and Continuity in Behavior

Stalin and Hitler were willing to kill enormous numbers of people in order to achieve their political goals. As Alan Bullock notes, "Stalin and Hitler were materialists not only in their dismissal of religion but also in their insensitivity to humanity as well."[16] In addition to the indirect murderous impact of their political programs, which killed tens of millions of people, they also implemented plans that directly killed just as large or even greater a number. With respect to their treatment of the Church, Stalin attacked it directly; Hitler made more of an effort to manipulate and use, rather than to immediately destroy, the Church. Despite Stalin's antagonism, he failed to eradicate the Church. Indeed, it continues to be strong in twenty-first-century Russia, having survived the Bolshevik onslaught and it has been revived and strengthened by Putin.[17] Germany has become more secular since World War II, but this is part of a general European trend of secularization rather than the impact of Hitler's attacks on the Church.[18]

Religion and the institution of the Church have proved to be extremely resilient and long-lasting.[19] The major religions, Judaism, Christianity, and Islam, have survived thousands of years, and are in effect the oldest business enterprises in human history. Each of the major religions are carried forward and propagated by powerful cultural carriers, which are extremely difficult to eliminate, in part because they are associated with narratives that are central to the cultural lives of societies and passed on from generation to generation. For example, the menorah, a multibranched candelabra, is an important cultural carrier signifying Judaism, and it is now the official emblem of the state of Israel. A lighted menorah has special significance for practicing Jews, as it is associated with the narrative of a miracle of a tiny quantity of oil lasting eight days to light the Temple's menorah during the celebration of the festival of Hanukkah about 2,200 years ago. For Christians, the cross is a powerful carrier, because it symbolizes the Crucifixion of Jesus Christ and is supported by narratives about the redeeming nature of his sacrifice for humanity. The extensive narratives associated with the cross are a central part of Christianity, and are passed on from generation to generation. In Islam, the *Kaaba* (located in Mecca, Saudi Arabia) is a central cultural carrier, representing the most sacred site and the direction in which practicing Muslims pray five times a day. The Kaaba is the center of the pilgrimage (*Hajj*) to Mecca, which all practicing Muslims should undertake if they are physically and financially able. Narratives about the Kaaba, the Hajj, and Mecca are part of the socialization of all Muslims across generations throughout the world.

The power of cultural carriers supporting religion is one important reason why revolutionaries have found it so difficult to eliminate the Church. For example, after the 1917 Russian Revolution, the Bolsheviks engaged in a systematic campaign against the Church, forcing ordinary practicing Christians and Church authorities to make public renunciations, but as Sheila Fitzpatrick explains:

> The kind of renunciation that most interested Soviet authorities was when priests renounced the cloth. Such renunciations, if done publicly, provided dramatic support for the Soviet position that religion was a fraud that had been discredited by modern science. Signed announcements that a priest was renouncing the cloth ... appeared from time to time as letters to the editor in the local press ...[20]

But even more dramatic were renunciations of the cloth by priests standing in front of the congregation in church, denouncing religion as fraudulent.

The Bolsheviks engaged in a long list of actions to try to end the influence of the Church:

> Schools were taken out of the hands of the Church, and religious education in schools was banned. Icons and other images were to be removed from all public buildings and processions were to be allowed only with the permission of the local soviet. The practice of religious rituals in state and public institutions was forbidden. Churches were deprived of their status as judicial personages and thus forbidden to possess property ... the registration of births, marriages, and deaths was also taken out of the hands of the Church and transferred to the soviets ... By the late 1920s, 673 monasteries ... had been dissolved and their 1.2 million hectares of land confiscated ... The Bolsheviks portrayed the clergy as inveterate reactionaries: posters depicted priests as drunkards and gluttons, monks and nuns as sinister "black crows", the faithful as innocent dupes of ruling-class lackeys.[21]

In addition, numerous churches were desecrated, emptied of valuables, and closed.

The three main elements of Soviet Union policy toward religion have been summed up by John Anderson in this way: "a socialization process aimed at the creation of the new Soviet (atheist) man; the administrative and legislative regulation of religious bodies with the ostensible intention of eventually seeing them disappear; coping with the responses of believers to official policies, if necessary by repressive means."[22] As a result of this assault, religious activities in the Soviet Union went largely underground.[23] Practicing Christians would meet in private homes to worship together, keeping their activities hidden from authorities. However, this did not mean that the sacred carriers of Christianity disappeared. The cross continued to be worn as jewelry, but often in secret.[24] The most important Christian cultural carrier that could not be easily changed were the large church buildings. Cathedrals were sometimes used as anti-religion museums in the Soviet anti-religious campaigns, but the existence of these vast religious buildings and the collective historic religious memories associated with them could not be completely suppressed.[25]

Indeed, the dormant power of the cultural carriers supporting the Russian Orthodox Church is evident in the rapid speed with which Putin managed to revive this Church in the twenty-first century. In other domains as well, patterns of behavior that were supposed to be eliminated reemerged as very much alive in the post-revolution period. An example of this is leadership and resource inequalities, which I turn to next.

Cultural Carriers, Leadership, and Resource Inequalities

A vast array of cultural carriers endorses the view that leaders are needed as decision-makers, and that different people should have access to unequal levels of power and resources. The alternative to leaders making the important decisions, and resources and power being unequally distributed, is a society in which decision-making is shared fairly equally among the people, as are power and resources. This kind of utopian society has been envisaged by various revolutionaries, artists, and writers, and in political terms it is captured by labels such as the "classless society" as envisaged by Karl Marx and the term *Utopia* as imagined three centuries earlier by Sir Thomas More (1478–1535).[26]

Of course, some revolutionaries begin with an ideology that *endorses and propagates* centralized leadership, as well as power and resource inequalities.

For example, the Iranian Revolution was quickly taken over by Khomeini and his extremist supporters, who were a numerical minority, but who used force to implement rule by a single male cleric (according to the principle of *velayat-e faghih*, discussed in Chapter 7). Given their ideological foundation, it is not at all surprising that Khomeini and his supporters forced post-revolution Iranian society to continue as a dictatorship with even larger group-based inequalities in power and resources. What is puzzling and surprising is cases such as the Bolsheviks, who were also a radical minority who used force to take over after the Russian Revolution, but in this case the Bolsheviks began with an ideology that had as its declared goal a classless society. Given this very different utopian goal, how is it that the outcome was not very different in Russia and Iran? How is it that the centralization of power in the hands of a single male dictator, and the unequal distribution of resources across different groups, also characterized Soviet society – even though the avowed goal was a classless society? It is in addressing this question that the important role of cultural carriers becomes apparent.

Cultural carriers support continuity in actual behavior and the actual organization of the material world. This continuity concerns what people actually do and the way power and resources are actually distributed in society. Continuity in actual behavior and the actual organization of the material world is often camouflaged by rhetoric, and this is particularly evident in the changes that take place in the stories and narratives used by regimes before and after revolutions. We are reminded of Vilfredo Pareto's (1848–1923) observation that elites use masks to hide the deeper nature of social organization from the non-elite (Pareto's views are discussed in Chapter 2 of this text). Elites use masks and idealistic rhetoric to mobilize non-elites, so they can "get rid of one aristocracy and replace it with another."[27] Of course, from this perspective revolutionaries want to get rid of the ruling aristocracy simply to take over as the ruling aristocracy themselves – the president changing places with the tsar in Russia, the Chairman changing places with the emperor in China, and the ayatollah changing places with the shah in Iran.

Myths, fairytales, stories about history, tales about national heroes – these are all part of the cultural carriers that normalize and support the continuation of the idea that leaders are necessary for making important decisions and determining the future direction of society. Many such narratives are about mythical national heroes, or actual historical figures who have become part of the national mythology, and their influence did not stop with revolution. For example, Russian tales of magic and the supernatural have continued their influence across the centuries, gliding under the radar of revolutionaries determined to change everything in line with their ideology.[28]

Revolutionaries have made great efforts to counter the influence of cultural carriers and prevent continuities in what they consider to be behavior that is not in line with the goals of the revolution. This has involved attempting to change the details of everyday life in society. For example, after the French Revolution, the traditional Gregorian calendar was replaced by a revolutionary calendar, with new names for months and each month divided into three ten-day periods. After the Iranian Revolution, the monarchist calendar was set aside, and more importance was given to the Islamic calendar. The names of cities, streets, buildings, and just about all other features of the built environment are changed after revolutions. Typically, the new names have to do with freedom, liberty, revival, and hope.

But the changes made after revolutions are often only at a surface level, and they tend to hide deep-level continuities. For example, after the French, Russian, Chinese, Iranian, and Cuban revolutions, a common trend was to reject titles ("Your Excellency," "Your Highness," and so on), and to use terms such as "citizen," "comrade," "brother," and "sister." After the revolution in Iran, some revolutionary students in my classes insisted on calling me "brother" rather than "*ostad*" ("professor") or "Dr." Also, names associated with former leaders became rarely used, and names associated with the new revolutionary leadership became popular (e.g., Nokolai became rare after the Russian Revolution; Fidel became commonly used in post-revolution Cuba). However, these surface-level changes hide a deeper-level continuity: First, a male leader holds absolute power; second, new titles are gradually ascribed to the new revolutionary leader. For example, in Iran the "King of Kings" and other royal titles were no longer used, but Khomeini acquired even more lofty titles, including ones that claim him to be *the* representative of God on earth.

This cycle of post-revolution rejection of titles and then gradual acquisition of new titles is described by Sheila Fitzpatrick in this way for the case of Russia:

> The Revolution had initially swept away all titles, ranks, and uniforms, regarding them as unnecessary and even absurd marks of status characteristic of an autocratic regime. Epaulettes, insignia, and even military ranks were banished from the Red Army for almost two decades ... The old uniforms of university and high school students disappeared. Civil service ranks were abolished, as were the different uniforms that had been worn by

officials in different ministries ... Then, in the mid 1930s, the tide turned. Titles, ranks, and uniforms were reinstated, and often bore a strong resemblance to their Imperial predecessors ... Communists who had moved up from the lower classes were particularly inclined to see their assumption of distinctions modeled on those of the old regime as simply a proof that the Revolution had finally triumphed: they now had what the old bosses used to have.[29]

This return to the old ways is irresistible because the revolutionaries themselves are entangled in social relationships that are regulated by difficult-to-detect and to-change cultural carriers. Napoleon replaced King Louis XVI, Lenin replaced Tsar Nicholas II, Mao Zedong eventually replaced Emperor Hsian-T'ung, Fidel Castro replaced President Fulgencio Batista, Khomeini replaced the Shah ... and in each case the new revolutionary leader became just as or even more powerful than his predecessor, with at least as many lofty titles ("Supreme Leader," "The Great Helmsman," and so on).

Concluding Comment

Revolutions tend to be misleading; they are like magic shows, in which smoke, mirrors, dazzling lights, distracting noises, elephants, clowns, and wild spells put people in a trance, at least for a while. People get carried along by the feverish rhetoric of revolution and the mesmeric images of an ideal world that seems just ahead of us, almost within reach. The exciting noise and clamor mislead us to imagine that the surface changes we are witnessing are leading to a transformed world, whereas at a deeper level solid, foundational continuities persist in behavior and in the organization of the world. We often misunderstand that what has been changed by the revolution is rhetoric, not actual action. Most importantly, the title of the leader has changed, but the role of leaders and their absolute power remains the same.

Cultural carriers create resistance to change, and they are powerful because they are the result of long-term developments and it is extremely difficult to change them in the short term. For example, classical literature, myths, fairy tales, and folk songs of a society develop over hundreds, sometimes thousands, of years. These are woven into the fabric of everyday life. Changing them requires tearing apart how things are done in everyday life, including how people think. But if these aspects of life are not changed, they serve to support the continuation of traditional forms of thinking and doing, including in important areas such as motivation, ownership, and work.

Cultural carriers serve as an invisible hand that pulls people back to how they thought and acted before the revolution. Some revolutionaries, such as Mao Zedong, recognize the power of this deep force and call for a perpetual revolution, so that the pull of cultural carriers can be forever resisted. But perpetual revolutions have been resisted; cultural carriers have proved to be too powerful across history.

CHAPTER 9

The Role of Personality in Revolutions

Historically, personality has been assumed to have a pivotal, determining role in revolutions, as reflected in the extensive academic and media coverage of the personalities of revolutionary leaders such as Robespierre, Lenin, Trotsky, Mao, Castro, Mandela, and Khomeini. The study of the personalities of revolutionary leaders is often assumed to be a fruitful path for gaining a more in-depth and accurate understanding of revolutions. There is undoubtedly some truth to this. After all, part of what happened in the lead-up to, during, and after the Russian, Chinese, South African, and Iranian revolutions is shaped by the personalities of Lenin, Mao, Mandela, and Khomeini, respectively. For example, after fourteen years of exile outside Iran, Khomeini returned to muzzle, imprison, exile, or kill those who opposed his will; in contrast, after twenty-seven years of imprisonment in South Africa, Mandela (aided by de Klerk) helped to improve the wounds inflicted by apartheid and saved his country from transforming into a dark dictatorship. The extreme repression in Iran and the relatively open system of South Africa partly reflects the different personalities of Khomeini and Mandela.

My discussion of the role of personality in revolutions diverges from, and improves upon, the traditional path in three ways. First, I propose that the consistencies in behavior that we refer to as personality arise from both intrapersonal and contextual characteristics. I discuss this proposition in the next section. Second, I consider the role of personality in supporting *continuity of behavior* across revolutions. That is, personality is one of the factors that leads to lower political plasticity in patterns of collective and individual behavior before and after revolutions. Third, in addition to considering (1) the personalities of revolutionary leaders, I also consider (2) the personalities of the people who surround the revolutionary leader and become the second-level leaders, (3) the loyal masses who follow and support the revolutionary leader, and (4) those who do not conform and obey according to the wishes of the revolutionary regime (these rebels are often a minority, at least to begin with).

Obviously, women have played an important role in revolutions, and discussions of the role of personality that exclude women are inadequate.[1] However, the leaders who came to power after major revolutions have been male, and so we have less information about the personality characteristics of females in this leadership role.

The Role of System M Personality and System E Personality in Behavioral Continuity

The traditional interpretation of personality is limited to what I have termed *System M ("Micro") personality*, which assumes that consistency in behavior arises from intrapersonal characteristics.[2] For example, Freud discusses the role of the id, the ego, and the superego in human personality development, and in human relationships broadly.[3] Freud also explores the role of certain *traits*, consistent tendencies in behavior such as narcissism, which are also assumed to be part of the internal characteristics of individuals and integral to their personalities. Twenty-first-century researchers have homed in on the so-called Big Five traits: openness to experience, conscientiousness, extroversion, agreeableness, and neuroticism (OCEAN). The assumption is that these five (supposedly universal) traits capture the personalities of all humans. The personality trait approach is in line with the "Great Man/Woman" theory of history, which assumes that historical developments are shaped by outstanding individuals, who have personality characteristics that are special and, in some ways, unique. This explanation is reductionist, in the sense that it reduces vast macro-level historical developments across and within nations to traits and other characteristics assumed to operate within individuals. Reductionism is one of the main shortcomings of mainstream psychological theory and research.[4]

The traditional *System M ("Micro")* approach to personality does not take into consideration the enormous role of contextual factors as a source of consistency in individual behavior, but this is incorporated in what I have terms *System E ("Extended") personality*.[5] For example, poverty and a subordinate position is an extremely powerful context that influences behavior, including in areas such as decision-making and other cognitive skills. In controlled experiments, financially poorer participants did less well on standardized cognitive tests when they were (even indirectly) reminded of money and their relatively impoverished material conditions.[6] Following this line of research, from the perspective of *System E ("Extended") personality*, the context is a major factor shaping consistency and continuity in the behavior of individuals before and after revolutions.

Consistency in behavior before and after revolutions is explained at least partly by the characteristics of the context remaining the same before and after revolutions. With respect to continuity in style of leader–follower relations, the context that enables a leader to have absolute power and control in dictatorial societies tends to be resilient and to reemerge after revolutions. It is with respect to both the power of context and continuity in context that we can explain why at a deep level, rather than the surface level of revolutionary rhetoric and symbolism, that both leaders and followers tend to behave in similar ways before and after revolutions.

The Personalities of Key Individuals and Groups in Revolutions

In this section, I distinguish between the personality characteristics of four different sets of individuals: the revolutionary leader, the second-level leaders who surround the revolutionary leader, the masses who (often adoringly) follow the revolutionary leader, and those who refuse to conform and obey in line with the demands of the revolution. Of course, these categories are to some degree artificial because they overlook the overlapping and fluid nature of categories. For example, it is not unusual for individuals who begin as supporters of the revolutionary leader and the revolution to change their minds and join the opposition, sometimes openly.

The Personalities of Revolutionary Leaders

> ... *Lenin was personally beyond challenge as leader of the Party. Everyone saw him as the senior figure ... it was unthinkable that anyone would criticize Lenin personally in the terms he used to reprimand others ... Lenin was a prophet among disciples: reprimands only went in one direction ... by 1920 Lenin had made himself into a kind of philosopher king ... he was conducting a nationwide seminar ... based on hypotheses which Lenin took as undeniable axioms. Indeed, the legitimacy he claimed for himself and his government did not arise from a clear popular mandate ... but from his philosophical claim to possess the correct policies and consciousness of the ruled, even if the ruled did not see it that way. He was, in this respect a secular equivalent of theocratic leaders who derive their legitimacy from the truth of their doctrines, not popular mandates.*[7]

How is it that only a few years after the 1917 revolution and the murder of Tsar Nicholas II (along with his family, in 1918), Lenin had become the undeniable and unchallengeable center of power – and arguably was reshaping Russian society in more fundamental ways than ever undertaken by Tsar Nicholas II or any other member of the Romanov dynasty over their 300-year rule? How is it that Lenin managed to concentrate so much power and prestige in his own person, so soon after the Bolsheviks took over in Russia with the avowed goal of reaching a classless society in which government and centralized leadership would disappear (because, after all, communist ideology sees the traditional function of government to be the protection of ruling-class interests and the repression of the lower classes. When there is no ruling class, then presumably there is no need for a central government)? To put it bluntly, how is it that in such a short time Lenin had become more of a tsar than the assassinated Tsar Nicholas II?

The same trend of continuity in leadership style, particularly in terms of the concentration of power in the hands of the dictator, is evident after other revolutions. For example, after the Chinese Revolution, Mao Zedong ruled in the style of the old Chinese emperors, including in the details of enjoying a narcissistic, egocentric social life, which included concubines and various pleasures forbidden to other Chinese people.[8] Having acquired the power, prestige, and lifestyle of the old emperors, Mao was now portrayed as a miraculous, prophetic leader, as Michael Lynch describes:

> Mao was projected as the outstanding interpreter of class struggle, the last and the greatest in the line of prophets of revolution that stretched from Marx, by way of Lenin and Stalin, to reach its culmination in him ... The Little Red Book, which first appeared in 1964, is best understood as China's secular bible ... The sayings of Confucius had once been invoked to settle legal and social disputes. It was now the thoughts of Chairman Mao that were the ultimate reference.[9]

Thus, only a short time after the old emperors of China were banished forever, emperor Mao emerged with so much power, mystique, and influence that would have made many of the old emperors envious.

The same trend was evident in post-revolution Iran, when power became completely concentrated in Khomeini's hands and he became the ultimate decider on absolutely *everything*. The ancient shahs would indeed have been envious. The rhetoric of revolution initially camouflaged Khomeini's dictatorial relationship with the people of Iran, but just beneath the misleading surface of this mesmerizing rhetoric was the reality of absolute power in the hands of a single male dictator (a tradition which continues with Khamenei). What was true for Lenin and Mao in terms of reprimands only going in one direction was doubly true for Khomeini – he could criticize all others, but no one could criticize him. Whereas Lenin (and later Mao) acted as the "secular equivalent of theocratic leaders who derive their legitimacy from the truth of their doctrines, not popular mandates" (as quoted above), Khomeini was positioned as the representative of God on earth, who did not need popular mandates because his word was the truth, not to be contested by any Iranian.

There are two steps in how the personality of the revolutionary leader helps to perpetuate dictatorship after revolutions. First, the context of the revolution helps to create what I have termed the *springboard to dictatorship*, the social and psychological characteristics that make society ready to accept a dictator and prepare the ground for the launching of a new dictatorship (often under the guise of a new revolutionary rhetoric, which might be Marxist, Islamic, fascist, nationalist, or some other). Second, the intrapersonal characteristics of the potential dictator enables him to outmaneuver his rivals (including by using extreme violence) and to spring to power. Thus, we see that whereas the context of the revolution created the opportunity for continuity in leadership style in Russia, China, and Iran, the details of the individual intrapersonal characteristics of Lenin, Mao, and Khomeini enabled them to step directly and emphatically into the role of supreme infallible leader. It is here that we recognize the power and importance of intrapersonal personality characteristics.

Elsewhere I have discussed the main components of the dictator personality.[10] The majority of efforts to identify the personality characteristics of dictators came after World War II, in large part because of the threat posed by Adolf Hitler, Benito Mussolini, and other dictators (e.g., Emperor Hirohito of Japan), and were highly influenced by psychoanalytic psychology.[11] But in assessing the personalities of dictators, we can go beyond the psychoanalytic approach by also considering the psychometric research leading to the identification of key traits,[12] as well as the cognitive research providing information about personality and styles of thinking and problem-solving.[13] I will now turn to discuss the key intrapersonal characteristics that lead to particular individuals becoming leaders through revolutions. Unfortunately, these also tend to be the personality characteristics of individuals who are most likely to become dictators (there are a few rare exceptions to this in history, such as George Washington and Nelson

Mandela – individuals who voluntarily stepped away from supreme power).

Pathological Narcissism: From Napoleon Bonaparte to Ruhollah Khomeini, pathological narcissism is central to the personalities of individuals who grab power after revolutions.[14] Pathological narcissism involves extreme self-centeredness, an overbearing sense of righteousness and entitlement, a belief that their path is the correct one and their views are the best, and a lack of empathy for the suffering others have to go through in order for their path to be followed. This personality style has in some cases (such as in China, Russia, and Iran) resulted in millions of people being killed because the great leader has programs that must be implemented at all costs – even though these plans are in practice disastrous for society, such as Bonaparte's international wars and invasion of Russia, Lenin's rushed collective farming schemes, Mao's so-called Great Leap Forward, and Khomeini's so-called Cultural Revolution and refusal to bring an end to the Iran–Iraq War (1980–8) at the earliest possible opportunity.

Craving for Power: Major revolutions involve mass uprisings of numerous different groups, with many different potential revolutionary leaders. How is it that from these many different possibilities, particular individuals and their groups become the absolute leaders of the revolution? For example, how is it that Lenin led the Bolsheviks to power in Russia, even though when the Tsar's regime collapsed very few would have predicted Lenin's meteoric rise and the dominance of the Bolsheviks? Among the factors that led to Lenin, Mao, Khomeini, and other individuals to become supreme revolutionary leaders is their extraordinarily strong craving for power. The motivation of individuals such as Napoleon to rise to power is among their most astonishing personality features. It is a motor that drives them on, to ignore all the costs and only focus on harnessing power in their own hands. This personality characteristic gives revolutionary leaders such as Napoleon, Lenin, Mao, and Khomeini a detachment, an aloofness that sets them apart from ordinary people. They seem untouched by events – mass suffering and dying, war, famine – nothing seems to affect them, as they maintain their focus on attaining absolute power (I recall Khomeini answering "*hichi*," nothing, in response to a reporter asking him what he felt after returning to Iran – the Shah's regime had just collapsed and Khomeini was about to grab power, but he felt nothing).[15]

Risk-Taking: The leaders who come to power through revolutions are extraordinary high risk-takers. There is the obvious risk of being killed or otherwise harmed by the regime that they are attempting to topple (in the case of Fidel Castro, there were also numerous attempts by the CIA to assassinate him after he came to power). They often have to endure many years of exile, as did Lenin and Khomeini (Mandela suffered twenty-seven years of imprisonment), as well as physical hardship, such as the 6,000-mile *Long March* (1934–5) undertaken by Mao, together with 90,000 other communists (only about 20,000 survived).[16] Mao's two-year-old son was too young to be taken on the Long March, and after they set off Mao and his wife never saw him again. After imprisonment and exile, Castro took the risk of returning to Cuba in 1956, and for the next three years he conducted guerrilla warfare against far larger and better-equipped government forces – until the collapse of the Batista regime in 1959.

Machiavellianism: The leaders who spring to power through revolutions tend to be high on *Machiavellianism*, the ability to influence and manipulate other people to do what one wants, without them necessarily becoming aware of this influence.[17] The measures of Machiavellianism developed by modern psychologists originate in the work of Niccolò Machiavelli (1469–1527). Highly Machiavellian individuals are ruthless, see the world as a dangerous place, adopt an attitude of "the ends justify the means," and have the ability to camouflage their true motives and methods. For example, Lenin was the main driving force behind the *Red Terror*, a campaign of extreme repression that resulted in the death, exile, and imprisonment of hundreds of thousands of Russians in the immediate post-revolution period, 1918–22. But although Lenin was happy to openly endorse numerous decrees and laws, he tried to make sure his name was not publicly associated with the Red Terror and acts of violence generally.[18] Similarly, the so-called *Great Leap Forward* (1955–9) was supposed to result in rapid industrialization in China, but actually caused mass famine.[19] Although Mao was the driving force behind the disaster, he maneuvered nimbly, tried to escape blame, and positioned himself to lead China to yet another disastrous project, the Cultural Revolution of the 1960s. Khomeini was just as high on Machiavellianism, managing to camouflage his real opinions, which were anti-democratic and against equal rights for women, until he had gained absolute power. His high Machiavellianism is also reflected in his manipulative use of the hostage-taking crisis (1979–80) and the Iran–Iraq War (1980–8), both disastrous for Iranian national interests, but extremely useful for Khomeini's personal goal of concentrating power in his own hands.

Intolerance for Ambiguity: Leaders who come to power through revolutions tend to be extraordinarily focused: Every fiber of their being is exclusively devoted to attaining power. An important part of this general approach is intolerance of ambiguity, a concept originating in the work of Else Frenkel-Brunswik (1908–58),[20] and explained by Stephen Bochner as having the following primary and secondary characteristics:

> Primary characteristics ... (a) rigid dichotomizing into fixed categories ... (b) seeking for certainty and avoiding ambiguity ... (c) inability to allow for the co-existence of positive and negative features in the same object ... (d) acceptance of attitude statements representing a rigid white-black view of life ... (e) a preference for the familiar over the unfamiliar ... (f) a positive rejecting of the different or unusual ... (g) resistance to reversal of apparent fluctuating stimuli ... (h) the early selection and maintenance of one solution in a perceptually ambiguous situation ... (i) premature closure ... Secondary characteristics: persons intolerant of ambiguity will be ... authoritarian ... dogmatic ... rigid ... closed minded ... ethnically prejudiced ... uncreative ... anxious ... extra-punitive ... aggressive.[21]

Twenty-first-century research on intolerance for ambiguity has further demonstrated the important role of categorical thinking and generalized prejudice against others who are perceived to be different.[22] Categorical thinking is at the core of the way Lenin, Mao, Castro, Khomeini, and other revolutionary leaders dogmatically insisted that only their path was correct, and that anyone who deviated from their path must be rejected – and killed if necessary. As Erich Weeded and Edward Muller note, "revolutionary struggles for power are often won by those contenders who are most ready to kill,"[23] and categorical thinking provides the cognitive platform for identifying and distancing those whom revolutionary leaders such as Lenin, Mao, and Khomeini decide have to be killed.

Illusions of Control and Grandeur: Leaders who come to power through revolutions face enormous, seemingly unsurmountable, challenges. After all, they first have to topple the regime in power, supported by a dangerous and often powerful and extensive security apparatus. In some cases, the ruling regimes have ruled for centuries and seem impossible to dislodge (e.g., the Romanovs ruled Russia for 300 years). For revolutionaries and particularly revolutionary leaders, the costs of being captured are terrifying – imprisonment, torture, exile, and death are the typical outcomes. What makes revolutionary leaders believe they can topple the ruling regime and come out on top? Even if the regime falls, there are numerous other revolutionary groups competing to take over as the next ruling regime. At the dawn of the Russian Revolution, the Bolsheviks had scores of competitors and there were many other individuals who might have overtaken Lenin and become the next national leader. The same is true for Mao at the dawn of the Chinese Revolution, for Castro at the dawn of the Cuban Revolution, and for Khomeini at the dawn of the Iranian Revolution. But part of what made Lenin, Mao, Castro, Khomeini, and some other revolutionary leaders different and special was their illusions of control and grandeur – unending, exaggerated, giant conviction that they could control events and their destiny to achieve greatness.[24]

But of course, most leaders who have illusions of control and grandeur end up with dirt in their hands rather than reaching the stars. For example, in the 1930s when Mao was struggling to keep his communist forces together during the Long March and the numerous battles that followed (many of which the communists lost), Sir Oswald Mosely (1896–1980) was leading the British Union of Fascists to try to inspire a fascist revolution in Britain. Watching films of Mosely make speeches at fascist rallies, it is clear he has learned through imitation to make gestures and movements like Hitler and Mussolini. It is also clear that he was suffering from illusions of control and grandeur – but these came to nothing because the fascist revolution never came to fruition in Britain, and Mosely spent many years in jail and in exile.[25] While Mao struggled on, led a revolution, and eventually came to dominate China, the fascist revolution in Britain did not materialize for Mosely.

Charisma: Another personality feature of leaders who come to power through revolutions is *charisma*, the mysterious quality some individuals possess that enables them to inspire, influence, and lead others to make sacrifices for a cause – from working hard and dedicating themselves to an organization to making enormous sacrifices for larger goals, such as giving up their lives for a revolution. Charisma is not unique to individuals who do good and have a constructive impact; it is also part of the personality of destructive individuals such as Mussolini, Hitler, Saddam Hussein, and Osama bin Laden. There is general agreement that revolutionary leaders tend to be charismatic, and that they somehow cast a spell on large populations and lead them to make enormous sacrifices.[26] Since at least the pioneering research of Max Weber (1864–1920), charismatic leadership has been seen to be social in nature, meaning that its power emerges through relationships *between* leaders and followers.[27]

It is particularly when a population faces great hardship and the leader must persuade people to make deep sacrifices for the revolutionary cause that the vital role of charisma becomes clear. For example, consider the terrifyingly harsh conditions of the Long March undertaken by Mao and the communists in the mid-1930s and the guerrilla warfare waged by Castro against the ruling Batista government in extremely harsh conditions in 1956–9 (until Batista fled Cuba). These undertakings were only possible through the charismatic influence of the revolutionary leader to persuade his followers to make life-and-death sacrifices. Twenty-first-century research has made some progress in identifying the details of what makes an individual charismatic, such as making eye contact in a way that moves followers.[28] But case studies of charismatic leaders suggest that it is the combination of contextual and personality factors that leads to charismatic influence (this reminds us of the distinction between *System E "Extended" personality*, focused on context, and *System M "Micro" personality*, focused on intrapersonal characteristics, discussed earlier in this chapter).

An example of a context which was used to highlight Hitler's charisma is the Nuremberg Nazi rallies of the 1930s, which were conducted outdoors at night, using technology to create a "cathedral of light" and the music of Richard Wagner (1813–83) to enhance the atmosphere. Stacey Reed points out that "so powerful were the effects of the aesthetic and psychological aspects of the rallies that they swept people up into a fervor of passion and support . . . "[29]. It is often commented that the "cathedrals of light" created by the Nazis had a religious flavor, and I think this means that the rallies moved people deeply and emotionally. The power of the context moved people.

The Personalities of the People Who Surround the Revolutionary Leader

Leaders who come to power through revolutions are surrounded and supported by numerous other people. Who surrounds the revolutionary leader and what are their personality characteristics? In answering these questions, I distinguish between three categories: (1) individuals who help topple the ruling regime and bring about the revolution, but are politically moderate relative to the radical revolutionary leader who comes to dominate after regime change; (2) individuals who are political extremists and support radical programs, sometimes even pushing the radical revolutionary leader to further extremism; and (3) individuals who act opportunistically and will change in whatever way necessary and move in any direction required in order to personally advance in the post-revolutionary society. There is some overlap across these groups. For example, some individuals who are moderate at the time of the revolution change over time to become far more radical, perhaps because they become one of the opportunists in the third category.

Political Moderates Relative to the Radical Revolutionary Leader

The expression "revolutions devour their own children," probably originated by the playwright George Buchner (1813–37) in reference to the French Revolution, comes to mind when we consider individuals in the first category (i.e., moderates who fail to maneuver swiftly enough to avoid being devoured).[30] The classic example of this is the thousands of people who had supported the French Revolution in one way or another, or at least moved along with the changes, but then found themselves victims in the Terror years (discussed in Chapter 3). The great French scientist Antoine Lavoisier (1743–94), who helped lay the foundations of modern chemistry, is an example. Lavoisier was an aristocrat who remained in France after the revolution, believing that science and the French *Académie des Sciences* could play an important role in post-revolution French society. Unfortunately, the aristocratic roots of both Lavoisier and the *Académie des Sciences* (founded in 1666 by King Louis XIV) resulted in him being guillotined, along with some other eminent French scientists.[31] A strong continuous theme in revolutions, from the French Revolution in the eighteenth century to the Iranian Revolution in the twentieth century, is the tendency for scientists and science to be attacked. This is in part because of the association between scientific research and the elite in societies – but also because the authoritarian pro-fascist movements that also rise up through revolutions are anti-science (and this includes failed attempts at revolutions, such as what was attempted by Donald Trump's supporters on January 6, 2021).

The Terror following the French Revolution was the brutal weapon of extremists against anyone even suspected of representing moderation in their position vis-à-vis the Revolution. As Simon Schama describes:

> The Terror went into action with impressive bureaucratic efficiency. House searches, usually made at night, were extensive and unsparing. All citizens were required to attach to their front doors a notice indicating all residents who lived inside. Entertaining anyone not on that list, even for a single night, was a serious crime ... From early December [1793] the guillotine went into action at a much greater tempo ... pride was taken in its mechanical efficiency ... thirty-two heads were severed in twenty-five minutes; a week later, twelve heads in just five minutes.[32]

Very similar "terror years" followed the Russian Revolution in 1917–22 and the Iranian Revolution in the early 1980s, during which large numbers of moderates who had been part of the revolution were unceremoniously devoured.

What can we say about the personalities of the moderates who themselves became victims during periods of terror following revolutions? When we review the lists of moderates who helped to bring about the Russian Revolution but were destroyed by Lenin (and later Stalin); who helped to bring about the Chinese Revolution but were destroyed by Mao; who helped to bring about the Cuban Revolution but were destroyed by Castro; and who helped to bring about the Anti-Shah Revolution in Iran but were destroyed by Khomeini, it is clear that they have diverse personality characteristics (of course, I am using the term "moderate" in a relative sense. These were only moderates relative to extremist revolutionary leaders). For example, consider just the "moderates" who accompanied Khomeini in his move from Paris to Tehran in 1978–9 and helped him transition to absolute power, but were very soon destroyed by him in different ways: These include Abolhassan Banisadr (1933–2021), the first president of Iran after the revolution, who was dismissed by Khomeini in 1981 and forced to live for the rest of his life under tight police protection in exile in France; Ibrahim Yazdi (1931–2017), deputy-prime minister and minister of foreign affairs after the revolution, forced to resign in 1979 and then repeatedly jailed until his death; Mehdi Bazargan (1907–95), the first prime minister after the Anti-Shah Revolution, forced to resign in 1979 and persecuted until his death; and Sadegh Ghotbzadeh (1936–82), foreign minister after the revolution, arrested, tortured, and killed by firing squad in 1982. Another important victim was Grand Ayatollah Hussein-Ali Montazari (1922–2009), who was in 1985 positioned as Khomeini's successor but in 1988 was cast out by Khomeini because he spoke out publicly against mass torture and executions (discussed in Chapter 7). Is there something common to all these moderates?

Probably the most important common characteristic of these kinds of moderates is that although they helped to topple the former regime, they were not willing to support the extremist post-revolution actions undertaken by leaders such as Lenin, Mao, Castro, and Khomeini. In Russia, the moderates fell from grace because they did not have the stomach for extremist actions, ranging from the assassination of the Tsar and his family to the forced collectivization of farms and mass relocation of populations. In China, the moderates incurred the wrath of Mao because they opposed, or at least did not enthusiastically support, what they saw to be destructive programs such as the Great Leap Forward and the Cultural Revolution. In Cuba, the moderates were seen as obstacles on the path to rapid and complete collectivization of all property and work organization. In Iran, the moderates stood against what they saw to be extremist actions against

Iranian national interests, such as the invasion of the US Embassy and hostage taking, as well as the refusal to end the Iran–Iraq War in 1982–3 (when Saddam Hussein signaled his readiness to negotiate a peace treaty – but Khomeini ensured the war continued until 1988, resulting in millions of needless deaths and injuries).

Extremist revolutionary leaders such as Lenin, Mao, Castro, and Khomeini come to see the moderates who helped them come to power as a burden in the post-revolution period, a limitation on their actions, a straitjacket they must break out of. On the one hand, the moderates do serve a useful function after the revolution because they can be blamed for whatever goes wrong, and they can even be accused of colluding with the enemy, being treasonous, and sabotaging extremist programs. On the other hand, power must be wrestled from the moderates and they must be pushed aside. Lenin was clear about this soon after the collapse of the Tsar's regime, specifically stating in a letter to the rest of his party: "The Bolsheviks ... can and *must* take state power into their own hands."[33] He wanted no power-sharing with other groups – who had helped to overthrow the Tsar, but were now considered by him as lacking the ideological purity of the Bolsheviks.

Mao was lethal in his efforts to drive and keep the moderates out of power. He saw them as enemies of the people, constantly working to pull China away from the path of perpetual revolution. From the 1940s until his death, he championed different "anti" movements (e.g., "anti-administrative corruption") that primarily targeted moderates, and hammered them as a way of frightening the rest of the population and keeping people in line.[34] Khomeini's attacks on moderates were absolutely lethal: Within a year after the revolution, he had either killed, imprisoned, or exiled just about all the moderates in the political sphere. Those attacked by Khomeini included moderate mullahs, such as the Grand Ayatollah Mohammad Kazem Shariatmadari (1906–86), who was essentially placed under house arrest and officially addressed as a mere "mister."

Political Extremists

Unlike the moderates who do better in times of peace and stability, extremist revolutionary leaders are greatly helped by war and turmoil; they thrive in conditions of violence and threat. Michael Lynch points out how Mao was shaped by the involvement of China in the Korean War (1950–3).

An interesting historical parallel presents itself. Thirty years earlier, revolutionary Russia had taken its shape not in accordance with the original plans of Lenin and the Bolsheviks but in response to the bitter civil war into which Russia was plunged from 1918 to 1920. The Soviet Union was born in violent conflict. So, too, was the PRC [People's Republic of China]. The Korean war demanded sacrifice and commitment. The effort left no opportunity for a smooth transition from the old China to the new.[35]

We can add that the historical parallel extends to Iran, which was plunged into war in 1980–8 (against its neighbor Iraq), a war that Khomeini refused to end earlier because he recognized that the war conditions benefited his extremist group and his style of leadership.

Political Opportunists

In Woody Allen's film *Zelig* (1983), the main character (Leon Zelig) is a man who transforms himself, sometimes in drastic ways, to become just like those around him. The third group who surround and support the extremist revolutionary leader have this chameleon-like ability to change themselves (sometimes overnight) and become fervent revolutionaries. These are often opportunists, with no solid principles other than to further their own interests, irrespective of what they have to do to be close to power – so as to benefit from the authority of the radical revolutionary leader. I witnessed a number of such individuals advancing among the "ranks of revolutionaries" after the coming to power of Khomeini in Iran. These individuals suddenly became fervent Muslims, spouted revolution-ary slogans, supported radical "revolutionary" actions, and in general did whatever it took to get into the corridors of power.

In psychological terms, these opportunistic individuals have a high self-monitoring personality, meaning that they monitor, regulate, and change the image that they present to better fit in with those around them.[36] Low self-monitors remain stable and true to themselves across situations: They are the ones who opposed both the dictatorial rule of the Shah and Khomeini, and were often persecuted by both dictators. Similarly, low self-monitors in Russia were persecuted by the Tsar and by the Lenin (and their heirs are persecuted by Putin).

Dictatorial regimes often find it extremely useful to employ chameleon-like high self-monitors, at both high and low levels of power. The reason is that these individuals have obvious weaknesses and can be more easily controlled. For example, after the revolution in Iran, local committees were set up in each community to work closely with the neighborhood mosques and maintain security (and also to keep power in the hands of the local mullahs, who would work closely with Khomeini's government). It was pointed out to me that a number of the "devout" committee members in our neighborhood in Tehran were thugs who until recently were known for their drunkenness, drug dealing, and other illegal activities. They now sported beards, dressed and talked like revolutionaries, and aggressively pushed local people to conform and obey as dictated by Khomeini. Many of these former thugs, high self-monitors, were later absorbed into the Revolutionary Guards that now control Iran. Information about their former (and ongoing) behavior that did not fit with being a devout Muslim was used by extremist followers of Khomeini as a saber over their heads, as a weakness that could be exploited when necessary. They could be relied upon to turn a blind eye to repression, corruption, outright robbery, and even murder when needed.

The Loyal Masses Who Follow and Support the Extremist Revolutionary Leader

Extremist revolutionary leaders who come to power are typically charismatic and capable of inspiring large followings. In this section, I address the following question: Do the millions who follow extremist revolutionary leaders such as Lenin, Mao, Castro, and Khomeini have certain distinct personality characteristics? We can get a good idea of their personality characteristics by paying close attention to the tactics used by extremist revolutionary leaders to mobilize these followers. At the heart of such tactics is displacement of aggression and a constant focus on threats, both internal and external.

Extremist revolutionary leaders repeatedly highlight the threats faced by "our people," of the dangerous attacks that are imminent, of the evil forces attempting to destroy us. These alleged threats are both from the outside and the inside, and often do objectively exist at some level – but they are grossly exaggerated and used manipulatively by extremist revolutionary leaders. Indeed, conspiratorial thinking is encouraged among followers, through descriptions that depict forces inside the country as collaborating with external forces to attack and try to bring down the revolutionary government. For Lenin, it was easy to highlight the link between internal and external threats because immediately after the 1917 revolution Russia was plunged into civil war, during which Britain and a number of other foreign countries made unsuccessful interventions to try to help the Whites defeat the communists.[37] Similarly, Mao, Castro, and Khomeini could all make the same claim: that external forces (particularly the United States) were conspiring with internal forces to bring down the revolutionary government (an example of such an intervention attempt is the *Bay of Pigs* fiasco, through which the United States attempted to topple the Castro government[38]). Invariably, the internal threats include – or are entirely made up of – minorities of various kinds.

It is when we examine the characteristics of the (fictional or real) internal threats targeted by Lenin, Mao, Castro, Khomeini, and other extremist revolutionary leaders, as well as the style of leadership adopted by these leaders, that we better understand the personalities of the millions of followers they attract. First, these revolutionary leaders invariably become dictators and demand that they must be unquestioningly obeyed. The justification for their establishing a dictatorship differ, at least on the surface: For example, Lenin, Mao, Castro, and other communist leaders established dictatorships based on the idea that they have led their societies to the stage of "dictatorship of the proletariat," and they are now ruling as dictators on behalf of the proletariat, and as part of the vanguard leading society to the next stage of the communist revolution. On the surface, Khomeini's justification for why he established a dictatorship is different: Based on his interpretation of Shi'a Islam (discussed in Chapters 7 and 8), society must be led by a *velayat-e faghih* – a wise cleric. Although these justifications for dictatorial rule differ on the surface (e.g., communist vs. Islamic), at a deeper level they are exactly the same: an authoritarian male leader is attempting to legitimize why he must be the dictator, and why society must unquestioningly follow his dictates.

An important faction among the followers of extremist revolutionary leaders consists of individuals with authoritarian personality characteristics (discussed in Chapter 8). The authoritarian personality was the focus of intensive study after World War II (1939–45), when Theodore Adorno (1903–69) led a group of researchers (which included the pioneer female scholar Else Frenkel-Brunswik, discussed earlier in this chapter) to examine the characteristics of individuals more prone to follow authoritarian leaders, such as Hitler. Extremist revolutionary leaders such as Lenin, Mao, and Khomeini tend to attract robust support from individuals with authoritarian personality characteristics. This support is gained particularly through strong aggressive actions by the extremist revolutionary leader against dissimilar others, perceived enemies of various kinds, who are part of the threatening world, working against "our revolution," "our people." Individuals high on authoritarianism fall in line to support the extremist revolutionary leader in attacks against dissimilar others, including fatal attacks that kill large numbers of the targeted group.

The particular targets of the extremist revolutionary leaders have differed, but the common theme that resonates with their authoritarian personality followers has been the outsider category of those targeted. The outsiders include the intellectuals, scientists, and broadly liberal thinkers who, sometimes openly, question the wisdom of leaders such as Lenin, Mao, and Khomeini. The outsiders also include ethnic minorities who often resist being incorporated into the national plans implemented by the extremist revolutionary leaders – whether it be Russification and collectivization through Lenin's leadership, or radical changes in culture and work processes in Mao's China, or Islamification (according to Khomeini's pro-dictatorship interpretation of Islam) in Iran. Another vitally important but often overlooked reason for the support extremist revolutionary leaders such as Khomeini win from authoritarian personalities is the explicit endorsement of treating women as third-class citizens.[39] Of course, it could be argued that in practice, Mao and some other extremist revolutionary leaders also reverted to traditional gender roles in their personal relations with women, despite their rhetorical support of equal rights.[40]

Those Who Do Not Conform and Obey According to the Wishes of the Revolutionary Regime

Not everyone supports extremist revolutionary leaders and their regimes. What are the personality characteristics of the nonconformists and the disobedient, those who refuse to go along with the revolutionary rhetoric and programs? At first glance, this seems like an impossible question to answer because of the varieties of extremist revolutionary leaders and the varieties of their opponents. However, all revolutionary movements have a common theme after regime change: extreme pressure on the people to fall in line behind the revolutionary leadership. Immediately after the revolution, this leadership tends to be relatively moderate – but soon the moderates are swept aside by radicals and an extremist revolutionary leader such as Lenin, Mao, Castro, or Khomeini takes control. Now, people are expected to follow the edicts of this extremist revolutionary leader – so we narrow our search to look for the personality characteristics of those who are more likely to disobey and refuse to conform to the extremist revolutionary leader, even under extreme pressure.

Psychological research on the relationship between personality characteristics and disobedience and nonconformity suggests certain systematic patterns.[41] Early research by Stanley Milgram found that participants who refused to obey orders to administer electric shocks to another person in his famous obedience to authority experiments (discussed in Chapter 4) also scored low on a measure of authoritarianism.[42] Low obedience was also found to be associated with lower authoritarianism by the Canadian scholar Bob Altemeyer, using his right-wing authoritarianism scale.[43] In addition, lower conformity has been shown to be associated with certain personality characteristics. For example, there is a negative association between *agreeableness*, the tendency to be cooperative and kind (one of the so-called Big Five personality traits, discussed earlier in this chapter), and nonconformity.[44] In other words, nonconformists are *less* agreeable. The bureaucratic personality is overconforming, but the unbureaucratic personality is nonconformist, acting according to internal principles rather than the often changing demands of authorities.[45] These research findings remind us of the insights of Hannah Arendt (1906–75) about the *banality of evil* – the idea that massive destruction and evil can arise from the actions of what on the surface are ordinary individuals with mundane personalities, carrying out what they see to be their normal responsibilities as dutiful citizens.[46]

Concluding Comment

I have argued that revolutions arise out of particular contexts, and these contexts present the extremist revolutionary leader with opportunities to rise to absolute power – just as dictatorships evolve when a springboard to dictatorship comes into place and presents opportunities for the potential dictator to spring to power.[47] However, as I have discussed in this chapter, the personalities of individuals also have a role in shaping revolutions – just as the personalities of potential dictators can influence and help bring into being the springboard to dictatorship. The extremist revolutionary leader has a set of personality characteristics that mark him (and throughout history they have been male leaders) as distinct and special – including pathological narcissism, high risk-taking, intolerance for ambiguity, categorical thinking, illusions of control, high Machiavellianism, and readiness to kill and injure others in enormous numbers in order to reach his goals. The extremist revolutionary leader fights his way to power and is willing to inflict enormous harm in order to get his way and achieve absolute power monopoly. All competitors, including the moderates who helped to bring about the revolution, are ruthlessly cut down in this push for power.

The extremist revolutionary leader develops an extensive support system, and personality characteristics also influence how this support system takes shape. The different groups in this support system are characterized by particular personality traits. The foundation of this support system are the millions who sacrifice themselves so that the extremist revolutionary leader can climb over their dead or injured bodies to reach absolute power, as well as the moderates who fail to take timely action to prevent the extremist revolutionary leader attaining power monopoly. Among the first group are many high authoritarians, but there are also those who are higher risk-takers and simply seek change in the hope of improvement. An important role is also played by the opportunists. These are the numerous individuals who make swift, chameleon-like changes, suddenly shifting with the new values of the revolution to become devout communists, fascists, Muslims, or whatever ideology the extreme revolutionary leader requires, in order to gain in personal status, prestige, and resources. Opportunists climb very high after revolutions.

PART IV

Reevaluating Revolutions

How should we evaluate the great revolutions? Surely not according to the rhetoric of revolutionaries, and particularly not the slogans thrown out by their extremist leaders. With their charisma and powerful magnetism, the likes of Lenin, Mao, Castro, and Khomeini will mislead us. Their triumphant rhetoric will lead us away from the chaotic realities of revolutions, the enormous destruction and the lives and opportunities lost. These extremist leaders help create the illusions that inspire and drive revolutionary movements. The first chapter in Part IV (Chapter 10) explores the five main illusions that serve as the motor for revolutions. The Illusion-Motivation Model of Revolution is presented in this chapter, with each illusion linked to a particular type of motivation that drives collective action forward. However, a point that I stress is that the use of the term "illusion" is not intended to have negative connotations in this context.

There is a cyclical quality to revolutions, identified and outlined by Vilfredo Pareto and others (as discussed in earlier chapters in this text). Some thinkers argue that revolutions are constrained and regulated, and even doomed, by fixed characteristics in human nature. What this means in terms of psychological science is that there are certain hardwired human characteristics that cause revolutions to evolve in particular ways and end up with particular outcomes. For example, this "human nature" argument is often used to explain the failure of communist societies that attempt to implement collectivist economic systems, based on collective ownership and collective incentives. I discuss and assess these issues in Chapter 11, and address the question: Does human nature doom revolutions?

An extraordinary feature of revolutions is their creativity. Indeed, in the Afterword I argue that revolutions can be interpreted as acts of collective creativity. This is an enormously promising and positive aspect of revolutions, which contrasts with the deep pain and suffering, the dashed hopes, that also arise.

CHAPTER 10

The Illusion-Motivation Model of Revolution

Revolutions are acts of desperation, sacrifice, as well as soaring hope and aspiration. A central psychological feature of revolutions is that they are born out of motivations shaped by different types of *illusions*, discrepancies between what people subjectively imagine and objective reality – the actual state of the world.[1] Although revolutions differ from one another in some ways, and no two revolutions are identical, there are also foundational similarities across revolutions. The Illusion-Motivation Model of Revolution postulates that there are important universal features of revolutions: all revolutions are similar in that they go through five developmental stages and are characterized by motivations shaped by particular illusions.

The five stages of the Illusion-Motivation Model of Revolution are hierarchical, stepwise, and universal. They are hierarchical in the sense that in order to get to the higher stage, the lower stage(s) must first be passed. For example, in order to get to stage 2, a revolution must first pass through stage 1, and in order to reach stage 3, a revolution must first pass through stages 1 and 2 in that order. Revolutions are stepwise, in the sense that the stages are passed through one at a time. It is not possible for a revolution to leap over stages: for example, a revolution could not leap from stage 1 to stage 4, and forgo development through stages 2 and 3. The five stages revolutions go through are universal, in that all revolutions experience the same sequence of stages in the same hierarchical order. What makes this model uniquely psychological is that each of the five stages of revolution are based on different subjective illusions, which shape motivations. These illusions are collectively constructed and collectively upheld in a society experiencing revolution.

Political plasticity regulates change in political behavior, including in the five stages of psychological change that are experienced by societies and extremist revolutionary leaders during revolutions. First, these five stages are themselves as a whole structured and regulated by political plasticity. Second, change within each of the five stages is also regulated and limited by political plasticity. It is through this influence that there emerge the universal features of the five-stage Illusion-Motivation Model of Revolution.

In this chapter, I use the discussion in the previous ten chapters as a foundation to formulate the Illusion-Motivation Model of Revolution. For example, in Chapters 2 and 3 I critically reviewed the main psychological models of collective action, distinguishing between models that assume material factors to be the driving force of collective action and those models which propose psychological factors to be the driving force. The factors discussed in these chapters as having a key role in models of collective action play a pivotal role in the Illusion-Motivation Model of Revolution.

Each of the stages in the Illusion-Motivation Model of Revolution is characterized by a particular psychological illusion. In this discussion, the use of the term "illusion" is not intended to have negative connotations. All humans are influenced by illusions in their everyday lives, and we are all biased in the ways in which we interpret the world – such as the self-serving biases shaped both by cognitive and motivational processes that help to maintain a positive sense of self and positive ingroup identity.[2] Illusions are prevalent in human social and political life; they help us to function and meet the demands of our individual and collective lives.[3] The particular illusions I discuss in this chapter are highly powerful and play a central role in how revolutions evolve; they shape the motivations that are the drivers of collective and individual actions in the process of revolutionary change, including regime change. However, there is a gap between these illusions and objective reality.

The Illusion-Motivation Model of Revolution is represented in diagrammatic form as a pyramid in Figure 10.1. The base of the pyramid is characterized by the broadest and most commonly shared illusion, which I term the *supreme revolutionary illusion*. All the different people trying to change the regime are swayed by this illusion (the different listed illusions are discussed in detail in this chapter). In the higher parts of the pyramid, the illusions are shared by fewer people, so that the *illusion of permanence* and the *illusion of control* are shared only by the ruling elite or, in the case of some revolutions, only by the extremist revolutionary leader. Regime change takes place at two places in this hierarchy of illusions: the first is between the *illusion of unity* and the *illusion of rationality*; the second is after the *illusion of permanence*. The general structure and flow of revolutions through the five stages is regulated by political plasticity (discussed in

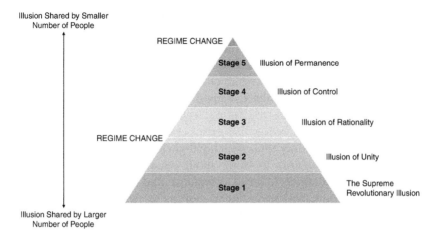

Figure 10.1 Diagrammatic representation of the Illusion-Motivation Model of Revolution.

Chapter 1). The implications of the Illusion-Motivation Model of Revolution are discussed at the end of this chapter.

The Supreme Revolutionary Illusion

"Nor must it be forgotten that the revolution, when it left Canton, was not only anti-feudal but anti-imperialist, and that the Communists are the only party now actively interested in the latter aim … They alone carry the banner of popular war against the Japanese."[4] George Taylor, here writing in 1936 about the situation in China, pointed out that the Chinese communists were spearheading the fight against foreign invaders, as well as their representatives in China, as depicted by the communists. This was during the long revolutionary process, which lasted about a quarter of a century from the 1920s until Mao Zedong declared the establishment of the People's Republic of China (PRC) in 1949. The Chinese communists galvanized and helped to direct the many different factions who came under the broad umbrella of the revolutionary movement. Throughout this long revolutionary struggle, the diverse array of people who pushed for revolution and regime change were under the spell of the *supreme revolutionary illusion*: the belief that all of them would benefit, and in equal ways, from regime change and the coming to power of a revolutionary government.

The *supreme revolutionary illusion* arises without intentional design out of the pre-revolutionary conditions and processes. In the sense that it arises without intentional design, it is automatic and inevitable. People are not aware of this illusion, and it is very seldom made explicit. This is because of practical necessities. Before regime change, all revolutionary forces that combine to make up the collective opposition are completely focused on the task of overthrowing the ruling regime. These opposition forces overlook the many differences that exist between themselves, and indeed discourage and even shun those who highlight such differences. Priority is given to unity in efforts to bring about regime change. In this pre-revolution period, there is broad acceptance and openness to different groups joining the anti-government movement, so that there will be more people pulling together against the ruling regime.

One of the key characteristics of revolutions that succeed in achieving regime change is the wide-ranging coalitions achieved – mostly through circumstances and without explicit planning ahead – by the revolutionaries in their fight against the ruling regime. The important role of coalitions in the success or failure of revolutions has been noted by a wide range of researchers, including Samuel Huntington (1927–2008), Charles Tilly (1929–2008), and numerous others.[5] In a detailed analysis of anti-regime protest movements across the globe between 1900 and 2013, Sirianne Dahlum found that authoritarian regimes have a greater likelihood of being overthrown by opposition movements made up of more diverse groups.[6] In the case of revolutionary movements, we can say that diversity of groups is a strength because it means that a broader spectrum of society is represented in the movement.

For example, the Anti-Shah Revolution of Iran has been recognized as achieving regime change through a wide coalition of opposition forces. The following assessment is typical of many others, interpreting the Iranian opposition as "the coalescence of a broad coalition of classes and groups in the course of 1978, including clerics (the *ulama*) and middle-class intellectuals in leadership positions, as well as a massive base of striking industrial workers, hard-pressed merchants and artisans of the bazaar economy, students, office workers, professionals, and urban lower-class women and men from the shantytowns of the major cities."[7] In my experience of Iran during that revolutionary period, there were only parts of the security forces and the peasantry that were not active in this broad opposition movement.

During the immediate pre-revolution stage, the focus and concentrated energy of the opposition groups is aimed at toppling the ruling regime. The exclusive motivation is to achieve regime change. The opposition groups are well aware that the ruling regime is working through its agents to try to fragment and create conflicts between the opposition groups – and the government agents have a lot of opportunities to achieve this. After all, there are enormous differences between the different factions and groups within the broad opposition movement (e.g., a wide range of both secular and religious groups were in the anti-Shah movement in Iran). But what keeps the different and varied opposition groups united is their usually unacknowledged illusion that they will all benefit fairly equally from regime change and the coming to power of a revolutionary government. This is the first and foundational illusion binding all revolutionary movements.

Illusion of Unity

From the American and French revolutions in the eighteenth century to the Arab Spring revolutions of the twenty-first century, a second common illusion underlying revolutions leading to regime change is the *illusion of unity* characteristic of opposition movements. The diverse revolutionary groups are so intensely motivated to fight and topple the ruling regime that this unity of purpose and motivation becomes magnified, expanded, and spreads to cover all their other activities. This can be likened to the *halo effect*, where how we see one character trait of an individual comes to dominate – spill over into – how we see everything else about that individual.[8] As a result, we ignore all the different negative aspects of the individual because these negative aspects remain hidden under the glow of the halo effect. Similarly, during the buildup to revolutions, differences and even contradictions between opposition groups remain unnoticed, as everyone focuses on the common and binding opposition and even hatred all groups feel toward the regime.

The result of the *illusion of unity* is that all kinds of differences between opposition groups are overlooked, even important ones that could paralyze a revolutionary movement if they actually received attention. This became blatantly obvious to me as we approached the Anti-Shah Revolution in Iran, when factions with diametrically opposite views and political positions all collaborated in order to topple the Shah. For example, included in the anti-Shah movement from the mid-1970s were Islamic extremists who wanted to establish a society governed strictly according to Islamic sharia law, liberated women who wanted to achieve a society where women enjoy freedoms and opportunities in parity with men, orthodox bazaari merchants who wanted a society with a free-market economy but were conservative in moral values and gender relations, and left-wing activists who wanted a society based on socialist principles and liberated values. The anti-Shah revolutionary movement would have come to a screeching halt if these groups had given attention to working out their differences instead of focusing on toppling the ruling regime.

Groups with similarly very different values and political positions make up the opposition in all the other major revolutions. For example, the opposition that brought down the French monarchy included sections of the nobility, the peasantry, the bourgeoisie, working-class urban dwellers, intellectuals – all with motivations, values, and goals that differed from one another in important ways. The *illusion of unity* galvanized their energies to topple the monarchy, and as long as the monarchy remained their differences were not given priority.[9] It is the breadth and strength of this *illusion of unity* that explains how groups with such foundational differences in interests come to collaborate and even sometimes sacrifice for one another.

The first two illusions, the *supreme revolutionary illusion* and the *illusion of unity*, are mass illusions, in that they are shared by most people that are part of the revolutionary movement. These two mass illusions, which can engage tens of millions of people, are influential prior to regime change. After regime change, the illusions that are most influential in the revolutionary movement are shared by a smaller circle of people, basically the ruling elite and the extremist revolutionary leader.

Illusion of Rationality (after Regime Change)

Immediately after regime change, relatively moderate leaders and factions take center stage – this has been true for the major revolutions from the American and French revolutions of the eighteenth century to the more recent Iranian Revolution (as discussed in Chapter 5).[10] Following the chaos of the revolution, there is a brief *opportunity bubble*, a short period when the new government authorities can step in and give constructive direction to change.[11] It is usually during this period that new constitutions are debated and sometimes endorsed, and broad discussions are undertaken about the future direction of society. On the surface, at least, these discussions are inclusive, and it appears that great efforts are made to involve different factions and political and cultural orientations within the debates.

There is a tension during this immediate post-revolution period between the destruction and chaos resulting from forced regime change and the attempts by the ruling moderates to govern in an inclusive, cooperative, and representative manner. After supporting regime change, people expect to be included and to have their interests and views represented. Indeed, one of the dangers during this period is that many people have overly high expectations about how much their views and interests can be represented at the national level. But there is an air of optimism, and the moderate leadership assumes that a rational approach will yield the necessary positive results for the revolution to succeed. During this opportunity-bubble period, the moderates attempt to balance the demands of the radicals with those of the conservatives. Unfortunately, the contradictory demands of different factions during the post-revolution opportunity-bubble period, together with the characteristics of the moderates themselves, severely limit progress.

Four sets of factors intersect to result in defeat for the moderates in the immediate post-revolution period. First, the rhetoric in the lead-up to regime change emphasized the rights rather than duties of people, and raised very high expectations among the general population.[12] Before regime change, revolutionary leaders constantly told people how their rights have been trampled on by the ruling regime and how their lives and material conditions would dramatically improve after regime change. In the immediate post-regime change period, the revolutionary leadership attempts to shift priorities from rights to duties, in order to persuade people that they now have to give priority to their duties to the larger society, and how in this new era people must make sacrifices for the revolution. But in practice this shift from rights to duties is not very persuasive because most people already have very high expectations for a better life, based on what they understand to be their individual and collective rights in society after regime change.

Second, the moderates are pushed and pulled by different political sides, including left- and right-wing radicals and cultural liberals and conservatives, to move in different directions. All these different groups were active in the opposition in the lead-up to regime change and feel entitled to have influence because they had a role (an essential one, according to them) in toppling the ruling regime. Of course, each political group celebrates and exaggerates their own role in bringing about the revolution and minimizes the role of competitor groups.

Third, the competing and often contradictory push and pull of different political groups makes it very difficult for the moderates to take decisive action because whatever action they propose is immediately opposed by some political groups with claims about their heavy sacrifices for the revolution. The moderates find themselves at a standstill, but the expectations of the masses remain very high and impossible to fulfill, in the short term at least.

Fourth, the opposition of different political groups to proposed actions by moderates reinforces the natural tendency of moderates to avoid programs and actions that are more decisive, radical, and (inevitably) divisive. The personality characteristics of moderates exacerbates this situation (moderates tend to have high tolerance for ambiguity, see multiple sides to issues, recognize the value of alternative moral systems, and are less likely to take decisive action, believing they have the correct answer). The result of these processes is that in the immediate post-revolution period, rising expectations among the people remain unfulfilled, and the moderate leadership looks inept and incapable of decisive action. The moderates maintain an *illusion of rationality*, but political and practical realities on the ground shatter this illusion.

Illusion of Control

The defeat of moderates in the immediate post-regime-change period coincides with, and is often causally connected to, a power-grab by revolutionary extremists. That is, seeing the dithering of the moderates and their inability to take decisive action, extremist group(s) take the opportunity to jump into the leadership position. The extremists often climb to power by sabotaging moderate programs, helping to create an atmosphere of chaos and fear, and bringing about gridlock. It is also at this stage that extremist revolutionary leaders – from Lenin to Khomeini – show their hand and openly grab power, pushing aside and eventually suffocating all alternative political groups and leaders. The coming to power of extremists after the initial post-revolution opportunity-bubble period is at least initially welcomed by many ordinary people as an opportunity to deal with a whole host of problems, including chaos and the reestablishment of order, ending the gridlock in which moderates (and the rest of society) have become trapped, enforcing national unity and putting an end to separatist movements, dealing with internal and external perceived threats, and restoring hope and repositioning the revolution positively.

In addition, the coming to power of an extremist revolutionary leader is associated with a cult of personality and the adoration of forceful, charismatic leadership (such as Napoleon, Lenin, Mao, Castro, and Khomeini). After the immediate post-revolution period of gridlock and inertia, many people sense a need for strong leadership. But extremists and extremist revolutionary leaders come to power with specific ideological goals, which require radical behavior changes in the population. For example, the Bolsheviks led by Lenin came to power with the goal of collectivizing Soviet society, and radical behavioral changes were required in order for collectivization to come to fruition. For example, people have to learn to be motivated by collective incentives rather than incentives for themselves as individuals; this means working hard so that the collective is rewarded rather than because of increased rewards directly to the self. The extremists all suffer the *illusion of control*, believing that they are capable of controlling behavioral changes in the population toward the direction of their extremist ideological goals. I will return to discuss this illusion after considering in more detail why revolutionaries overtake moderates in the immediate post-regime-change period.

Reports from all the major revolutions show that the period immediately following regime change is chaotic and disorderly. The security forces have been disbanded and are in disarray, and even the police are not functioning properly. Military barracks and police stations have been attacked and sometimes burned to the ground during the fight to bring down the former regime. Law and order is in the hands of ordinary citizens, who often band together to protect their own neighborhoods. On the one hand, this is an exciting time because people suddenly find they are free to express themselves and take actions that were previously suppressed by the ruling regime. On the other hand, there is disarray because people have not yet worked out the limits of their freedoms and how each individual and group needs to take care not to encroach on the freedoms and rights of other individuals and groups. The chaos and unlimited freedoms of this period lead many people to want the reestablishment of order in society.

Related to the chaos and disorganization in the post-revolution period is the gridlock that has trapped the moderates in charge of government and everyone else along with them. Landowners and peasants, factory owners and factory workers, conservative women and liberated women, radical students and traditional-minded bureaucrats – all the different groups that *saw themselves* as part of the revolutionary movement (even though some of them did not play a decisive role) now pull in different directions, resulting in gridlock. The moderates in charge are not able to overcome this gridlock, and their leadership is incapable of taking the decisive action needed for people to at least feel as if their society is moving forward. By their nature, the moderates do not want to take action that seems to trample on the rights of any groups. The extremists – and particularly extremist revolutionary leaders – have no qualms about taking such actions.

Regime change and the freedoms of the immediate post-revolution period create new opportunities for different types of separatist movements to mobilize and try to achieve independence from the nation-state. These separatist movements are often based on ethnicity, language, religion, and other similar bases, but remain crushed and under control as long as the central government remains strong. With the collapse of the ruling regime and the coming to power of a post-revolution government led by moderate elements, the central government struggles to enforce national unity and to control separatist movements. Also, internal and external enemies of the revolution take the opportunity to encourage and support separatist movements.

In the context of this chaotic post-revolution period, the extremists have one key advantage – they have no hesitation in taking decisive action, even if it means using widespread violence. They break the gridlock. When they take over the government from the moderates, extremists immediately take action against separatist movements, as well as against those they identify as internal and external threats. At this stage, the extremists opportunistically use the excuse of fighting separatism and dealing with threats to national security and unity to persecute and obliterate their political opponents.

Extremists who take over the government also act decisively to reposition the revolution positively, throttling critical and dissenting voices. This narrowing of perspectives and voices is associated with the *illusion of control* suffered by extremists, believing that they can control and shape human behavior to fit with their ideological goals. Because the extremists eliminate opposition groups and control the public narratives in society, the *illusion of control* is very strong among them: They come to see their own ideologically driven narratives as social reality. For example, the illusion of control is at the base of the facade of collective farms and collective life in the Soviet Union, the facade of industrial progress during the so-called Great Leap Forward in China, and the facade of righteous, corruption-free, improved governance and standard of living in Iran.

Illusion of Permanence

The final stage of the Illusion-Motivation Model of Revolution is characterized by the *illusion of permanence*, the belief that the revolutionary society – Napoleonic France, Soviet communism, Maoist communism, Cuban communism, Khomeini Islamism, and others – will continue forever. This illusion builds on two platforms: The first is the *illusion of control* that evolved as a collective characteristic (mostly among the ruling elite) in the fourth stage of the Illusion-Motivation Model of Revolution, and the second is the individual characteristic of the personality of extremist revolutionary leaders – which makes them particularly susceptible to experiencing the *illusion of permanence*.

The *illusion of control* characteristic, which is the fourth stage of the Illusion-Motivation Model of Revolution, cements the collective belief – at least among the ruling elite – that society is progressing according to the requirements of the accepted revolutionary ideology. This collective belief is socially constructed and collectively upheld, and it determines what the ruling elite accept as "truth" in society. Those who challenge this truth are in different ways punished and cast aside. These are the dissidents, the outcasts who are persecuted, jailed, and killed in the Soviet Union, in communist China, in Iran – and other closed societies.

The mass media, the education system, and all public narratives in revolutionary societies reflect and represent what is acceptable truth according to extremist revolutionary leaders and the ruling elite. The high levels of conformity and obedience achieved by the ruling elite in revolutionary societies strengthen the *illusion of control*, and serve as a solid platform for extremist revolutionary leaders (and the ruling elite who surround them) to come under the sway of the *illusion of permanence*. What I have described in this chapter is the collective basis for the *illusion of permanence*, but there is also a strong individual basis related to the personality of extremist revolutionary leaders, which I will turn to discuss now.

Extremist revolutionary leaders who come to power after the defeat of moderates in the immediate post-revolution period have a number of distinct personality characteristics (as discussed in Chapter 9). These personality characteristics include pathological narcissism, craving for power, high level of risk-taking, high Machiavellianism, low tolerance for ambiguity, illusions of control and grandeur, and charisma. The combination of these personality characteristics, together with the absolute power enjoyed by extremist revolutionary leaders after the collapse of the moderates and the extraordinarily high adulation and cult of personality that develop around them, sets up the launching pad for the *illusion of permanence*. There is a quasi-religious characteristic to this illusion as experienced by extremist revolutionary leaders.

By "quasi-religious" in this context I mean that the bond between extremist revolutionary leaders and their followers results in both the leaders and followers being emotionally moved to such a great degree that they experience a form of transcendence, a feeling that they have traveled together beyond the normal, and outside the boundaries of the physical world. I witnessed this in the case of Khomeini when he was giving live speeches, surrounded by adoring crowds who would collectively convulse and weep and laugh, and be moved to surge forward and try to touch the rim of his robe or, if he dropped his handkerchief, to be fortunate enough to touch or hold the cloth with which the leader wiped his brow. In every sense of the term, these leader–follower interactions were moving, transformative, and inspirational experiences.

Of course, it could be claimed that this kind of adulation is also well known in Western societies. For example, consider how crowds have reacted emotionally – the hysteria, the screaming, the shaking and sobbing – to the performances of popular stars such as Elvis Presley (and, in an earlier era, Frank Sinatra). Elvis would only need to wipe his brow with a handkerchief and it would become an object of adoration among hysterical, screaming fans. What is similar in these kinds of performances across different cultures is the shared experience of transcendence by both the performer-leader and the audience-followers: being moved to an experience and place beyond the immediately physical.

Being the object of adoration and the center of a super-charged personality cult moves extremist revolutionary leaders, from Napoleon to Lenin to Mao to Castro to Khomeini – to come fully under the spell of the *illusion of permanence*. Extremist revolutionary leaders come to have a self-perception of being of unique historical importance, of having an impact on the world that is significant and forever. Being an extension of themselves, the revolutionary societies they dominate and dictate to also come to be seen by extremist revolutionary leaders as significant and forever. They believe that they and their societies have changed the world, and they have become part of what is permanent.

In most cases, extremist revolutionary leaders end their lives without experiencing regime change again – one that would bring to an end the revolutionary society they helped to establish. Lenin, Mao, Castro, and Khomeini all passed away at a time when the revolutionary societies they helped to establish were still surviving and developing (Napoleon lived to witness the end of revolutionary France, and the return to the Bourbon monarchy). Thus, in most cases extremist revolutionary leaders have died while still under the spell of the *illusion of permanence*.

The Illusion-Motivation Model of Revolution

The Illusion-Motivation Model of Revolution has a number of important implications, which I now briefly consider. First, the broadest and most important implication concerns the predictable pattern of changes that arise with revolutions. This predictability provides opportunities for planning ahead. Second, predictability raises the possibility of sidestepping problems. Third, the possibility is also raised that political plasticity can be influenced, so as to bring about a more progressive, pro-democracy type of change and outcome.

Predictability of Behavioral Patterns during Revolutions

A number of researchers have noted the systematic unfolding of events leading up to, during, and after revolutions.[13] Going beyond this, the Illusion-Motivation Model of Revolution proposes a common and predictable sequence of psychological processes which results in particular patterns of political behavior. At the core of these psychological processes are the five illusions discussed in this chapter, each of which has motivational consequences. First, in the lead-up to collective mobilization and regime change, the *supreme revolutionary illusion* and the *illusion of unity* result in individuals and groups overlooking their (often substantial) political differences and concentrating completely on collaborating with everyone who is willing to help bring about regime change. The challenge of what to do about the foundational differences between opposition groups, and how these differences will be reflected in and worked out by the post-revolution government, is set aside until after regime change has been achieved.

The *illusion of rationality* that characterizes the (relatively) moderate government in the immediate post-revolution period results in three behavioral tendencies that eventually lead to gridlock, inaction, collapse of moderate groups, and the rise of extremist leadership. First, the relatively moderate post-revolution government avoids taking action that would upset any significant political group. Second, this government attempts to be inclusive in its programs, resulting in many contradictory movements and groups exerting pressure in different and often competing directions. A third behavioral tendency of this government is to try to share decision-making, and avoid building up or relying upon a strong leader, an individual who could dominate the national stage and take decisive action against those who might weaken the nation-state (such as minorities seeking independence).

After the collapse of the relatively moderate group who took center stage immediately after the revolution, the extremists who come to power are characterized by the *illusion of control*, which is associated with a very high level of confidence and convergent thinking (the extremists engage in problem-solving in a narrow-minded way, swayed by extremist ideology). In short, the extremists firmly believe – and become utterly devoted to this worldview – that their radical solutions provide a shortcut to historic national progress. The style and content of their cognition result in actions that are often highly radical and involve great risks for the nation – such as the Cultural Revolution in China in the late 1960s, and the invasion of the US Embassy and the hostage taking of US diplomats in Iran (1979–80).

The *illusion of permanence* that characterizes the lives of extremist revolutionary leaders (and some of the elites that surround them) results in actions that are increasingly separated from the world that the rest of society inhabits and their perceptions of reality. Extremist revolutionary leaders reach a stage when there seems no limit to their power; the glory and adulation showered on them also seems unbounded. It is in this situation that they take even greater risks, in the belief that their power is so great that they can do no wrong. This is Napoleon attempting to spread the revolution by invading Russia (1812) – and discovering, too late, that the French military has not correctly prepared for the Russian winter. The result was disastrous for the French military, and eventually for Napoleon. This is Lenin launching land reform programs without the necessary preparations, resulting in low agricultural production, food scarcity, and widespread famine. This is Mao launching industrialization through the Great Leap Forward, and discovering that national industrialization cannot come about through millions of chaotic, small-scale changes. This is Castro rushing forward with nationalization policies, without the careful planning necessary to increase the chances of success – with the result of economic stagnation rather than robust growth for Cuba. This is Khomeini risking rash steps (such as taking US diplomats hostage, pursuing aggressive policies with neighboring countries, and attempting to export his brand of revolution to other nations) to distance Iran from Western powers so that it becomes increasingly isolated and more exclusively dependent on Russia and China. All these risky steps are taken by extremist revolutionary leaders in full confidence that the revolutionary societies they lead will last forever.

Concluding Comment

I firmly believe in the dictum that the most practical thing is a good theory. There have been numerous theoretical explanations of revolutions, but the foundational role of psychology has been neglected in these theories.[14] A number of researchers, particularly Ted Gurr, have been labeled as adopting a psychological approach to explaining revolutions, and they have undoubtedly made valuable contributions, particularly by exploring the role of relative deprivation in collective action.[15] However, psychological factors and processes are not just important in the lead-up to regime change; they are of foundational importance in what happens during and after regime change and, very importantly, the long-term experiences, successes, and defeats of revolutionary societies. The Illusion-Motivation Model of Revolution puts psychology at the center of revolutionary changes, from collective mobilization to regime change and the post-revolution society.

In the next chapter, I argue that psychological factors and human nature do not necessarily doom revolutions. However, psychological factors and political plasticity influence how fast, how much, and in what ways behavioral changes can (and cannot) be brought about through revolutions. The five major illusions I have identified are integral to revolutions, and they are part of the political plasticity that influences changes in the process of revolution, regime change, and what comes after. Some of these illusions – such as the *supreme revolutionary illusion* and *the illusion of unity* – facilitate change in the process of revolution, but some illusions – such as the *illusion of control* and the *illusion of permanence* – result in inefficiency, disorder, and even decay and defeat.

CHAPTER II

Does Human Nature Doom Revolutions?

Given the idealistic goals with which major revolutions begin, goals which none of them have achieved so far, is it accurate to describe revolutions as failures? Among the revolutions that have been the main focus of this book, the French and Russian revolutions led to societies that collapsed, and although societies that evolved directly from the Chinese, Cuban, and Iranian revolutions are still standing, they have turned into dark dictatorships – so it could be argued that they have also failed.

A simple test of the outcome of revolutions is to ask the following question about the society that resulted from the revolution: "Would I want to live in this society?" My answer is that, having come to know Chinese, Cuban, and Iranian societies, I regard them as fairly closed dictatorships and I would definitely not want to live in any of them (although I consider Chinese society to be the most promising of these three). An alternative would have been for me to focus on revolutions that were more successful and resulted in societies that are relatively open. Two examples would be the Dutch Revolution in the sixteenth century against the Spanish and the eighteenth-century American Revolution against the British.[1] But these both involve rebellion against a foreign power, and should not be considered in the same category as the French, Russian, Chinese, Cuban, and Iranian revolutions. With a continued focus on these five revolutions, the central question I address in this chapter is, does human nature doom revolutions?

From a psychological perspective, I interpret human nature as consisting of those human psychological characteristics that are relatively fixed and extremely difficult to change. Are there aspects of human psychology that are highly resistant to change, and that result in the failure of revolutions? It is useful to consider this question through deeper consideration of what we mean by human nature.

170

The term human nature is often used to refer to characteristics that are inborn, and in cognitive science terminology these are hardwired characteristics inside individuals. But is it correct to interpret at least some psychological characteristics of human nature as forever fixed and unchanging? An alternative interpretation is that in historical time, all human nature does undergo transformation. This is akin to the idea in cognitive neuroscience that even what is hardwired in neural networks can change over the long term. This is also in line with an epigenetic perspective, where developmental trajectories are probabilistic and at least some gene expression is dependent on environmental factors and interactions between genes, and between genes and the environment.[2] In the very long term, then, even what we assume to be human nature does change over historical time, in part through interactions with changing environmental conditions. Even human nature is not fixed forever.

Neither is what I have called hardwiring outside people forever fixed and unchanging.[3] Hardwiring outside people includes the built environment (e.g., architecture, town planning, historic buildings) that is shaped by humans and, in turn, shapes human behavior. Hardwiring outside people also includes the normative system (norms, values, rules, and so on) that is shared in society through narratives and that regulates human behavior. This hardwiring outside people is already present when we are born, and it continues after our departure from this world. Of course, there are some changes during our lifetime in the built environment and in the normative systems that regulate behavior, but there are also continuities. For example, the basic design of cities and houses, including the traditional middle-class family house of three to four bedrooms, continues across generations. Also, the symbolic importance of certain historic buildings (e.g., cathedrals, homes of national leaders – the White House, 10 Downing Street, and so on) continues. But there are also foundational shifts in hardwiring outside people: for example, consider the dramatically changed norms in attitudes toward gay people since the 1960s.

We can conceive of a continuum, where "completely hardwired" is at one extreme and "completely softwired" is at the other extreme (see Figure 11.1).[4]

Completely Hardwired _____Completely Softwired

Figure 11.1 A continuum of behaviors, from completely hardwired to completely softwired, with almost all behaviors located somewhere between these two extremes.

The location of different behaviors on the completely hardwired–completely softwired continuum can change over time. Thus, in response to the question "Does human nature doom revolutions?" we must distinguish between short-term and long-term processes. When revolutionary goals require rapid changes in those aspects of human behavior that are closer to the hardwired end of the continuum, then it is more likely that these goals will not be reached. On the other hand, when revolutionary goals require changes in behavior that are closer to the softwired end of the continuum, then it is more likely that the necessary behavioral changes can be achieved toward reaching revolutionary goals.

The success or failure of revolutions, then, has to be assessed in relation to the goals espoused by the revolutionaries who come to power after regime change. In the first part of the discussion in this chapter, I critically review the goals of revolutions. I argue that certain revolutions have more feasible goals than do others. In the second part, I explore whether revolutions are doomed by certain characteristics of human nature, and specifically those aspects of human psychology that are most resistant to change.

The Goals of Revolutions

> ... no single acting group, whether a class or an ideological vanguard, deliberately shapes the complex and multiply determined conflicts that bring about revolutionary crisis and outcomes. The French Revolution was not made by a rising capitalist bourgeoisie or by the Jacobins; the Russian Revolution was not made by the industrial proletariat or even by the Bolshevik party. If the purpose is to explain in cross-nationally relevant terms why revolutions break out in some times and places and not others, and why they accomplish some changes and not others, we cannot achieve this by theorizing as if some grand intentionality governs revolutionary processes.[5]

Any assessment of the success of a revolution must take into consideration the goals of the revolution. Did the revolution succeed in achieving the goals set out by the revolutionaries? Of course, there was not complete agreement about goals among all the revolutionary leaders of the major revolutions, and some utopian goals were never seen as practical or even attempted.[6] Nevertheless, the main generally accepted goals of each revolution can be identified. This means that each revolution has to be assessed on a case-by-case basis, in terms of its particular goals. But two challenges immediately arise. The first is pointed out by Theda Skocpol (quoted above): We have to be careful to avoid assuming that some "grand intentionality governs revolutionary processes." Keeping this in mind, we can still identify certain goals put forward by revolutionaries and evaluate to what extent these goals have been met. A second challenge is that in addition to examining the success of each revolution according to the goals espoused by revolutionaries, we should also identify some universal criteria according to which we assess all revolutions.

Assessments of revolutions inevitably are based on criteria around human rights, justice, and economic and political progress, and such criteria inevitably are influenced by cultural biases. In terms of adopting universal criteria for assessing revolutions – at least those of the twentieth and twenty-first centuries – I propose that the United Nations Universal Declaration of Human Rights, adopted by the General Assembly of the United Nations Organization in 1948, should serve as a foundation.[7] The United Nations Universal Declaration of Human Rights can be criticized as being too focused on individual rights and neglectful of both collective rights and individual and collective duties. This bias perhaps arose because the Declaration was shaped through the leadership of Western thinkers and politicians in meetings held in the United States after World War II. However, despite certain cultural biases, the Declaration has the advantage of identifying core rights as universal and of having been endorsed by all nations. Of course, I do not propose that the French Revolution (or other revolutions prior to the twentieth century) be assessed in light of the United Nations Universal Declaration of Human Rights.

However, an even more challenging task is to assess the goals of a revolution in relation to human psychology: Given the psychological characteristics of human beings, how viable are the goals adopted by the revolutionaries? Even though empirical research is not always available to address this question in specific areas of behavior, we can still find some guides in the empirical psychological literature. Of course, we can also use as a guide the actual practical experiences of revolutionaries in trying to implement programs to reach their revolutionary goals. There is always the possibility that flaws in their program design and implementation, rather than low political plasticity in certain domains of behavior, have prevented revolutionaries from reaching their goals. However, the success or failure of revolutionaries in reaching their goals is also a reflection of human psychological characteristics, to some extent independent of the quality and implementation of particular programs. With these points in mind, I briefly review the main goals of the five revolutions that serve as the focus of our discussions.

The French Revolution: The publicly declared ideal goals of the French Revolution are captured in the slogan *Liberté, Égalité, Fraternité* ("Liberty, Equality, Fraternity"). Even at the time of the French Revolution, there were passionate disagreements between different groups of supporters of the Revolution, including outside of France, about the ideals that should be pursued. The period of Terror (1793–14) and the chaos and international war (until the final defeat of Napoleon in 1815) that followed led to many thinkers turning against the French Revolution, including the English Romantic poets Percy Bysshe Shelly (1792–1822) and William Wordsworth (1770–1850) – who had been strong supporters initially.[8] Edmund Burke (1729–97) also became highly critical of the French Revolution, pointing to the likelihood of the chaos and disorder of the revolution resulting in a military leader emerging as dictator (which did happen with Napoleon crowning himself as emperor in 1799, two years after Burke's death).[9]

Perhaps the greatest success of the French Revolution was in the international impact it had, through the spread of new ideas about governance. For example, new ideas about religious toleration, spread particularly through the writings of Voltaire (1694–1778), and the theory of the separation of judiciary, legislative, and executive powers, influenced in particular by Montesquieu (1689–1755), came to shape developments in America and, eventually, around the world.[10] After this, national constitutions evolved to enshrine the separation of powers. Napoleon's invasion of Spain and other major countries helped spread this and other revolutionary ideas, even though Napoleon himself embodied more the dictatorial tradition that the French Revolution was supposed to have left behind.[11] It is particularly in the area of leadership that the French Revolution raises questions about human psychology, and I discuss this topic in a more in-depth manner later in this chapter.

The Russian Revolution: In looking back on the twenty-fifth anniversary of the Russian Revolution on November 7, 1942, William Chamberlin argued that

> The Revolution, in its original form, challenged at least five deep-rooted human instincts ... the institution of private property, which was supposed to be replaced by a collectivist socialist system of economy ... it challenged religion ... it challenged the feeling of nationalism, because in its first phase it was militantly internationalist and avowedly subordinated the interests of Russia to those of the world revolution ... It challenged the family, which it rejected as something "bourgeois," bound up with the capitalist order of society ... It challenged the whole individualist-liberal trend in politics and

in human relations which was characteristic of the century before the First World War.[12]

Chamberlin then asks, "How far has the Soviet régime of 1942 adhered to these ideals of 1917?"[13] The answer he provides is that in the areas of private property and religion, the ideals of 1917 were still adhered to, in the sense that the state remained committed to a position of supporting collectivization and not allowing private ownership, as well as supporting Marxist materialist atheism. But in the domains of a uniform standard of living and lack of inequality, patriotism, and the family, by 1942 the ideals of 1917 had been abandoned. That is, in the Soviet Union there was already in 1942 very wide variation in people's incomes and other resources (this variation had increased further by the time of the Soviet collapse in 1990). A Soviet elite now lived in relative luxury. Some Soviet citizens enjoyed far greater power and resources. Although they did not have private owner-ship, they did have access to grand homes, holiday resorts, motorcars, and other luxuries. Second, particularly as a result of the need to achieve massive mobilization during World War II, nationalism (rather than internationalism) became a high priority for the ruling Soviet elite (later in this chapter, we shall see that the same trend is evident in the case of the Iranian Revolution). Third, the Soviet attitude toward the family moved away from the 1917 ideal. Divorce was made more difficult and expensive, motherhood and having children became venerated and monetarily rewarded by the state, and family stability was encouraged.

The Chinese Revolution: In an important sense, the year 1949 when Mao Zedong declared the creation of the People's Republic of China (PRC), was only the start of the revolution in China. This is particularly because from 1949 until his death in 1979, Mao attempted to implement a number of enormous national programs that would, according to him, safeguard the Chinese Revolution through perpetual revolution (discussed in Chapter 7).[14] The most important of these programs were the Great Leap Forward and the Cultural Revolution. Both of these programs reflect contradictions between ideals and actual practices in China, between lofty revolutionary goals and often chaotic applied programs on the ground.

Mao saw a need for perpetual revolution because he believed there would be a tendency for backsliding and a return to capitalist ways, particularly among the educated professional classes. Those with greater power, status, skills, resources, and prestige would find ways to separate themselves from the ordinary masses, the people with relatively little education and resources. In the ideal, the masses would be involved in planning and implementing revolutionary programs that would keep the revolution alive. In practice, however, the process of change was directed from above. As Wang Gungwu argues:

> In theory, China was in revolution under a visionary leadership guided by scientific Marxist ideology and functioning through what was called democratic centralism. Therefore, every citizen was about to experience revolutionary change. In reality, however, the revolution was determined and controlled by the Party. It soon became clear that most people were controlled by members of the Party at every level and therefore were more the objects of education and indoctrination than active participants.[15]

An assessment of the extent to which revolutionary ideals have been met in China must deal with the actual operations of the Communist Party, and the enormous wealth inequalities that have evolved in Chinese society. This includes in the rural areas, where post-Mao changes brought back different forms of privatization and the demise of collective ownership.[16] Although portraits of Karl Marx, Mao Zedong, and other revolutionaries who supported egalitarianism and collectivization are prominently on display in China, in practice Chinese society is characterized by the growth of a wealthy middle class, as well as that of a far wealthier super-rich elite. But these wealth differences are not necessarily reflected in official statistics; rather, they are part of a "gray" unacknowledged area.[17] However, despite the enormous wealth of the Chinese elite, the power of the Party and the Chinese state is overwhelming. China is home to the world's second largest number of US dollar billionaires, but the state has the power to suddenly step in and intervene in the economy – including to control the activities of billionaires, who in this sense only have a fragile fortune.[18]

Thus, the development of an economy with capitalist characteristics (private property, group-based economic inequalities, billionaires, and so on), alongside a political system dominated by the Communist Party which dictates to the masses, reflects the enormous gap between idealistic goals and actual realities in China.

The Cuban Revolution: On the ideal of internationalism, the Cuban Revolution stands in contrast to the Russian Revolution. The Russian Revolution began in 1917 with the ideal of internationalism, but by World War II reverted to giving priority to nationalism. In contrast, the Cuban Revolution has continued to give highest priority to internationalism, using as a guide the words of the Cuban author and hero José Martí (1853–95) *"Patria Es Humanidad"* ("Homeland is Humanity"). This internationalist ideal was prioritized by Fidel Castro (1926–2016), Che Guevara (1928–67), and other Cuban leaders, and is reflected in the huge investment made in international revolutionary projects and movements by the Cuban government.[19] For example, Cuba invested heavily in fighting South Africa's Apartheid regime in Angola, from 1975 to 1991. Cuba's internationalism is seen by Cuban leaders as integral to the fight for the survival of the Cuban Communist regime; as Che Guevara put it: "Every drop of blood spilled in a land under whose flag one has not been born is an experience gathered by the survivor to be applied later in the struggle for the liberation of one's own country. And every people that liberates itself is a step in the battle for the liberation of one's own people."[20]

But Cuban revolutionary ideals have been increasingly difficult to maintain at home, especially since the 1990s and the end of help to Cuba from the Soviet Union. Following the overthrow of the dictator Fulgencio Batista (1901–73) in 1959, the Cuban revolutionary movement, supported by the Soviet Union, experienced a honeymoon period from the 1960s to the 1980s. Nationalization and collectivization were undertaken on a broad basis so that collective behavior became normalized and the new convention, while free and expansive health and education programs were set up for the masses.[21] Women and ethnic minorities were given far greater opportunities to participate in political and community life. But the collapse of the Soviet Union in 1990 cut most of the external support for Cuban socialism, resulting in economic hardships and greater international isolation. Younger Cubans continue to suffer from lack of opportunities, and they have contributed to anti-government protests and criticisms.[22] Basic freedoms and civil liberties are denied to people in Cuba and, in this sense, critics argue that revolutionary ideals have not been fulfilled. However, there is some evidence that older Cubans have continued to be supportive of the ideals of the Cuban Revolution.[23]

In some important respects, the fate of ideals in the Cuban Revolution is similar to the situation in post-revolution Iran.

The Iranian Revolution: Some of the publicly declared ideals of the Anti-Shah Revolution in Iran changed dramatically from 1979, as regime change was taking place, to 1980, when Khomeini and his extremist supporters ousted their political competitors and took monopoly control of Iran. Examples of ideals changing are in the domain of, first, leadership and, second, the role of women. Prior to regime change the idea of leadership through *velayat-e faghih*, basically a clerical dictator (discussed in Chapter 7), was only well known within a limited circle of Khomeini's followers. However, after regime change and during the confirmation of the new revolutionary national constitution, which enshrined rule by *velayat-e faghih*, this form of leadership was more widely discussed and (finally) became well known, at least among the better-educated population in Iran. Government ideals with respect to the role of women also shifted during this period, with forced hijab (the Islamic covering women must put on) being symbolic of the far more restricted role women now play in the public sphere. One of the other publicly declared ideals that was highly prominent in the initial period after the revolution was captured by the slogan, *"Na Sharghi, Na Gharbi"* ("Neither East, Nor West"). This slogan reflects the ideal of Iran being independent of both communist (eastern) and capitalist (western) powers. The Iranian Revolution was also associated with a number of other ideals, including pan-Islamism (rather than nationalism), individual liberties, free speech, and a corruption-free society.

Practical experiences and limitations since the 1980s have meant that these ideals have remained unfulfilled. First, the Iran–Iraq War (1980–8), which involved Muslims fighting Muslims, forced the Iranian government to rely far more on nationalism and less on pan-Islamism (this is similar to the Soviets having to rely on nationalism to mobilize Russians to expel German invaders during World War II). The mullahs have acted to support Shi'a governments and movements, including the minority Shi'a government of Bashar al-Assad in Syria and Hezbollah forces in Lebanon and Iraq. But they have failed to exert influence in the much larger Sunni Arab world (almost 90 percent of all 1.7 billion Muslims are Sunni, and less than 10 percent are Shi'a) and there is now more sectarianism in the Islamic world, in part because of Iranian government policies.[24] The reestablishment of dictatorship, through *velayat-e faghih*, has meant that basic freedoms, including free speech, have become severely restricted and corruption has increased, as reflected in objective international assessments.[25]

The ideal of independence reflected in the slogan "Neither East, Nor West" has also proved impossible to uphold. The Anti-Shah Revolution was also in key respects anti-Western and especially anti-American, and the mullahs have strengthened this anti-Western and anti-American bias since 1979 – in part by enshrining this bias in the new national constitution.[26] Iran has become increasingly dependent on Russia and China, and more distant from the United States and other Western nations. Although some see the Russia–China–Iran entente as illusory, Iran has moved closer to

China politically and economically, and is one of the few countries directly helping Russia in its invasion of Ukraine, which began in 2022.[27]

In summary, then, the idealist goals of major revolutions mostly remain unfulfilled. The French and Russian revolutions resulted in societies that collapsed, without fulfilling initial revolutionary ideals. The Chinese, Cuban, and Iran revolutions have led to societies that persist, but in ways that are far from the ideals set out after regime change and the start of the revolutionary society. China, Cuba, and Iran function as dictatorships, but in their defense the revolutionaries of these countries would claim that their present form of government is a defensive posture in response to attacks from the United States and other capitalist countries. Next, I turn to consider the extent to which the ideals identified by revolutionaries in France, Russia, China, Cuba, and Iran are in line with, or contradicted by, human psychological characteristics. In other words, to what extent did human psychology doom revolutionary goals?

Human Nature and Limitations on Revolutionary Goals

"All human history is nothing but a continuous transformation of human nature."[28] The goal of revolutionaries is to put forward an ideal and try to shape human behavior toward that ideal. But such changes might be limited by human nature, which raises questions about the flexibility of human nature. Karl Marx (quoted above) suggests that the transformation of human nature is ongoing throughout human history. By implication, the task of revolutionaries is to give particular directions to this transformation. That is, revolutionaries are attempting to transform human nature in line with their ideologies. For example, Marxist revolutionaries attempt to change people so as to establish the dictatorship of the proletariat and eventually arrive at a classless society, and Islamic revolutionaries try to transform people toward building what they see as an ideal Islamic state.

In this section, I examine four ways in which human nature seems to doom revolutions, or at least place heavy limitations on them. First, I discuss the coming to power of extremist revolutionary leaders and their supporters, with the result that a dictatorship is established. Second, I argue that the coming to power of extremists in a closed post-revolution society results in "ends justify the means" policies, as well as corruption. Third, I point out that leader–follower relations after revolutions become highly traditional and top–down. Fourth, I argue that collectivization and similar policies fail because revolutionaries are not able to set up the conditions for the successful implementation of such policies. Of course, these judgments are on the basis of experiences with past revolutions. There is always the possibility that in the future, revolutionaries will learn from history and overcome the limitations I have identified.

Extremists Come to Power

A persistent pattern that has been identified after regime change through revolutions is the initial setting up of a temporary government by moderates, which survives for a short time but is followed by the obliteration of the moderates by extremists and the establishment of a dictatorship under an extremist revolutionary leader such as Napoleon, Lenin, Mao, Castro, or Khomeini. In the earlier discussion on the role of personality in revolutions (Chapter 9), I argued that the extremist revolutionary leaders who come to power after revolutionary regime change, together with their extremist followers, are characterized by authoritarian personality characteristics. These personality characteristics – which include categorical thinking, intolerance for ambiguity and intergroup differences, ethnocentrism, high conformity and obedience to authority – are associated with closed rather than open societies, dictatorship rather than democracy.

Extremist revolutionary leaders adopt a leadership style that results in power being completely concentrated in their hands and those of their supporters, with all other competing groups being destroyed and their leadership ending up in jail, killed, or in hiding abroad. This move to establish a dictatorship is justified by extremist revolutionary leaders according to ideology which purports to be in the interests of the people, using explanations such as "dictatorship of the proletariat," where a vanguard representing the proletariat establish a dictatorship on behalf of the proletariat (Russia, China, Cuba), and *velayat-e faghih*, where a supreme clerical leader is the ultimate decider on all issues, acting on behalf of the nation on the basis of his interpretation of Islam (Iran). This ideology becomes the dominant ideology in society, at least until the dictatorship falls.

Two points need to be emphasized regarding the pattern of behavior I have highlighted, with moderates coming to power briefly in the post-revolution period and then being suffocated and pushed aside by extremist revolutionary leaders and their followers. First, this pattern of behavior can only be understood if we adopt a Gestalt approach and remember that, in this case at least, the whole is more than the sum of its parts. The behavior of the moderates, the extremists, and the majority of ordinary people in society must be considered through their interactions and co-dependencies – not in isolation. The personality characteristics of the moderates and the extremists (discussed in Chapter 9) take shape through interactions with other groups, and in particular the personality and actions of the extreme revolutionary leader takes shape in the context of revolution and the opportunistic and risk-taking behavior it both allows and enables. Second, this pattern of behavior surfaces again and again during and after revolutions, and serves to limit the success of revolutions. Revolutionaries who are also supporters of democracy must plan ahead to try to prevent this pattern being repeated, so that yet another revolution does not result in an extremist revolutionary leader founding a dictatorship.

"Ends Justify the Means" and Corruption

> It was a well-established practice of the socialists to couch their propaganda in religious and peasant terms. The populists of the 1870s had often used the ideas of Christian brotherhood to preach socialism to the peasantry. And the same theme was taken up by the socialist parties in 1917. Pamphlets for the peasants presented socialism as a sort of religious utopia . . .[29]

In assessing the extent to which the goals of the major revolutions were achieved and how this reflects on human nature, we should keep in mind that in some foundational ways there were continuities in the methods used by revolutionaries in France, Russia, China, Cuba, and Iran to try to reach their goals. To take the example of Russia, as Orlando Figes (quoted above) points out, the socialists systematically couched their materialist political ideology in religious rhetoric – despite the Soviet Union adopting an atheist position and rejecting formal religion. Thus, although the formal Church saints and prophets were rejected by the Soviet state, Lenin and later Stalin were presented through religious imagery and symbolism. This trend itself reflects on human nature because it demonstrates that change in post-revolution periods has to be considered as complex and multilayered.

The adoption and use of religious imagery by the atheist authorities in the Soviet Union is one of many examples of extremists in post-revolution France, Russia, China, Cuba, and Iran using an "ends justify the means" strategy to grab and monopolize power. The ultimate objective of the extremist revolutionary leader is to establish himself as the final word on everything, using any means necessary. This is reflected in the similarly harsh and violent systems of repression put into place by Lenin (and later Stalin), Mao, Castro, and Khomeini in their efforts to achieve power monopoly. But a consequence of this approach is the rapid and pervasive spread of corruption.

Corruption is a dominant characteristic of dictatorships[30] (I am not suggesting that more democratic societies are not vulnerable to some level of manipulation and corruption[31]). More democratic societies with independent judiciaries are generally less corrupt, although this relationship is complex and changes over the course of democratic development.[32] However, objective international indices of corruption, such as the Corruption Perception Index (CPI), generally show that the most corrupt societies tend also to be the most closed, dictatorial ones.[33] A major reason for this is that absolute rule and power monopoly by the extremist revolutionary leader provides a protective umbrella for his family, friends, and supporters to become increasingly corrupt with impunity (this relates to the earlier discussion of corruption and culture in Chapter 8). Nobody dares to criticize the extremist revolutionary leader's family, friends, and supporters for corruption, because they will end up being jailed or killed. The consequence is what I have called "trickle down corruption."[34] In most cases corruption is associated with increasing inefficiency and eventual collapse, such as in the case of the Soviet Union, but so far China has managed to continue with economic growth despite having a high level of corruption.[35] Of course, China has combined a dictatorship (ostensibly on behalf of the proletariat) with a state-controlled capitalist economy.

Strongman Leader–Follower Relations

The most commonly repeated pattern of behavior following anti-dictatorship revolutions is the replacement of one strongman by another, and one dictatorship by another. The ideology and symbolic representation of the strongman changes after revolutionary regime change, but leader–follower relations remain the same. For example, in France King Louis XVI was replaced by Emperor Napoleon, but the absolute power of the leader continued. In Iran I saw Khomeini replace the Shah and end up with a power monopoly that was just as total, and actually even more terrible and cruel in consequences, especially for Iranian women.

The continuation of the same style of leader–follower relations before and after revolutions reflects low political plasticity that is associated with interconnected patterns of behavior involving both the extremist revolutionary leader and his followers.[36] The styles of behavior of leaders and followers are interconnected, and change in leader–follower relations can only come about when the whole changes. For example, a followership that has learned over centuries to interact with and follow dictatorial leadership can more quickly and easily switch from following one strongman to another strongman than switch from following a strongman to a leader with a more democratic style. In order for a followership to switch from strongman leader to a more democratic leader, new cognitive and behavior patterns have to be learned, and new skills in evaluating and interacting with leadership have to be developed. These new styles of thinking and doing take time and need a supportive context in order to develop – time and context that are not available in the immediate post-revolution period, with the extremist revolutionary leader and his followers pushing hard to oust the moderates and grab power.

There are a few rare cases in history when after a revolution a leader finds himself with the opportunity to continue in perpetuity in power and even take on the title of king, but he decides to step aside and not monopolize power (the rare cases of Oliver Cromwell, George Washington, and Nelson Mandela are cited in Chapter 8). However, the general trend in history, supported by evidence from psychology experiments, is that power corrupts and absolute power corrupts absolutely.[37] Napoleon, Lenin, Mao, Castro, and Khomeini monopolized power until the end of their lives (close to death, Castro handed power to his brother Raúl, when his health would not allow him to rule any longer).

The post-revolution opportunity bubble (discussed in Chapter 10) provides a transient and brief opportunity for people to develop a followership style that is more in tune with democratic leadership. But this opportunity has to be taken quickly, and there needs also to be some pro-democracy leadership to help the masses move in a democratic direction and acquire the psychological characteristics needed for democratic citizenship.[38] The starting point for democratic citizenship is the ability to begin interactions and dialogues with the acknowledgment that "I could be wrong," and then move on to acquire other additional psychological characteristics that enable the citizen to participate in and support a democracy (I discuss these characteristics in detail elsewhere[39]). But limitations in political plasticity mean that this psychological development can only take place when appropriate context and opportunity become available.

Collectivization and Other Policy Failures

In discussing the goals of revolutions earlier in this chapter, I concluded that the major revolutions have generally failed to reach their most important goals. For example, collectivization was not successful in the Soviet Union, and the turn in China to capitalism and private ownership suggests that collectivization has also failed in at least the main economic sectors of that country. Although intergenerational class mobility is still healthy in China compared to major industrialized nations, policy experimentation has declined under Xi Jinping and state–labor relations are generally authoritarian.[40] Cuba has attempted to continue with a basic program of collectivization, but largely because of economic stagnation there has been some movement by the Cuban government toward allowing privatization of small businesses in a few sectors in the twenty-first century.[41] Cuba is also faced with the challenge of ending interethnic inequalities, including in the domains of economic and political power. Although some progress was made in meeting this challenge, the return to privatization in Cuba is associated with a return to social and economic inequalities along ethnic lines, suggesting that ethnic inequality is stubbornly resistant to change.[42]

How should we interpret the experiences of the Soviet Union, China, Cuba, and other communist societies with collectivization? Supporters of capitalism argue that research on *social loafing*, the tendency of people to work less hard in a group than when they work by themselves, demonstrates that humans are more strongly motivated by individual incentives than collective ones.[43] Furthermore, supporters of capitalism argue that the motivation to accumulate private property is the essential motor for economic growth, and this explains the economic superiority of the capitalist West and the demise of the Soviet Union and other communist societies that implement collective rewards and collective ownership. From this perspective, then, collectivization is doomed to fail because it goes against basic human psychological characteristics that have either very low political plasticity or none at all.

But an alternative argument is that under certain conditions, humans work better in collectives and in response to collective rewards; this is reflected in the research literature on *social laboring*, which demonstrates increased efforts in response to collective incentives.[44] There are also conditions in capitalist societies where social laboring rather than social loafing takes place, such as the example of eight people in a rowing crew racing against other rowing crews, or the members of a business team competing against other business teams. In these intergroup competitions, individuals could loaf and automatically collect their rewards as part of the team, but instead they typically are inspired to work even harder for a collective reward. Thus, even in capitalist societies there are conditions in which a form of collectivization works very well to increase productivity. But if this is the case, why has collectivization failed in communist societies?

One possible reason for the failure of collectivization in communist societies has to do with corruption. Serious large-scale attempts at collectivization have only been attempted in communist dictatorships, which are notorious for having high levels of corruption (as we discussed earlier in this chapter). For social laboring and collectivization to work effectively, individuals must have a relatively high level of dedication and trust in the group, which is far less likely to happen if a society suffers high levels of corruption – which closed societies inevitably do, as discussed in this chapter.

Concluding Comment

My assertion, then, is that the psychological stepping stones leading to and from revolutions are associated with certain patterns of behaviors, which are often destructive and supportive of dictatorship rather than democracy. The disturbing behavioral pattern found after revolutions includes the rise of an extremist revolutionary dictator (Napoleon, Lenin, Mao, Castro, Khomeini), a sharp restriction on individual freedoms, and a rise in corruption and despotism. Why does this pattern arise and become repeated, to ruin the utopian revolutionary dreams of the wide spectrum of people who typically supported the revolution prior to regime change, such as those in France, China, Russia, Cuba, and Iran? Richard Stites points out that in the case of Russia:

> revolutionary utopianism was replaced by Stalin's "utopia in power" ... the old dreams and their experimental variants in the 1920s were repudiated by those in power in favor of an ideology of bureaucratic state centrism and a theology of the Stalin personality cult. The pathos of the radical idealist rotting away in a revolutionary prison is one of the great themes in the literature of the Stalin purges.[45]

What Stites says about revolutionary dreams and the Russian Revolution is true for the other major revolutions (we just need to replace "Stalin" with Mao, Castro, Khomeini, and so on).

But I do not conclude that human nature, in the form of key psycho-logical characteristics that are resistant to change, necessarily dooms revolutions. Rather, human nature results in restrictions on behavioral changes in the short term, and consequently makes it more probable that revolutionary ideals will not be reached fast enough to avoid the springing to power of an extremist revolutionary leader (Napoleon, Lenin, Mao, Castro, Khomeini) intent on establishing a dictatorship with himself as dictator. Revolutionaries who are supportive of democracy must plan ahead, on the basis of practical and realistic limitations. For example, there is a high probability that extremists and an extremist revolutionary leader will attempt to grab and monopolize power after revolutionary regime change. This means that pro-democracy forces are confronted with a dilemma: either they use aggression to prevent the extremist revolutionary leader from coming to power or they submit to aggression and accept the coming dictatorship.

The dilemma facing pro-democracy forces after revolutions may seem simple to solve on paper. However, as I experienced after the Iranian Revolution, in practice pro-democracy forces are confronted by what seems to be an insoluble dilemma. On the one hand, pro-democracy forces are competing with extremists who are determined to use any means possible to establish a dictatorship under the rule of the extremist revolu-tionary leader, but on the other hand pro-democracy forces are influenced by their political ideology and individual personality characteristics to use peaceful and democratic means to power. In post-revolution Iran, the outcome of this dilemma was that (relatively) moderate leaders such as Mehdi Bazargan and others (discussed in Chapters 5 and 7) felt forced to resign from political office because they could not carry out or endorse extremist and violent tactics (ranging from hostage taking to torture to assassinations). The result was a power vacuum that was quickly filled by Khomeini and his extremist followers, single-mindedly focused as they were to monopolize power – a characteristic they shared with the Bolsheviks in Russia.[46]

Afterword: Revolutions as Acts of Collective Creativity

> *Resistance graffiti presents an artistic form of opposition that is unique in its form from other graffiti ... Resistance graffiti ... has the unique ability to fuse aesthetics and politics, offering a new form of democratic participation in public space and fosters the emergence of a powerful revolutionary culture. Artists ... use playful and self-reflective sets of semiotic strategies to engage their audience.*[1]

As Sarah Awad and her colleagues (quoted above) point out, resistance graffiti played an important part in the Egyptian Revolution that brought down the Hosni Mobarak (1928–2020) regime after thirty years in power. Resistance graffiti is a reflection of the creativity displayed in revolutions, and I witnessed many examples of resistance graffiti that was used by the anti-Shah movement in Iran in the late 1970s. The term *conflict graffiti* has also been used to reflect the wider role of graffiti in conflict zones, with people showing resistance while grappling with violence, in both Western and non-Western societies.[2] This is just one example of resistance tactics; Gene Sharp (1928–2018) identified around 200 methods of nonviolent actions used by collective movements, reflecting tremendous creativity in many different domains of non-normative activity.[3] Creativity during revolutions is at the three levels of *micro* (intrapersonal), *meso* (organization and small group), and *macro* (large-scale societal transformations).[4] However, it is at the meso and macro (i.e., collective) rather than the micro (individual) levels that creativity during revolutions flourished most fully.

But creativity during revolutions is not exclusive to anti-government movements. Rather, creativity is a characteristic of *both* the revolutionary movements trying to bring about regime change and those defending the ruling regime and trying to prevent revolution. On the one hand, those in the revolutionary movement show creativity in how they demonstrate their opposition to, and disapproval of, the ruling regime. They sometimes do this secretly, for example by painting graffiti under the cover of darkness, by surreptitiously sabotaging regime projects, and by leaving varieties of signs of their displeasure and opposition without divulging their identities (increasingly, this is done using electronic communications). On the other hand, they also use direct and public displays of opposition, by taking part in demonstrations in broad daylight and by going on strike to bring work and production to a halt.

On the other hand, the ruling regime and its supporters use a wide and sometimes innovative range of tactics to try to weaken the revolutionary movement and strengthen the regime, in their efforts to prevent regime change. These include overt tactics, such as openly using police and other security forces to attack, intimidate, arrest, and even kill people who are part of the revolutionary opposition, but also covert tactics, such as using their agents to spy on, interfere with, and disrupt the activities of opposition groups without them knowing. In the twenty-first century, the use of covert tactics to combat revolutionaries on the Internet has dramatically expanded, because of the increasingly important role of electronic communications in revolutionary movements.[5] Government agents in many different countries routinely pose as agitators and revolutionaries in electronic interactions, in order to spy on, ensnare, capture, and destroy the authentic agitators and revolutionaries.

The weapons available to the ruling regime and the revolutionary opposition are in important ways very different. The ruling regime has available state-sponsored violence, with the secret police, the military, and numerous other security agencies available to inflict violence on the revolutionary opposition.[6] Moreover, the ruling regime uses the formal justice system to "legally" criminalize the activities of the revolutionary opposition, so that the punishment of this group (through fines, banishment, jailing, executions) is carried out through the judicial system. The revolutionary opposition do sometimes have access to guns, explosives, and other such weapons, but the physical violence they can inflict on the ruling regime is far less serious than what the regime can inflict on them. Violence by the revolutionary opposition is immediately labeled by the ruling regime as "terrorism" and "illegal," and is dealt with through the state security apparatus and the formal judicial system. However, the revolutionary opposition also has other collective tactics that can become far more effective and are more difficult to nullify when they gain momentum, such as civil disobedience, including mass marches and general strikes across an entire nation.[7]

Varieties of Collective Creativity in Revolutions

A visitor to Tehran in 1978 would have witnessed a strange collective behavior in many parts of the city after sunset. People would open their windows and shout "Allah Akbar" (God is Great) or "Marg Bar Shah" (Death to the Shah) or some similar slogan into the dark night air. Their voices would carry from one neighborhood to the next, creating a continuous string of rebellious sounds around Tehran. It was not clear how this collective practice started, but it helped to create unity in the revolutionary anti-Shah movement, and it was not something the authorities could prevent. Neither could the military dictatorship of Argentina (in power 1976–83) prevent the gathering of the mothers and grandmothers of the Plaza de Mayo, who came together in silence to bring attention to the many thousands of political activists who disappeared at the hands of regime security forces during the dictatorship.[8] Nor could the apartheid regime of South Africa prevent the gathering of the Black Sash women, who gathered in public to display their rejection of apartheid.[9] When I was teaching at the University of Caracas, Venezuela, I witnessed demonstrators using pots, pans, and other kitchen utensils to magnify their collective voice as they marched in the streets against the increasingly repressive regime of Hugo Chavez (1954–2013). Ordinary people show enormous creativity in the forms of resistance they construct in their everyday lives, from subtle ways of dressing in support of rebellion, to satirical resistance graffiti, to explicit and public condemnation of the rulers.[10]

Revolutionaries can sometimes be fortunate when the ruling regime is forced to limit the weapons and tactics it can use against them to quell rebellion. For example, when Jimmy Carter became the president of the United States in 1977, the emphasis he placed on human rights forced the Shah of Iran to moderate his repression and give more room to the opposition to maneuver. Because the Shah was so heavily reliant on United States support, the slightest change of policy in the White House dramatically influenced events in Iran. There have been different interpretations of President Carter's exact role in the downfall of the last Shah of Iran, but there is general agreement that his policies changed how the Shah dealt with the opposition, and very probably made the Shah's regime more vulnerable to collapse.[11]

Another important example of how revolutionaries can sometimes be fortunate when the ruling regime is forced to limit the weapons and tactics it can use is the case of the Russian Revolution in 1905 as compared to 1917.[12] The Russian Revolution of 1905 had the same ingredients as the

Russian Revolution of 1917: the same enormous and widespread dissatisfaction with the Tsar's regime, the same economic problems and huge
mismanagement at home, and the same defeat in foreign wars. But there
was an important difference: The 1904–5 Russian–Japan war was quickly
brought to an end, and although Russia was defeated, the military was now
available and brought back to be used by the Tsar to successfully defend his
regime at home. But at the time of the 1917 Russian Revolution, the
Russian military was fully engaged in World War I (1914–18) and could
not be brought back to defend the Tsar's regime. Indeed, the Tsar himself
had taken command of the war effort and was blamed for repeated Russian
defeats at the war front. Consequently, Lenin and other revolutionaries
benefited from the fact that a large part of the Russian military and security
forces were occupied at war and not available to defend the Tsar and his
government back in St. Petersburg, Moscow, and other major cities.

Enlightenment and Violence

Revolutionary forces and the ruling regime both require, and have shown,
creativity in two particular areas: first, in communicating with and influencing or "enlightening" the masses to support their particular cause
and, second, in the judicious use of threats or actual use of violence to
intimidate and, if possible, destroy the opposition. Lenin was particularly
astute in the combination of timing and violence he adopted, according to
the idea of "Overthrow by force when the time is ripe."[13] The use of
violence by communists to achieve revolution has been stressed, in part
through the glorification of Che Guevara (1928–67) and other armed
revolutionaries committed to international revolutionary movements.[14]
But in this regard, it is worth quoting Mao, so as to not lose sight of the
integrative use of different strategies by communist revolutionaries: "stres-
sing armed struggle does not mean abandoning other forms of struggle; on
the contrary, armed struggle cannot succeed unless coordinated with other
forms of struggle."[15]

The term "enlightenment" is itself controversial with regard to revolutions, because what one side regards as "enlightenment" generally tends to
be regarded as misleading propaganda by the opposition. The Marxist
concept of false consciousness (discussed in Chapter 1 and 2) suggests that
the masses need to be enlightened so as to escape the dominant ideology in
society, which has been introduced by the rulers to justify their rule (this
relates to our discussion in Chapter 2 of this book of system justification
theory, and the idea that the ruling elite control the dominant ideology in

society and use it to influence people to believe that the present societal and political arrangements are fair). For example, Maoist insurgencies in Peru and Nepal combined programs for enlightening the masses, as well as using violent terrorism as a way to spark and spur on rebellion.[16]

A challenge shared by both revolutionaries and the ruling elite is to bridge the gap that inevitably exists between themselves, as an educated and relatively affluent urban elite, and the masses, who tend to be less well educated, less affluent, and more rural. This gap persists even after revolutions, so that after regime change revolutionaries find themselves trying to communicate with the masses who are now in a revolutionary society but not necessarily thinking and acting as revolutionaries. For example, after the 1917 Russian Revolution, the Bolsheviks found that their efforts to enlighten the Russian masses were not very effective, with the result that the revolutionaries tended to look down on the Russian population as ignorant and uncultured, particularly in the villages.[17]

One line of argument is that in order for enlightenment toward democracy to be achieved, a minimum standard of material living must first be met. Christian Welzel and Ronald Inglehart argue that:

> Virtually everyone wants freedom and autonomy, but people's priorities reflect their socioeconomic conditions, and they therefore place the highest subjective value on their most pressing needs. Since material sustenance and physical security are the first requirements for survival, people assign them top priority under conditions of scarcity; with growing prosperity, people become more likely to emphasize autonomy and self-expression values.[18]

An implication is that when revolutionaries are attempting to mobilize collective action in a low-income society, they must give priority to material benefits that would result from the revolution and regime change. But after the revolution has succeeded in bringing about regime change, the revolutionaries will still be faced with the challenge of improving material living conditions. Preaching to the peasants about the ideals of revolution, as the Bolsheviks did after the 1917 Russian Revolution, will not inspire the peasants and the urban poor if the preaching is not accompanied with direct material benefits. But the long-term economic trends in the Soviet Union (and elsewhere) did not bring the expected benefits to the masses.[19]

Given the documented increase in wealth concentration in the world, with more and more of the total wealth in the hands of a smaller and smaller number of people, and the increased difference between governments and people with respect to the availability and use of violence, it is not surprising that civil disobedience has also increased. Kurt Schock notes that:

> ... large-scale campaigns of civil resistance with maximalist political object-ives occurred with greater frequency across the 20th century. Some factors that may have contributed to this include an increasing disparity in the means of violence between citizens and the state in most countries, cross-national diffusion of methods of non-violent action, cross-national transfer of generic knowledge about non-violent action, processes of learning, and an increasing recognition of the effectiveness of nonviolent resistance and the relationship between means and ends.[20]

Working in the tradition of Henry Thoreau (1817–1962), Mahatma Gandhi (1869–1948), and Martin Luther King (1929–68), some thinkers are very optimistic about the possibility for progress toward more open societies through nonviolent resistance. They argue that nonviolent resist-ance is more effective than violent resistance, even against aggressive and repressive dictatorships.

Nonviolent resistance is certainly more in line with the values of democracy, and it would be morally advantageous if nonviolent means could be used to achieve democratic ends. However, China, Russia, North Korea, Iran, and other dictatorships are closely collaborating and support-ing one another, and they are sharing information and techniques for sustaining effective repression.[21] These dictatorial regimes have demon-strated that they are ready and able to use extreme violence – and to do so in creative ways when necessary – in order to destroy democratic move-ments within their borders and also, when possible, outside their borders. Consequently, nonviolent resistance movements must achieve an extraor-dinarily high level of cohesion, efficiency, and expansiveness to succeed to move the world toward actualized democracy. Toward this end, nonvio-lent resistance movements must become more coordinated and collabora-tive globally. There is already some progress in this regard, through collaboration between the tens of millions of expatriates who have fled Russia, China, Russia, North Korea, Iran, and other dictatorships, and are participating in democratic movements. These movements must better develop their networks to influence changes within dictatorships, in order to create movement toward more open societies and open minds.

Notes

Preface

1 The question of what happens after revolutions has received some – but scant – attention in the media and by academics (Greenberg, 2014; see also www.wnyc .org/crowdsourcing/what-happens-after-revolution/report/).

1 A Psychological Perspective on the Puzzle of Revolution

1. Psychological research has shown how bloodshed has been justified by leaders of violent twentieth-century revolutions (Martin, Scully, & Levitt, 1990).
2. For continuity in behavior across long time periods, see Moghaddam (2023).
3. Huntington (2003, p. 38).
4. Goldstone (2003). See Tanter and Midlarsky (1967) for other ways of categorizing revolutions.
5. This relates to discussions of political plasticity in Moghaddam (2023).
6. Le Bon (1913).
7. Brinton (1965).
8. Wagoner, Moghaddam, and Valsiner (2018).
9. For example, see the *Handbook of Revolutions in the 21st Century* (Goldstone, Grinin, & Korotayev, 2022).
10. Agostini and van Zomeren (2021); Louis et al. (2020).
11. Wagoner, Moghaddam, and Valsiner (2018).
12. Le Bon (1913, p. 25).
13. As one of hundreds of examples, see the discussions in Telios, Thoma, and Schmid (2020).
14. Moghaddam (2023).
15. See chapter 2 in Moghaddam (2023).
16. For a standard account of hardwiring in the brain, see Gazzaniga, Ivry, and Mangun (2019).
17. Moghaddam (2022).
18. Moghaddam (2022).

19. Following in the tradition of Lev Vygotsky (1896–1934), Jerome Bruner (1915–2016), and Rom Harré (1927–2019), among others.
20. Goldstone (1982).
21. Selbin (1993).
22. Noueihed and Warren (2012). Brownlee, Masoud, and Reynolds (2015) distinguish between hereditary and nonhereditary Arab Spring regimes; regime change came in the latter (Egypt, Libya – foreign-imposed change, Tunisia, and Yemen).
23. Ahmad (2020).
24. Beissinger (2022, p. 4).
25. For example, Weede and Muller (1998).
26. For example, Richards (2004) includes the Iranian Revolution in his study of major revolutions in world history.
27. As I have pointed out, "2,500 years ago in Athens, free men born in Athens, not women or slaves, could vote. Approximately 2,200 years later, the American Revolution gave rise to a new republic, the United States, in which free men, not women or slaves, could vote. In this sense, the American Revolution only advanced the United States to similar levels of democracy enjoyed in ancient Athens. It was not until 1920 that women gained the right to vote in the United States, and, in practice, it was not until after the Civil Rights Act of 1964 and the improved status of minorities that African Americans and other minority group members could actually cast votes in significant numbers and in relative safety" (Moghaddam, 2019, p. 52).
28. For Color Revolutions, see Beachain and Polese (2010); for the Nazi Revolution, see Mitchell (1997).
29. Moghaddam (2023).
30. See Milani (2015) and other discussions in Baker and Edelstein (2015).
31. For a recent discussion of this literature, see Louis et al. (2020).
32. Sherif (1966); McKenzie and Twose (2015).
33. Zald and McCarthy (2002).
34. Taylor and McKirnan (1984).
35. Sidanius et al. (2004).
36. Wilson (1975); Dawkins (1989).
37. Jost and Banaji (1994).
38. Tajfel and Turner (1979).
39. Pyszczynski, Solomon, and Greenberg (2004).
40. Stouffer et al. (1949).
41. Lind (2020).
42. For a review, see Moghaddam (2008).
43. For example, see Lizzio-Wilson et al. (2021).
44. See chapters 5 and 6 in Desnoyers (2017).

2 Psychological Theories and Revolution: Material Factors as Drivers

1. Marx (1977, p. 214).
2. Lenin (1972, Vol. 11, p. 344).
3. For example, Sargent and Velde (1995).
4. For a review of these theories, see Moghaddam (2008).
5. See the related discussion in Billig (1976) of groups-for-themselves and groups-in-themselves.
6. Jost (1995) discusses six types of false consciousness.
7. See Fasenfest (2021) for a critical discussion of the corporate university.
8. Chatterjee (2012) presents a more nuanced interpretation of false consciousness and feminism.
9. Evolutionary psychology is well represented by Buss (2019).
10. Moghaddam (2015).
11. Sherif (1951, 1956, 1966); Sherif and Sherif (1953, 1969); Sherif et al. (1961); Sherif, White, and Harvey (1955).
12. For examples, see Brief et al. (2005); Echebarria-Echabe and Guede (2003); Lundy and Darkwah (2018); McKenzie and Twose (2015); Terhune and Matusitz (2016); Zárate et al. (2004).
13. Sherif (1966, p. 63).
14. Sherif (1966, p. 12; original emphasis).
15. Capozza and Brown (2015).
16. See Blake and Mouton (1961) for an early example, and Swaab et al. (2021) for a more recent example.
17. McCarthy and Wolfson (1996); McCarthy and Zald (1977).
18. McCarthy and Zald (1977, pp. 1217–1218).
19. Reda, Sinanoglu, and Abdalla (2021).
20. Breuer, Landman, and Farquhar (2015).
21. Klandermans (1984).
22. Piketty (2014).
23. Piketty (2014).
24. Friesen et al. (2018); Jost (2018); Osborne, Sengupta, and Sibley (2018).
25. Jost, Banaji, and Nosek (2004, p. 908).
26. Festinger (1957).
27. See discussions in Harmon-Jones (2019).
28. Hafer et al. (2020); Lerner (1980).
29. See Jost and Kay (2005) for more examples.
30. Friesen et al. (2018, p. 3).
31. Moghaddam (2022).
32. Darwin (1993).
33. Degler (1991).

34. Wilson (1975).
35. Dawkins (1989).
36. Allen and Chagnon (2004, p. 40).
37. Van den Berghe (1987, pp. 18–19).
38. Chagnon (1997).
39. Dowell et al. (2010).
40. Sidanius and Pratto (1999).
41. Sidanius et al. (2004, p. 862).
42. Jost, Banaji, and Nosek, 2004, p. 912).
43. Sidanius and Pratto (1999, p. 265).
44. Becker, Hubbard, and Murphy (2010).
45. There is an enormous body of research literature on these topics; for examples see Hessami and da Fonseca (2020) and Kroska and Cason (2019).
46. Lucas and Kteily (2018).
47. See Moghaddam (2023, pp. 154–161).
48. See Pareto's four volumes on *The Mind and Society* (1935). Marshall (2007) is also insightful on Pareto's contributions to social and political psychology.
49. Taylor and McKirnan (1984).
50. Pareto (1935, Vol. 3, pp. 1422–1423).
51. Plato (1987, Book III, 415b, c, d).
52. Pareto (1935, Vol. 3, p. 1430).
53. Jost (2018).
54. Wright, Taylor, and Moghaddam (1990).
55. Wright, Taylor, and Moghaddam (1990).
56. Sherif et al. (1961, p. 94).
57. See Gaertner et al. (2000).

3 Psychological Theories and Revolution

1. Holmes (2019, p. 65).
2. Social comparison theory was introduced by Festinger (1954), and has led to research on relative deprivation and social comparison (Kim et al., 2018).
3. Holmes (2019, p. 72).
4. Taylor and Moghaddam (1994, chapter 2).
5. Freud (1957, p. 288).
6. Vance-Cheng et al. (2013).
7. For a fuller discussion, see Taylor and Moghaddam (1994), chapter 2.
8. Freud (1955, p. 116).
9. For empirical evidence of similarity-attraction at the intergroup level, see Osbeck, Moghaddam, and Perreault (1997).
10. Freud (1961, p. 114).

11. Le Bon (1897).
12. Freud (1955, p. 122).
13. Fitzpatrick (2017, p. 121).
14. Unfortunately, the United States moved to overthrow Mossadegh in large part because of the perception that the Soviet-backed Tudeh Party was positioned to take control of Iran, and the Shah remained the best defender of US interests in Iran (Gasiorowski, 2019).
15. For an evaluation of the leaderless strategy used in Hong Kong, see Lai and Sing (2020).
16. McGeever (2017).
17. Vince (2020, p. 132).
18. Vince (2020, p. 2).
19. Tajfel and Turner (1979).
20. See Israel and Tajfel (1972); Taylor and Moghaddam (1994), chapter 4).
21. Rhodes and Baron (2019).
22. Kallens, Dale, and Smaldino (2018).
23. This research was part of the "new look" movement, headed by Jerome Bruner (1915–2016); Tajfel (1959), Tajfel and Wilkes (1963).
24. Campbell (1956).
25. Pettigrew, Allport, and Barnett (1958); Rabbie and Horwitz (1969).
26. The first publications reporting the minimal group paradigm were Tajfel (1970) and Tajfel et al. (1971).
27. See discussions in Brown and Pehrson (2020); Tajfel (1984).
28. Moghaddam and Stringer (1986).
29. Melvern (2020).
30. Louër (2022).
31. Moghaddam (2018).
32. See Moghaddam (2022) for discussions of the neglect of social class in Western psychology.
33. Wright, Taylor, and Moghaddam (1990).
34. For different kinds of creativity, see Van Bezouw, van der Toorn, and Becker (2021).
35. Taylor and Moghaddam (1994, p. 88).
36. We have to be careful not to assume that non-Western countries are all collectivistic, and that the United States is comparatively more individualistic. For example, see Takano and Osaka (2018) for a critical assessment of the traditional account of the United States versus Japan on individualism.
37. Drury and Reicher (2000); Thomas, McGarty, and Mavor (2016).
38. Wood (2003).
39. Van Zomeren, Postmes, and Spears (2008).

40. See Setiawan, Scheepers, and Sterkens (2020); Thomas et al. (2020).
41. For example, see Thomas, Mavor, and McGarty (2016).
42. Lerner (1980).
43. For reviews, see Ellard, Harvey, and Callan (2016); Hafer and Sutton (2016).
44. For example, Smith et al. (2011).
45. Smith (1985).
46. Choma et al. (2012).
47. Piketty (2014).
48. Furnham (2003).
49. Messick and Cook (1983); Walster, Walster, and Berscheid (1978).
50. For example, Gavrilets and Fortunato (2014); McKown (2013).
51. Runciman (1966).
52. Moghaddam (2004).
53. Moghaddam and Riley (2005).
54. Gurney and Tierney (1982).
55. See Smith et al. (2012).
56. Tocqueville (1955).
57. Power (2018).
58. Festinger (1954).
59. Festinger (1954, p. 117).
60. Festinger (1954, p. 118).
61. Festinger (1954, p. 124).
62. Buunk and Mussweiler (2001);Gerber, Wheeler, and Suls (2018); Kim et al. (2018); Tennen and Affleck (2000).
63. Hopkins (1764/1992, p. 54).
64. Boucher (1775, p. 203).
65. Naraghi (2015) has documented some of these shifts.
66. Quoted in Pérez-Stable (2012, p. 63).
67. Pérez-Stable (2012, p. 160).
68. Walton (2009).

4 The Tipping Point in Regime Collapse

1. Quoted in Smith (2017, p. 111).
2. Joint Economic Committee Majority Staff Chairman (2015).
3. Khan, Irfan, and Khan (2021, p. 93).
4. Dodge (2005, p. 710).
5. Stiglitz and Bilmes (2008).
6. Aron (2011, p. 65).
7. For example, see Marples (2004); Suny (1993).
8. Friedheim (2007).

9. The "tipping point" concept has been discussed by others in the context of revolutions (e.g., D'Anieri, 2006).
10. Garrioch (2002, p. 283).
11. Garrioch (2002, p. 189).
12. Garrioch (2002, p. 166).
13. Garrioch (2002, p. 231).
14. Garrioch (2002, p. 251).
15. Garrioch (2002, p. 246).
16. Garrioch (2002, p. 302).
17. Lefebvre (2005).
18. Amirahmadi and Kiafar (1987).
19. Gordji-Bandpay (1985).
20. Milani (2011, p. 100).
21. Milani (2011, p. 100).
22. Haliday (1979, p. 19).
23. Matin-Asgari (2012, p. 360).
24. See chapter 3 in Kurzman (2004).
25. Green (1984, p. 166).
26. Awad and Wagoner (2018, p. 191).
27. Holmes (2019, p. 47).
28. Lachmann (1997), Skocpol (1979), and others support this proposition, which I have discussed in more detail in Moghaddam (2013).
29. Marx and Engels (1967/1848).
30. In each case, I give the starting date of the revolutions.
31. Lane (1996).
32. Trimberger (1978).
33. Milgram (1974).
34. Da Costa et al. (2021).
35. Voss, Cable, and Voss (2006).
36. Pareto (1935, III, p. 1431).
37. Levitsky and Ziblatt (2018, p. 213).
38. Levitsky and Ziblatt (2018, p. 212).
39. Haberman (2022); Woodward and Costa (2021).
40. Levitsky and Ziblatt (2018, pp. 23–24).
41. Moghaddam (2019).
42. Merridale (2017).
43. Quoted in Smith (2017, p. 111).
44. Fulbrook (1995, p. 144).
45. Kurzman (2004).
46. Axworthy (2013, p. 131).
47. Khomeini (1979).

48. Axworthy (2013); Naraghi (2015).
49. Brenton (2017).
50. For example, Lee Baker (2005) describes the case of Terror in Dijon, France, which to some degree differed from national trends in France.

5 Psychological Processes Underlying Revolutionary Regime Change

1. Shakespeare (1993).
2. For example, see Lammers, Stapel, and Galinsky (2010); see also Moghaddam (2016, pp. 104–107; 2019, pp. 43–44, 123–127).
3. Pace (2005).
4. Moghaddam (2018, p. 4).
5. Levitsky and Way (2022).
6. Levitsky and Way (2022, p. 349).
7. The vast majority of research on system justification theory has been conducted in relatively open societies (see the review by Jost, 2018).
8. Moghaddam (2013).
9. This is predicted by psychological research on conformity and obedience (Moghaddam, 2005, chapters 15 and 16).
10. Quoted in Vanek and Mücke (2016, p. 20).
11. See chapter 4 in Fulbrook (1995).
12. Amarasinghe (2021).
13. Wigell (2021).
14. Figes (2007, p. 180).
15. Figes (2007, p. 180).
16. See Sherif (1966). Also, there is experimental evidence showing that external threat results in a highlighting of intragroup similarity and less tolerance for within group diversity (Davies, Steele, & Markus, 2008; Rothgerber, 1997).
17. Price (2002).
18. Crawford (2017).
19. Skocpol (1979).
20. Milani (2013).
21. Brenton (2017, p. 7).
22. Krastev and McPherson (2007).
23. Moghaddam (in press).
24. Vanek and Mücke (2016, p. 169).
25. Tackett (2015, p. 4).
26. Bullock (1991, p. 91).
27. Bullock (1991, p. 55).
28. Jordan (2012, p. 97).

29. Jordan (2012, p. 150).
30. Walton (2009, p. 37).
31. Jahanpour (1984).

6 Psychological Stepping Stones to Revolution

1. For a more in-depth discussion of a societies to cells approach, see Moghaddam (2022).
2. Godineau (1998, p. 97, original emphasis).
3. See chapter 6 in Taylor and Moghaddam (1994).
4. Leese (2011, p. 108).
5. This distinction was initially discussed in the context of commercial advertising (Petty, Cacioppo, & Schumann, 1983).
6. Scully and Levitt (1990).
7. Panning (1983, pp. 328–329).
8. Gerber, Wheeler, and Suls (2018).
9. Baldwin and Mussweiler (2018).
10. Power, Madsen, and Morton (2020).
11. Chandra and Foster (2005).
12. Baldwin and Mussweiler (2018).
13. See chapter 6 in Moghaddam (2022).
14. Anderson (1999).
15. Griffin and Oheneba-Sakyi (1993).
16. Farber (1983).
17. The focus here is on perceptions of legitimacy (Tyler, 2006).
18. Beetham (2013, pp. 19–36).
19. Van der Toorn, Tyler, and Jost (2011).
20. Tyler (2001).
21. Bickman (1974).
22. Moghaddam (2021).
23. Moghaddam (2002).
24. See chapters 15 and 16 in Moghaddam (2005).
25. LeVine and Campbell (1972).
26. Haeri (2014).
27. Rahimzadeh (2020).
28. Wood, Quinn, and Kashy (2002).
29. Brandenberger (2017) provides a more complex picture of events, which provides a semi-defense of Stalin's position.
30. Markwick (2001).
31. Hughes (2006).
32. Frings (1997).

33. Söllner (2013).
34. Berman and Fox (2023).
35. Blackwood and Louis (2012) articulate these traditions very well.
36. Jasko et al. (2019).

7 Behavioral Continuity and Attempts at Perpetual Revolution

1. Vanek and Mücke (2016, p. 65).
2. Razavi (2009).
3. Mittler (2014).
4. Wang (2021) discusses the possible side-effects of violence during the Cultural Revolution in China.
5. In the case of China, there have been serious reassessments of the Cultural Revolution (Branigan, 2023). The Cultural Revolution in Iran has also attracted some attention (Razavi, 2009).
6. Fischer (1980) provides a good account of seminary education at that time.
7. Khalaji (2016).
8. Delano and Knottnerus (2018).
9. Tackett (2000).
10. Quoted in Lynch (2017, p. 172).
11. Coarse and Wang (2012).
12. This Latin phrase is attributed to Juvenal (Decimus Junius Juvenalis), a Roman poet (see Courtney, 1980, for a commentary on Juvenal's satires).
13. Dabphet (2018); John (2009); Löwy (2010); Osborn (2007); Trotsky (2010).
14. Stoppard (2006).
15. Trotsky (2010).
16. Quoted in Nichol (2010, p. 12).
17. Smith (2017, p. 162).
18. Pepper (1999).
19. Trotsky (2005).
20. See Bird (2018) for an insightful discussion of culture as permanent revolution.
21. Ferdowsi (2016).
22. See chapter 7 in Moghaddam (2023).
23. Michael (1977).
24. Shirk (1984, p. 70).
25. Simms and Nichols (2014).
26. Lout and Wilk (2014).
27. Hay (2013) is a good source for general information about the Khmer Rouge era.
28. Tan (1984, p. 4).

29. Goldstein and Hiebert (2016).
30. Mok (2020, p. 18).
31. Tsai (1999, p. 42).
32. Watson (1984, p. 8).
33. Li and Yang (2005).
34. For China, see Hung and Chiu (2003); for Iran, see Azadi, Mirramezani, and Mesgaran (2020).
35. Osborn (2007, p. 130).
36. Dittmer (1973).
37. See Moghaddam (2023) for a discussion of hard-wiring outside individuals.

8 Cultural Carriers and the Failure of Revolutionaries to Reshape Behavior

1. Moaddel (2022).
2. The readings in Little (2009) provide reassessments of Cromwell.
3. Pincus and Robinson (2011).
4. Moghaddam (2002).
5. Lout and Wilk (2014).
6. For the background on Cuba, see Alvarez (2000) and Horowitz (1987); for more recent changes, see González-Corzo (2019).
7. Quoted in Bullock (1991, p. 260).
8. For the original authoritarian personality research, see Adorno et al. (1950); for more recent discussion, see Dean and Altemeyer (2020). For pioneering research on authoritarianism in the family, see Schaffner (1948). More recent relevant research includes explorations of different parenting styles, including the authoritarian style (Baumrind, 1991). There is debate as to what extent an authoritarian parenting style is universal and to what extent it varies across cultures (Mason et al., 2004; Sorkhabi & Mandara, 2013). My view is that there is consistency in style of parenting across authoritarian societies with surface differences in expressed ideology.
9. Some of the contradictions and complexities of family relations in Iran are discussed in Bøe (2015); see also Moghaddam (2013, p. 138).
10. Glaeser, Ponzetto, and Schleifer (2007).
11. Figes (2007, p. 20).
12. Daneshpour and Hassandokht Firooz (2022).
13. Sharlet (1984, p. 135).
14. Yadav and Mukherjee (2016) provide a critical account of corruption in dictatorships.
15. See the international corruption index: www.worldeconomics.com/Indicato r-Data/Corruption/Corruption-Perceptions-Index.aspx.

16. Bullock (1991, p. 382).
17. Anderson (2007).
18. Wolf (2008).
19. Moghaddam (2023, chapter 6).
20. Fitzpatrick (1999, p. 128).
21. Smith (2017, pp. 242–243).
22. Anderson (1994, p. 3).
23. Corley (1996).
24. Figes (2007, pp. 44–45) recounts the sad experience of a little child who was attacked for wearing a cross around her neck, even though it was hidden beneath her clothes.
25. Timasheff (1955).
26. Levitas (1990) discusses a variety of utopias. More's *Utopia* (1965, first published 1516) abandons private property more than three centuries before Marx.
27. Pareto (1971, p. 93).
28. Haney (2001).
29. Fitzpatrick (1999, p. 106).

9 The Role of Personality in Revolutions

1. Mullaney (1984).
2. Moghaddam (2022, chapter 4).
3. Freud (1953–1964).
4. Moghaddam (2022).
5. Moghaddam (2022, chapter 4).
6. Moghaddam (2022, chapter 2).
7. Read (2005, p. 262).
8. Salisbury (1992).
9. Lynch (2017, pp. 227–228).
10. Moghaddam (2013).
11. For example, Gilbert (1950); Langer (1972).
12. For example, see Ringwald et al. (2022).
13. For example, Volkova and Rusalov (2016).
14. For a review of discussions on narcissism and pathological narcissism, see Miller et al. (2017); Pincus and Lukowitsky (2010). I conceptualize normal and pathological narcissism as being at the ends of the same continuum.
15. This is also reported in Western publications (e.g., Axworthy, 2013, p. 141).
16. Lynch (2017, p. 105).

17. Christie and Geis (1970) originated the modern research which continues to explore how Machiavellianism is related to locus of control (Aldousari & Ickes, 2021).
18. Pipes (1990, p. 795)
19. Teiwes and Sun (1999).
20. Frenkel-Brunswik (1949).
21. Bochner (1965, p. 394).
22. Forsberg, Nilsson, and Jørgensen (2019).
23. Weede and Muller (1998, p. 330).
24. Moghaddam and Studer (1998).
25. Lewis (1987).
26. Bell (2020); Willner (1984).
27. Swatos (1981, p. 124).
28. Maran et al. (2019).
29. Reed (2015, p. 76).
30. This expression was probably first used in Buchner's (1835/2011) play *Danton's Death*.
31. Smeaton (1993).
32. Schama (1989, pp. 781–782).
33. Quoted in Read (2005, p. 178; original emphasis).
34. See Chen and Chen (1953) for a discussion of early "anti" movements.
35. Lynch (2017, p. 193).
36. Day et al. (2002).
37. Somin (2018).
38. Jones (2008).
39. The Nobel Peace Prize winner Shirin Ebadi (2016) presents a balanced discussion of human rights in Iran, with a particular focus on women.
40. Salisbury (1992).
41. Bègue et al. (2015); Blass (1991).
42. Elms and Milgram (1966).
43. Altemeyer (1981).
44. For example, see DeYoung, Peterson, and Higgins (2002).
45. DeHart-Davis (2007).
46. Arendt (2006).
47. Moghaddam (2013).

10 The Illusion-Motivation Model of Revolution

1. My late friend and colleague Rom Harré (1986) would no doubt remind me that it is more correct to conceptualize varieties of realism rather than assume one form of external reality.

2. Shepperd, Malone, and Sweeny (2008).
3. Moghaddam and Studer (1998).
4. Taylor (1936, p. 537).
5. See Dix (1984); Huntington (1968); Tilly (1973).
6. Dahlum (2022).
7. Foran and Goodwin (1993, p. 213).
8. Forgas and Laham (2016).
9. Schama (1989) provides a lively account of the interweaving opposition groups and individuals involved in the French Revolution.
10. Goldstone (1982, p. 191).
11. Moghaddam and Breckenridge (2011). A number of other authors have pointed out that after revolutions, new governments have very little time to deal with the chaos and restore order toward democracy (e.g., see Gard-Murray and Bar-Yam, 2015).
12. Moghaddam (2004).
13. For example, see the list of common events proposed by Goldstone (1982, pp. 189–192).
14. Discussions in Goldstone, Grinin, and Korotayev (2022) are a good start.
15. See Gurr (1970), and chapter 6 in Taylor and Moghaddam (1994).

11 Does Human Nature Doom Revolutions?

1. See the readings in Darby (2001) for the successful Dutch revolt against the Spanish.
2. See Moghaddam (2022, p. 31).
3. Moghaddam (2023).
4. From Moghaddam (2023).
5. Skocpol (1985, pp. 86–87).
6. See Stites (1989), particularly chapters 8–10, for examples of utopian revolutionary goals.
7. See the discussions in Finkel and Moghaddam (2005).
8. Shelley's *Laon and Cyntha* (Molinari, 2004) and Wordsworth's *The Prelude* (Radcliffe, 1994) reflect this trend.
9. Burke and Mitchell (2009).
10. Schinz (1923).
11. Robinson (1990) assesses the impact of the French Revolution on Spanish America.
12. Chamberlin (1942, p. 5).
13. Chamberlin (1942, p. 5).
14. Michael (1977); Osborn (2007).
15. Gungwu (1990, p. 40).

16. There have been pockets of resistance to privatization in rural areas (Yan, Bun, & Siyuan, 2021).
17. For example, see Callick (2013).
18. Xu (2022).
19. Saney (2009).
20. Quoted in Harris (2009, p. 36).
21. For collective behavior as conventional, see Aguirre (1984); for Cuban healthcare, see Fitz (2020) and also Geloso and Pavlik (2021).
22. Bye (2017).
23. Strug (2009).
24. Abdo (2017).
25. See the international corruption index: www.worldeconomics.com/Indicato r-Data/Corruption/Corruption-Perceptions-Index.aspx.
26. Pesaran (2008).
27. Grajewski (2022) refers to an illusory entente between Iran, China, and Russia.
28. Quoted in Cheng (2009, p. 1).
29. Figes (1997, p. 343).
30. See Moghaddam (2019, pp. 43–44, 123–127).
31. See readings in Le Cheminant and Parrish (2011).
32. Rock (2009).
33. See www.transparency.org/en/cpi/2022.
34. Moghaddam (2019).
35. Ang (2020).
36. See chapter 3 in Moghaddam (2023).
37. Lammers, Gordijn, and Otten (2008); Lammers, Stapel, and Galinsky (2010).
38. See Moghaddam (2016, chapter 2).
39. Moghaddam (2016).
40. For social mobility, see Zhou and Xie (2019); for policy experimentation, see Teets and Hasmath (2020); and for state–labor relations see Howell and Pringle (2019).
41. There is controversy and disagreement about how progress in Cuba should be assessed. There is no doubt that on issues and health and social services, Cuban society has advanced very well. However, according to more traditional criteria of economic performance, Cuba has had far less success (Zimbalist, 2018).
42. Hansing and Hoffman (2020).
43. See Moghaddam (2023, pp. 96–100).
44. Van Dick, Tissington, and Hertel (2009).
45. Stites (1989, p. 8).
46. Selznick (1952) focuses a lot on the motivation of the Bolsheviks to monopolize power.

Afterword: Revolutions as Acts of Collective Creativity

1. Awad, Wagoner, and Glaveanu (2017).
2. Lennon (2021).
3. Sharp (1973).
4. Moghaddam and Covalucci (2018).
5. See www.wired.com/story/iran-cyber-army-protests-disinformation/.
6. Greitens (2016) provides an insightful assessment of state violence.
7. Allen (2017) provides a strong defense of civil disobedience in global context, with a leaning toward philosophical rather than practical matters.
8. Arditti (1999).
9. Burton (2010).
10. Chaudhary et al. (2017).
11. For example, see Milani (2011, 2015) and Trenta (2013).
12. See Skocpol (1976, p. 183).
13. Becker (1937, p. 356).
14. See readings in Black (1965) for discussions of the relationship between the strategic use of violence and communism.
15. Quoted in Namboodiripad (1976, p. 61).
16. Marks and Palmer (2006).
17. Badcock (2006).
18. Welzel and Inglehart (2008).
19. Piketty (2014).
20. Schock (2013, p. 279).
21. Diamond, Plattner, and Walker (2016); Dukalskis (2017).

References

Abdo, G. (2017). *The new sectarianism: The Arab uprisings and the rebirth of the Shi'a-Sunni divide.* New York: Oxford University Press.

Adorno, T. W., Frenkel-Brunswik, E., Levinson, D. J., & Sanford, B. W. (1950). *The authoritarian personality.* New York: Harper & Row.

Agostini, M., & van Zomeren, M. (2021). Toward a comprehensive and potentially cross-cultural model of why people engage in collective action: A quantitative research synthesis of four motivations and structural constraints. *Psychological Bulletin, 147*(7), 667–700.

Aguirre, B. E. (1984). The conventionalization of collective behavior in Cuba. *American Journal of Sociology, 90,* 541–566.

Ahmad, T. (2020). The enduring "Arab Spring": Change and resistance. *Indian Foreign Affairs Journal, 15,* 91–107.

Aldousari, S. S., & Ickes, W. (2021). How is Machiavellianism related to locus of control: A meta-analytic review. *Personality and Individual Differences, 174,* 110677.

Allen, M. (2017). *Civil disobedience in global perspective: Decency and dissent over borders, inequities and government secrecy.* New York: Springer.

Allen, W. E., & Chagnon, N. A. (2004). The tragedy of the commons revisited. In Y. T. Lee, C. McCauley, F. M. Moghaddam, & S. Worchel (Eds.), *The psychology of ethnic and cultural conflict* (pp. 23–47). Westport, CT: Praeger.

Altemeyer, B. (1981). *Right-wing authoritarianism.* Winnipeg, Ontario: University of Manitoba Press.

Alvarez, J. (2000). Differences in agricultural productivity in Cuba's state and nonstate sectors: Further evidence. *Cuba in Transition, 10,* 98–107.

Amarasinghe, P. (2021). The depiction of "orthodoxy" in post-Soviet space: How Vladimir Putin uses the church in his anti-Western campaign? *Open Political Science, 4,* 74–82.

Amirahmadi, H., & Kiafar, A. (1987). Tehran: Growth and contradictions. *Journal of Planning Education and Research, 6,* 167–177.

Anderson, C. A. (1999). Attributional style, depression, and loneliness: A cross-cultural comparison of American and Chinese students. *Personality and Social Psychology Bulletin, 25,* 482–499.

Anderson, J. (1994). *Religion, state and politics in the Soviet Union and successor states.* New York: Cambridge University Press.

Anderson, J. (2007). Putin and the Russian Orthodox Church: Asymmetric symphonia? *Journal of International Affairs, 61*, 185–201.

Ang, Y. Y. (2020). *China's gilded age: The paradox of economic boom and vast corruption.* New York: Cambridge University Press.

Arditti, R. (1999). *Searching for life: The grand-mothers of the Plaza de Maya and the disappeared children of Argentina.* Berkeley, CA: University of California Press.

Arendt, H. (2006). *Eichmann in Jerusalem: A report on the banality of evil.* New York: Penguin Books. First published in 1963.

Aron, L. (2011). Everything you think you know about the collapse of the Soviet Union is wrong. *Foreign Policy, 187*, 64–70.

Aurelius, M. (1964). *Meditations.* (Trans. M. Staniforth). Harmondsworth: Penguin.

Awad, S. H., & Wagoner, B. (2018). Image politics of the Arab uprising. In B. Wagoner, F. M. Moghaddam, & J. Valsiner (Eds.), *The psychology of radical social change: From rage to revolution* (pp. 189–217). Cambridge: Cambridge University Press.

Awad, S. H., Wagoner, B., & Glaveanu, V. (2017). The street art of resistance. In N. Chaudhary, N. P. Hviid., G. Marsico, & J. W. Villadsen (Eds.), *Resistance in everyday life: Constructing cultural experiences* (pp. 161–180). New York: Springer.

Axworthy, M. (2013). *Revolutionary Iran: A history of the Islamic Republic.* New York: Oxford University Press.

Azadi, P., Mirramezani, M., & Mesgaran, M. B. (2020). Migration and brain drain from Iran. Working Paper 9, *Stanford Iran 2040 Project,* Stanford University. https://iranian-studies.stanford.edu/iran-2040-project/publica tions/migration-and-brain-drain-iran.

Badcock, S. (2006). Talking to the people and shaping revolution: The drive for enlightenment in revolutionary Russia. *The Russian Review, 65*, 617–636.

Baker, K. M., & Edelstein, D. (Eds.) (2015). *Scripting revolution: A historical approach to the comparative study of revolutions.* Stanford, CA: Stanford University Press.

Baker, L. (2005). The French Revolution as local experience: The Terror in Dijon. *The Historian, 67*, 694–711.

Baldwin, M., & Mussweiler, T. (2018). The culture of social comparison. *Proceedings of the National Academy of Science: Psychological and Cognitive Science, 115*, E9067–E9074.

Baumrind, D. (1991). The influence of parenting style on adolescent competence and substance use. *The Journal of Early Adolescence, 11*, 56–95.

Beachain, D. O., & Polese, A. (2010). What happened to the colour revolutions? Authoritarian responses from former Soviet spaces. *Journal of International and Area Studies, 17*, 31–51.

Becker, F. B. (1937). Lenin's application of Marx's theory of revolutionary tactics. *American Sociological Review, 2*, 353–364.

Becker, G. S., Hubbard, W. H. J., & Murphy, K. M. (2010). Explaining the worldwide boom in higher education of women. *Journal of Human Capital, 4*, 203–241.

Beetham, D. (2013). *The legitimation of power*. New York: Palgrave Macmillan. 2nd ed.

Bègue, L., Beauvois, J. L., Courbet, D., Oberlé, D., Lepage, J., & Duke, A. A. (2015). Personality predicts obedience in a Milgram paradigm. *Journal of Personality, 83*, 299–306.

Beissinger, M. R. (2022). *The revolutionary city: Urbanization and the global transformation of rebellion*. Princeton, NJ: Princeton University Press.

Bell, D. A. (2020). *Men on horseback: The power of charisma in the age of revolution*. New York: Picador.

Berman, G., & Fox, A. (2023). *Gradual: The case for incremental change in a radical age*. New York: Oxford University Press.

Bickman, L. (1974). The social power of a uniform. *Journal of Applied Social Psychology, 4*, 47–61.

Billig, M. G. (1976). *Social psychology and intergroup relations*. London: Academic Press.

Bird, R. (2018). Culture as permanent revolution: Lev Trotsky's *Literature and Revolution*. *Studies in East European Thought, 70*, 181–193.

Black, C. E. (Ed.) (1965). *Communism and revolution: The strategic use of political violence*. Princeton, NJ: Princeton University Press.

Blackwood, L. M., & Louis, W. R. (2012). If it matters for the group then it matters to me: Collective action outcomes for seasoned activists. *British Journal of Social Psychology, 51*, 72–92.

Blake, R. R., & Mouton, J. S. (1961). Reactions to intergroup competition under win-lose conditions. *Management Science, 7*, 420–435.

Blass, T. (1991). Understanding behavior in the Milgram obedience experiment: The role of personality, situations, and their interactions. *Journal of Personality and Social Psychology, 60*, 398–413.

Bochner, S. (1965). Defining intolerance of ambiguity. *The Psychological Record, 15*, 393–400.

Bøe, M. (2015). *Family law in contemporary Iran: Women's rights activism and Shari'a*. London: I.B. Tauris & Co.

Boucher, J. (1775). *On civil liberty, passive obedience, and non-resistance*. https://sites.miamioh.edu/empire/files/2022/08/1775-Boucher-On-Civil-Liberty-Passive-Obedience-and-Non-Resistance.pdf.

Brandenberger, D. (2017). Stalin's rewriting of 1917. *The Russian Review, 76*, 667–689.

Branigan, T. (2023). *Red memory*. New York: W. W. Norton.

Brenton, T. (2017). Introduction. In T. Brenton (Ed.), *Was revolution inevitable? Turning points in the Russian Revolution* (pp. 1–10). New York: Oxford University Press.

Brenton, T. (2017). The short life and early death of Russian democracy: The Duma and the Constituent Assembly. In T. Brenton (Ed.), *Was revolution inevitable? Turning points of the Russian Revolution* (pp. 142–162). New York: Oxford University Press.

Breuer, A., Landman, T., & Farquhar, D. (2015). Social media and protest mobilization: Evidence from the Tunisian revolution. *Democratization, 22,* 764–792.

Brief, A. P., Umphress, E. E., Dietz, J., Burrows, J. W., Butz, R. M., & Scholten, L. (2005). Community matters: Realistic group conflict theory and the impact of diversity. *The Academy of Management Journal, 48,* 830–844.

Brinton, C. (1965). *The anatomy of revolution.* 2nd ed. New York: Vintage Books. First published in 1938.

Brown, R., & Pehrson, S. (2020). *Group processes: Dynamics within and between groups.* Hoboken, NJ: Wiley Blackwell.

Brownlee, J., Masoud, T., & Reynolds, A. (2015). *The Arab Spring: Pathways of repression and reform.* New York: Oxford University Press.

Buchner, G. (2011). *Danton's death.* London: Methuen Drama. First published in 1835.

Bullock, A. (1991). *Hitler and Stalin: Parallel lives.* New York: Vintage Books.

Burke, E., & Mitchell, L. G. (2009). *Reflections on the revolution in France.* New York: Oxford University Press. First published in 1790.

Burton, M. (2010). The Black Sash story: Protest and service recorded in the archives. *English Academic Review, 27,* 129–133.

Buss, D. M. (2019). *Evolutionary psychology: The new science of the mind.* New York: Routledge. 6th ed.

Buunk, B. P., & Mussweiler, T. (2001). New directions in social comparison research. *European Journal of Social Psychology, 31,* 467–475.

Bye, V. (2017). Cuba's critical juncture: Main challenges. *Iberoamericana – Nordic Journal of Latin American and Caribbean Studies, 46,* 109–118.

Callick, R. (2013). *The party forever: Inside China's modern Communist elite.* New York: Palgrave Macmillan.

Campbell, D. T. (1956). Enhancement of contrast as a composite habit. *Journal of Abnormal and Social Psychology, 56,* 350–355.

Capozza, D., & Brown, R. (Eds.) (2015). *Social identity processes: Trends in theory and research.* London: Sage.

Chagnon, N. A. (1997). *Yanomamo.* New York: Harcourt Brace. 5th ed.

Chamberlin, W. H. (1942). The Russian Revolution 1917–1942. *The Russian Review, 2,* 3–9.

Chandra, S., & Foster, A. W. (2005). The "Revolution of rising expectations," relative deprivation and the urban social disorders of the 1960s: Evidence from state-level data. *Social Science History, 29,* 299–332.

Chatterjee, I. (2012). Feminism, the false consciousness of neoliberal capitalism? Informalization, fundamentalism, and women in an Indian city. *Gender, Place & Culture: A Journal of Feminist Geography, 19,* 790–809.

Chaudhary, N., Hviid. N. P., Marsico, G., & Villadsen, J. W. (Eds.) (2017). *Resistance in everyday life: Constructing cultural experiences.* New York: Springer.

Chen, T. H. E., & Chen, W. H. C. (1953). The "three-anti" and "five-anti" movements in Communist China. *Pacific Affairs, 26,* 3–23.

Cheng, Y. (2009). *Creating the "new man:" From enlightenment ideals to socialist realities*. Honolulu, HI: University of Hawaii Press.

Choma, B., Hafer, C. L., Crosby, F. J., & Foster, M. D. (2012). Perceptions of personal sex discrimination: The role of belief in a just world and situational ambiguity. *Journal of Social Psychology, 152*, 568–585.

Christie, R., & Geis, F. L. (1970). *Studies in Machiavellianism*. New York: Academic Press.

Coarse, R., & Wang, N. (2012). *How China became capitalist*. New York: Palgrave Macmillan.

Corley, F. (1996). *Religion in the Soviet Union: An archival reading*. Basingstoke: Macmillan Press.

Courtney, E. (1980). *A commentary on the satires of Juvenal*. London: Athlone Press.

Crawford, D. (2017). The last tsar. In T. Brenton (Ed.), *Was revolution inevitable? Turning points of the Russian Revolution* (pp. 66–90). New York: Oxford University Press.

D'Anieri, P. (2006). Explaining the success and failure of post-communist revolutions. *Communist and Post-Communist Studies, 39*, 331–350.

Da Costa, S., Delfino, G., Murattori, M., et al. (2021). Obedience to authority, cognitive and affective responses and leadership style in relation to a non-normative order: The Milgram experiment. *Revisita de Psycologia, 39*.

Dabphet, S. (2018). "Mao Zedong Thought" and the cultural revolution. *International Journal of East Asian Studies, 22*, 22–38.

Dahlum, S. (2022). Joining forces: Social coalitions and democratic revolutions. *Journal of Peace Research*. https://doi.org/10.1177/00223433221138614.

Daneshpour, M., & Hassandokht Firooz, S. (2022). Women, life, freedom: The new unveiling of feminism. *Journal of Feminist Family Therapy, 34*(3–4), 390–394.

Darby, G. (Ed.) (2001). *The origins and development of the Dutch revolt*. London: Routledge.

Darwin, C. (1993). *The origin of species by natural selection or the preservation of favored races in the struggle for life*. New York: Modern Library. First published in 1859.

Davies, P. G., Steele, C. M., & Markus, H. (2008). A nation challenged: The impact of foreign threat on America's tolerance for diversity. *Journal of Personality and Social Psychology, 95*, 308–318.

Dawkins, R. (1989). *The selfish gene*. Oxford: Oxford University Press. 2nd ed.

Day, D. V., Schleicher, D. J., Unckless, A. L., & Hiller, N. J. (2002). Self-monitoring personality at work: A meta-analytic investigation of construct validity. *Journal of Applied Psychology, 87*, 390–401.

De Lagasnerie, G. (2020). The concepts of revolution. In T. Telios, D. Thoma, & U. Schmid (Eds.), *The Russian revolution as ideal and practice* (pp. 227–241). Cham: Palgrave Macmillan.

Dean, J. W., & Altemeyer, B. (2020). *Authoritarian nightmare: Trump and his followers*. New York: Melville House.

Degler, C. N. (1991). *In search of human nature: The decline and revival of Darwinism in American social thought.* New York: Oxford University Press.

DeHart-Davis, L. (2007). The unbureaucratic personality. *Public Administration Review, 67,* 892–903.

Delano, D. L., & Knottnerus, J. (2018). The Khmer Rouge, ritual and control. *Asian Journal of Social Science, 46,* 79–110.

Desnoyers, C. A. (2017). *Patterns of modern Chinese history.* New York: Oxford University Press.

DeYoung, C., Peterson, J. B., & Higgins, D. M. (2002). Higher-order factors in the Big Five predict conformity: Are there neuroses of health? *Personality and Individual Differences, 33,* 533–552.

Diamond, L., Plattner, M. F., & Walker, C. (Eds.) (2016). *Authoritarianism goes global: The challenge to democracy.* Baltimore, MD: Johns Hopkins University Press.

Dittmer, L. (1973). The structural evolution of "criticism and self-criticism." *The China Quarterly, 56,* 708–729.

Dix, R. H. (1984). Why revolutions succeed & fail. *Polity, 16,* 423–446.

Dodge, T. (2005). Iraqi transitions: From regime change to state collapse. *Third World Quarterly, 26,* 705–721.

Dowell, R. D., Ryan, O., Jansen, A., et al. (2010). Genotype to phenotype: A complex problem. *Science, 328,* 469.

Drury, J., & Reicher, S. (2000). Collective action and psychological change: The emergence of new social identities. *British Journal of Social Psychology, 39,* 579–604.

Dukalskis, A. (2017). *The authoritarian public sphere: Legitimization and autocratic power in North Korea, Burma, and China.* London: Routledge.

Ebadi, S. (2016). *Until we are free: My fight for human rights in Iran.* New York: Random House.

Echebarria-Echabe, A., & Guede, E. F. (2003). Extending the theory of realistic conflict to competition in institutional settings: Intergroup status and outcome. *The Journal of Social Psychology, 143,* 763–782.

Ellard, J. H., Harvey, A., & Callan, M. J. (2016). The justice motive: History, theory, and research. In C. Sabbagh & M. Schmitt (Eds.), *Handbook of social justice theory and research* (pp. 127–143). New York: Springer.

Elms, A., & Milgram, S. (1966). Personality characteristics associated with obedience and defiance toward authoritarian commands. *Journal of Experimental Research on Personality, 2,* 289–292.

Farber, S. (1983). The Cuban Communists in the early stages of the Cuban Revolution: Revolutionaries or reformists? *Latin American Research Review, 18,* 59–83.

Fasenfest, D. (2021). Reflections on the decline of academia: Large problems and small minds. *Critical Sociology, 47,* 1057–1063.

Ferdowsi, A. (2016). *Shahnameh: The Persian book of kings.* (Trans. D. Davis). New York: Penguin.

Festinger, L. (1954). A theory of social comparison processes. *Human Relations, 7,* 117–140.

Festinger, L. (1957). *A theory of cognitive dissonance.* Stanford, CA: Stanford University Press.

Figes, O. (1997). The Russian Revolution of 1917 and its language in the village. *The Russian Review, 56,* 323–345.

Figes, O. (2007). *The whisperers: Private life in Stalin's Russia.* New York: Picador.

Finkel, N. J., & Moghaddam, F. M. (Eds.) (2005). *The psychology of rights and duties: Empirical contributions and normative commentaries.* Washington, DC: American Psychological Association.

Fischer, M. M. J. (1980). *Iran: From religious dispute to revolution.* Cambridge, MA: Harvard University Press.

Fitz, D. (2020). *Cuban health care: The ongoing revolution.* New York: Monthly Review Press.

Fitzpatrick, S. (1999). *Everyday Stalinism – Ordinary life in extraordinary times: Soviet Russia in the 1930s.* New York: Oxford University Press.

Fitzpatrick, S. (2017). *The Russian revolution.* New York: Oxford University Press. 4th ed.

Foran, J., & Goodwin, J. (1993). Revolutionary outcomes in Iran and Nicaragua: Coalition fragmentation, war, and the limits of social transformation. *Theory and Society, 22,* 209–247.

Forgas, J. P., & Laham, S. M. (2016). Halo effects. In R. F. Pohl (Ed.), *Cognitive illusions: Intriguing phenomena in judgement, thinking and memory* (pp. 276–290). New York: Psychology Press. 2nd ed.

Forsberg, E., Nilsson, A., & Jørgensen, Ø. (2019). Moral dichotomization at the heart of prejudice: The role of moral foundations and intolerance of ambiguity in generalized prejudice. *Social Psychological and Personality Science, 10,* 1002–1010.

Franz, M. (1977). *Mao and the perpetual revolution.* Woodbury, NY: Barron's Educational Series.

Frenkel-Brunswik, E. (1949). Intolerance of ambiguity as an emotional and perceptual personality variable. *Journal of Personality, 18,* 108–143.

Freud, S. (1953–1964). *The standard edition of the complete psychological works of Sigmund Freud.* (Ed. & Trans. J. Strachey, Vols 1–24). London: Hogarth Press. First published in 1886–1939.

Freud, S. (1955). Group psychology and the analysis of the ego. In J. Strachey (Ed. & Trans.), *The standard edition of the complete psychological works of Sigmund Freud* (Vol. 18, 67–143). London: Hogarth Press. First published in 1921.

Freud, S. (1957). Thoughts for the times on war and death. In J. Strachey (Ed. & Trans.), *The standard edition of the complete psychological works of Sigmund Freud* (Vol. 14, 271–302). London: Hogarth Press. First published in 1915.

Freud, S. (1961). Civilization and its discontents. In J. Strachey (Ed. & Trans.), *The standard edition of the complete psychological works of Sigmund Freud* (Vol. 21, 64–145). London: Hogarth Press. First published in 1930.

Friedheim, D. V. (2007). Regime collapse in the peaceful East German revolution: The role of middle level officials. *German Politics, 2,* 97–112.

Friesen, J. P., Laurin, K., Shepherd, S., Gaucher, D., & Kay, A. C. (2018). System justification: Experimental evidence, its contextual nature, and implications for social change. *British Journal of Social Psychology, 58,* 315–339.

Frings, K. V. (1997). Rewriting Cambodian history to "adapt" it to a new political context: The Kampuchean People's Revolutionary Party's historiography (1979–1991). *Modern Asian Studies, 31,* 806–847.

Fulbrook, M. (1995). *Anatomy of a dictatorship: Inside the GDR 1949–1989.* New York: Oxford University Press.

Furnham, A. (2003). Belief in a just world: Research progress over the past decade. *Personality and Individual Differences, 34,* 577–817.

Gaertner, S. L., Dovidio, J. F., Banker, B. S., Houlette, M., Johnson, K. M., & McGlynn, E. A. (2000). Reducing intergroup conflict: From superordinate goals to decategorization, recategorization and mutual differentiation. *Group Dynamics: Theory, Research, and Practice, 4,* 98–114.

Gard-Murray, A. S., & Bar-Yam, Y. (2015). Complexity and the limits of revolution: What will happen to the Arab Spring? In P. Vos Fellman, Y. Bar-Yam, & A. A. Minai (Eds.), *Conflict and complexity: Countering terrorism, insurgency, ethnic and regional violence* (pp. 281–292). New York: Springer.

Garrioch, D. (2002). *The making of revolutionary Paris.* Berkeley, CA: University of California Press.

Gasiorowski, M. J. (2019). U.S. perceptions of the Communist threat in Iran during the Mossadegh era. *Journal of Cold War Studies, 21,* 185–221.

Gavrilets, S., & Fortunato, L. (2014). A solution to the collective action problem in between-group conflict and within-group inequality. *Nature Communications, 5,* 3526. https://doi.org/10.1038/ncomms4526.

Gazzaniga, M. S., Ivry, R. B., & Mangun, G. R. (2019). *Cognitive neuroscience: The biology of the mind.* New York: W.W. Norton. 5th ed.

Geloso, V., & Pavlik, J. B. (2021). The Cuban Revolution and infant mortality: A synthetic control approach. *Explorations in Economic History, 80,* 1–9, 101376.

Gerber, J. P., Wheeler, L., & Suls, J. (2018). A social comparison theory meta-analysis 60+ years on. *Psychological Bulletin, 144,* 177–197.

Gilbert, G. M. (1950). *The psychology of dictatorship.* New York: Ronald Press.

Glaeser, E. L., Ponzetto, G. A. M., & Schleifer, A. (2007). Why does democracy need education? *Journal of Economic Growth, 12,* 77–99.

Godineau, D. (1998). *The women of Paris and their French Revolution.* (Trans. K. Streip). Berkeley, CA: University of California Press.

Goldstein, J. D., & Hiebert, M. S. (2016). Strange legacies of the Terror: Hegel, the French Revolution, and the Khmer Rouge Purges. *The European Legacy, 21,* 145–167.

Goldstone, J. A. (1982). The comparative and historical study of revolutions. *Annual Review of Sociology, 8,* 187–207.

Goldstone, J. A. (Ed.) (2003). *Revolutions: Theoretical, comparative, and historical studies.* Belmont, CA: Wadsworth Learning.

Goldstone, J. A., Grinin, L., & Korotayev, A. (Eds.) (2022). *Handbook of revolutions in the 21st century*. Cham: Springer.

González-Corzo, M. (2019). Agricultural production and land productivity in Cuba. *Cuba in Transition, 29*, 109–112.

Gordji-Bandpay, E. (1985). *The redistribution effects of government fiscal policy in Iran (1970–1980)*. PhD thesis, American University, Washington, DC. https://dra.a merican.edu/islandora/object/thesesdissertations%3A2191?solr_nav%5Bid%5D= b58a511209ac152cbfde&solr_nav%5Bpage%5D=91&solr_nav%5Boffset%5D=11.

Grajewski, N. (2022). An illusory entente: The myth of a Russia-China-Iran "Axis." *Asian Affairs, LIII*, 164–183.

Green, J. D. (1984). Countermobilization as a revolutionary form. *Comparative Politics, 16*, 153–169.

Greenberg, J. (2014). *After the revolution: Youth, democracy, and the politics of disappointment in Serbia*. Stanford, CA: Stanford University Press.

Greitens, S. C. (2016). *Dictators and their secret police: Coercive institutions and state violence*. New York: Cambridge University Press.

Griffin, W. E., & Oheneba-Sakyi, Y. (1993). Sociodemographic and political correlates of university students' causal attributions of poverty. *Psychological Reports, 73*, 795–800.

Gungwu, W. (1990). Outside the Chinese Revolution. *The Australian Journal of Chinese Affairs, 23*, 33–48.

Gurney, J. N., & Tierney, K. J. (1982). Relative deprivation and social movements: A critical look at twenty years of theory and research. *The Sociological Quarterly, 23*, 33–47.

Gurr, T. R. (1970). *Why men rebel*. Princeton, NJ: Princeton University Press.

Haberman, M. (2022). *Confidence man: The making of Donald Trump and the breaking of America*. New York: Penguin Press.

Haeri, S. (2014). *The law of desire: Temporary marriage in Shi'i Iran*. Syracuse, NJ: Syracuse University Press. Revised edition.

Hafer, C. L., & Sutton, R. (2016). Belief in a just world. In C. Sabbagh & M. Schmitt (Eds.), *Handbook of social justice theory and research* (pp. 145–160). New York: Springer.

Hafer, C. L., Busseri, M. A., Rubel, A. N., Drolet, C. E., & Cherrington, J. N. (2020). A latent factor approach to belief in a just world and its association with well-being. *Social Justice Research, 33*, 1–17.

Haliday, F. (1979). *Iran: Dictatorship and development*. London: Penguin Books.

Haney, J. V. (2001). *Russian wondertales*. (Ed. & Trans. J. V. Haney). Armonk, NY: M.E. Sharpe.

Hansing, K., & Hoffman, B. (2020). When racial inequalities return: Assessing the restratification of Cuban society 60 years after revolution. *Latin American Politics and Society, 62*, 29–52.

Harmon-Jones, E. (Ed.) (2019). *Cognitive dissonance: Reexamining a pivotal theory in psychology*. Washington, DC: American Psychological Association. 2nd ed.

Harré, R. (1986). *Varieties of realism: A rationale for the natural sciences*. Oxford: Basil Blackwell.

Harris, R. L. (2009). Cuban internationalism, Che Guevara, and the survival of Cuba's socialist regime. *Latin American Perspectives, 36,* 27–42.

Hay, J. (Ed.) (2013). *Cambodia: Genocide & persecution.* New York: Cengage.

Hessami, Z., & da Fonseca, M. L. (2020). Female political representation and substantive effects on policies: A literature review. *European Journal of Political Economy, 63,* 1–9.

Hill, C. (2021). *The world turned upside down: Radical ideas during the English Revolution.* London: Penguin. Penguin reprint. First published in 1972.

Holmes, A. A. (2019). *Coups and revolutions: Mass mobilization, the Egyptian military & the United States from Mubarak to Sisi.* New York: Oxford University Press.

Hopkins, S. (1992). Parliament is abusing the rights of Americans. In W. Dudley (Ed.), *The American revolution: Opposing viewpoints* (pp. 54–64). San Diego, CA: Greenhaven Press.

Horowitz, I. L. (Ed.) (1987). *Cuban communism.* New Brunswick, NJ: Transaction Books.

Howell, J., & Pringle, T. (2019). Shades of authoritarianism and state-labor relations in China. *British Journal of Industrial Relations, 57,* 223–246.

Hughes, C. (2006). Rewriting the cultural revolution: From centre to periphery. *The China Quarterly, 188,* 1098–1108.

Hung, E. P. W., & Chiu, S. W. K. (2003). The lost generation: Life course dynamics and *Xiagang* in China. *Modern China, 29,* 204–236.

Huntington, S. (1968). *Political order in changing societies.* New Haven, CT: Yale University Press.

Huntington, S. (2003). Revolution and political order. In J. A. Goldstone (Ed.), *Revolutions: Theoretical, comparative, and historical studies* (pp. 37–45). Belmont, CA: Wadsworth Learning.

Israel, J., & Tajfel, H. (Eds.) (1972). *The context of social psychology.* London: Academic Press.

Jahanpour, F. (1984). Iran: The rise and fall of the Tudeh party. *The World Today, 40,* 152–159.

Joint Economic Committee Majority Staff Chairman (2015). *War at any price? The total economic costs of the war beyond the Federal Budget.* Createspace Independent Publishing Platform. Available online www.jec.senate.gov/report s/110th%20Congress/War%20At%20Any%20Cost%20-%20The%20Total% 20Economic%20Costs%20of%20the%20War%20Beyond%20the%20Federa l%20Budget%20(1826).pdf.

Jones, H. (2008). *Bay of Pigs.* New York: Oxford University Press.

Jordan, D. P. (2012). *Napoleon and the revolution.* New York: Palgrave Macmillan.

Jasko, K., Szastok, M., Grzymala-Moszczynska, J., Maj, M., & Kruglanski, A. (2019). Rebel with a cause: Personal significance from political activism predicts willingness to self- sacrifice. *Journal of Social Issues, 75,* 314–349.

John, S. (2009). *Bolivia's radical tradition: Permanent revolution in the Andes.* Tucson, AZ: University of Arizona Press.

Jost, J. T. (1995). Negative illusions: Conceptual clarification and psychological evidence concerning false consciousness. *Political Psychology, 16,* 397–424.

Jost, J. T. (2018) A quarter century of system justification theory: Questions, answers, criticisms, and societal applications. *British Journal of Social Psychology, 58,* 263–314.

Jost, J. T., & Banaji, M. R. (1994). The role of stereotyping in system justification and the production of false consciousness. *British Journal of Social Psychology, 33,* 1–27.

Jost, J. T., & Kay, A. C. (2005). Exposure to benevolent sexism and complimentary gender stereotypes: Consequences for specific and diffuse forms of system justification. *Journal of Personality and Social Psychology, 88,* 498–509.

Jost, J. T., Banaji, M. R., & Nosek, B. A. (2004). A decade of system justification theory: Accumulated evidence for conscious and unconscious bolstering of the status quo. *Political Psychology, 25,* 881–919.

Kallens, P. A. C., Dale, R., & Smaldino, P. E. (2018). Cultural evolution of categorization. *Cognitive Systems Research, 52,* 765–774.

Khalaji, M. (2016). The Shiite clergy post-Khamenei. *Research Notes,* The Washington Institute for Near East Policy, No. 37, October.

Khan, M. I., Irfan, A., & Khan, A. W. (2021). Retreat of an empire or an of an era; Aftermath of US withdrawal from Afghanistan. *Competitive Social Science Research Journal (CSSRJ), 2,* 92–105.

Khomeini, R. (1979). *Islamic government.* Joint Publications Research Service. New York: Manor Books.

Kim, H., Callan, M. J., Gheorghiu, A. I., & Skylark, W. J. (2018). Social comparison processes and the experience of relative deprivation. *Journal of Applied Social Psychology, 48,* 519–532.

Klandermans, B. (1984). Mobilization and participation: Social-psychological expansions of resource mobilization theory. *American Sociological Review, 49,* 583–600.

Krastev, I., & McPherson, A. (Ed.) (2007). *The anti-American century.* Budapest: Central European University.

Kroska, A., & Cason, T. C. (2019). The gender gap in business leadership: Exploring an affect control theory explanation. *Social Psychology Quarterly, 82,* 75–97.

Kurzman, C. (2004). *The unthinkable revolution in Iran.* Cambridge, MA: Harvard University Press.

Lachmann, R. (1997). Agents of revolutions: Elite conflicts and mass mobilization from the Medici to Yeltsin. In J. Foran (Ed.), *Theorizing revolutions* (pp. 71–98). London: Routledge.

Lai, Y. H., & Sing, M. (2020). Solidarity and implications of a leaderless movement in Hong Kong: Its strengths and limitations. *Communist and Post-Communist Studies, 53,* 41–67.

Lammers, J., Gordijn, E. H., & Otten, S. (2008). Looking through the eyes of the powerful. *Journal of Experimental Social Psychology, 44,* 1229–1238.

Lammers, J., Stapel, D. A., & Galinsky, A. D. (2010). Power increases hypocrisy: Moralizing in reasoning, immorality in behavior. *Psychological Science, 21*, 737–744.

Lane, D. (1996). The Gorbachev Revolution: The role of the political elite in regime disintegration. *Political Studies, 44*, 4–23.

Langer, W. C. (1972). *The mind of Adolf Hitler: The secret wartime report.* New York: Basic Books.

Le Bon, G. (1897). *The crowd: A study of the popular mind.* London: T. Fisher Unwin.

Le Bon, G. (1913). *The psychology of revolution.* (Trans. B. Miall). London: T. Fisher Unwin. First published in 1894.

Le Cheminant, W., & Parrish, J. M. (Eds.) (2011). *Manipulating democracy: Democratic theory, political psychology, and mass media.* New York: Routledge.

Leese, D. (2011). *Mao cult: Rhetoric and ritual in Mao's cultural revolution.* New York: Cambridge University Press.

Lefebvre, G. (2005). *The coming of the French Revolution.* (Trans. R. R. Palmer). Princeton, NJ: Princeton University Press. First published in French in 1939 and in English in 1947.

Lenin, V. (1972). *Collected works.* (Trans. B. Isaacs). Moscow: Progress Publishers.

Lennon, J. (2021). *Conflict graffiti: From revolution to gentrification.* Chicago, IL: University of Chicago Press.

Lerner, M. J. (1980). *The belief in a just world: A fundamental delusion.* New York: Plenum Press.

LeVine, R. A., & Campbell, D. T. (1972). *Ethnocentrism: Theories of conflict, ethnic attitudes, and group behavior.* New York: John Wiley.

Levitas, R. (1990). *The concept of utopia.* New York: Peter Lang.

Levitsky, S., & Way, L. (2022). *Revolutions and dictatorships: The violent origins of durable authoritarianism.* Princeton, NJ: Princeton University Press.

Levitsky, S., & Ziblatt, D. (2018). How wobbly is our democracy? *The New York Times*, January 27. www.nytimes.com/2018/01/27/opinion/sunday/democracy-polarization.html.

Lewis, D. S. (1987). *Illusions of grandeur: Mosely, fascism, and British society.* Manchester: Manchester University Press.

Li, W., & Yang, D. T. (2005). The Great Leap Forward: Anatomy of a central planning disaster. *Journal of Political Economy, 113*, 840–877.

Lind, E. A. (2020). *Social psychology and justice.* New York: Routledge.

Little, P. (Ed.) (2009). *Oliver Cromwell: New perspectives.* New York: Palgrave Macmillan.

Lizzio-Wilson, M., Thomas, E. F., Louis, W. R., et al. (2021). How collective action failure shapes group heterogeneity and engagement in conventional and radical action over time. *Psychological Science, 32*, 519–535.

Louër, L. (2022). *Sunnis and Shi'a: A political history.* (Trans. E. Rundell). Princeton, NJ: Princeton University Press.

Louis, W., Thomas, E., McGarty, C., Lizzio-Wilson, M., Amiot, C., & Moghaddam, F. M. (2020). The volatility of collective action: Theoretical analysis and empirical data. *Political Psychology, 41*, 35–74.

Lout, R. B., & Wilk, S. L. (2014). Working harder or hardly working? Posting performance eliminates social loafing and promotes social laboring in workshops. *Management Science, 60*, 1098–1106.

Löwy, M. (2010). *The politics of combined and uneven development: The theory of permanent revolution.* Chicago, IL: Haymarket Books. Revised version of 1981 publication.

Lucas, B. J., & Kteily, N. S. (2018). (Anti-) egalitarianism differentially predicts empathy for members of the advantages versus disadvantaged groups. *Journal of Personality and Social Psychology, 114*, 665–692.

Lundy, B. D., & Darkwah, K. (2018). Ensuring community integration of Lusophone West African immigrant populations through needs assessment, human security, and realistic conflict theory. *International Migration & Integration, 19*, 513–526.

Lynch, M. (2017). *Mao.* Oxford: Routledge. 2nd ed.

Maran, T., Furtner, M., Liegl, S., Kraus, S., & Sachse, P. (2019). In the eye of the leader: Eye-directed gazing shapes perceptions of leaders. *The Leadership Quarterly, 30*, 101337.

Marks, T. A., & Palmer, D. S. (2006). Radical Maoist insurgents and terrorist tactics: Comparing Peru and Nepal. *Low Intensity Conflict & Law Enforcement, 13*, 91–116.

Markwick, R. D. (2001). *Rewriting history in Soviet Russia: The politics of revisionist historiography 1956–1974.* New York: Palgrave Macmillan.

Marples, D. R. (2004). *The collapse of the Soviet Union, 1985–1991.* London: Routledge.

Marshall, A. J. (2007). *Vilfredo Pareto's sociology: A framework for political psychology.* London: Routledge.

Martin, J., Scully, M., & Levitt, B. (1990). Injustice and the legitimization of revolution: Damning the past, excusing the present, and neglecting the future. *Journal of Personality and Social Psychology, 59*, 281–290.

Marx, K. (1977). *Selected writings.* (Ed. & Trans D. McLellan). Oxford: Oxford University Press.

Marx, K., & Engels, F. (1967). *Communist manifesto.* New York: Pantheon. First published in 1848.

Mason, C. A., Walker-Barnes, C. J., Tu, S., Simons, J., & Martinez-Arrue, R. (2004). Ethnic differences in the affective meaning of parental control behaviors. *The Journal of Primary Prevention, 25*(1), 59–79.

Matin-Asgari, A. (2012). The Pahlavi era: Iranian modernity in global context. In T. Daryaee (Ed.), *The Oxford handbook of Iranian history* (pp. 346–364). New York: Oxford University Press.

McCarthy, T. D., & Wolfson, M. (1996). Resource mobilization by local social movement organizations: Agency, strategy, and organization in the movement against drunk driving. *American Sociological Review, 61*, 1070–1088.

McCarthy, T. D., & Zald, M. N. (1977). Resource mobilization and social movements: A partial theory. *American Journal of Sociology, 82*, 1212–1241.

McGeever, B. (2017). Revolution and antisemitism: The Bolsheviks in 1917. *Patterns of Prejudice, 51*, 235–252.

McKenzie, J., & Twose, G. (2015). Applications and extensions of realistic conflict theory: Moral development and conflict prevention. In A. Dost-Gozkan & D. Sonmez Keith (Eds.), *Norms, groups, conflict, and social change: Rediscovering Muzafer Sherif's psychology* (pp. 307–324). London: Transaction Publishers.

McKown, C. (2013). Social equity theory and racial-ethnic achievement gaps. *Child Development, 84*, 1120–1136.

Melvern, L. (2020). *Intent to deceive: Denying the genocide of the Tutsi.* New York: Verso.

Merridale, C. (2017). *Lenin on the train.* New York: Metropolitan Books.

Messick, D. M., & Cook, K. S. (Eds.) (1983). *Equity theory: Psychological and sociological perspectives.* New York: Praeger.

Michael, F. (1977). *Mao and the perpetual revolution: An illuminating study of Mao Tse-tung's role in China and world communism.* Hauppauge, NY: Barron's Educational Series.

Milani, A. (2011). *The shah.* New York: Palgrave Macmillan.

Milani, A. (2013). *The Persian Sphinx: Amir Abbas Hoveyda and the riddle of the Iranian Revolution.* Washington, DC: Mage Publishers.

Milani, A. (2015). Scripting a revolution: Fate or fortuna in the 1979 revolution in Iran. In K. M. Baker & D. Edelstein (Eds.), *Scripting revolution: A historical approach to the comparative study of revolutions* (pp. 307–324). Stanford, CA: Stanford University Press.

Milgram, S. (1974). *Obedience to authority: An experimental view.* New York: Harper & Row.

Miller, J. D., Lynam, D. R., Hyatt, C. S., & Campbell, W. K. (2017). Controversies in narcissism. *Annual Review of Clinical Psychology, 13*, 1.1–1.25.

Mitchell, A. (1997). *The Nazi Revolution.* New York: Houghton Mifflin. 4th ed.

Mittler, B. (2014). *A continuous revolution: Making sense of cultural revolution culture.* Boston, MA: Harvard University Asia Center.

Moaddel, M. (2022). Secular shift among Iranians: Findings from cross-national and longitudinal surveys. Unpublished manuscript, Department of Sociology, University of Maryland (College Park).

Moghaddam, F. M. (2002). *The individual and society: A cultural integration.* New York: Worth.

Moghaddam, F. M. (2004). The cycle of rights and duties in intergroup relations: Interobjectivity and perceived justice re-assessed. *New Review of Social Psychology, 3*, 125–130.

Moghaddam, F. M. (2005). *Great ideas in psychology: A cultural and historical introduction.* Oxford: Oneworld.

Moghaddam, F. M. (2008). *Multiculturalism and intergroup relations: Psychological implications for democracy in global context.* Washington, DC: American Psychological Association Press.

Moghaddam, F. M. (2013). *The psychology of dictatorship*. Washington, DC: American Psychological Association Press.

Moghaddam, F. M. (2015). Conclusion: A scholar between and beyond. In A. Dost-Gozkan & D. Sonmez Keith (Eds.), *Norms, groups, conflict, and social change: Rediscovering Muzafer Sherif's psychology* (pp. 365–373). London: Transaction Publishers.

Moghaddam, F. M. (2016). *The psychology of democracy*. Washington, DC: American Psychological Association Press.

Moghaddam, F. M. (2018). *Mutual radicalization: How groups and nations push each other to extremes*. Washington, DC: American Psychological Association Press.

Moghaddam, F. M. (2019). *Threat to democracy: The appeal of authoritarianism in an age of uncertainty*. Washington, DC: American Psychological Association Press.

Moghaddam, F. M. (2021). The psychology of bureaucracy: A normative account inspired by Rom Harré. *Journal for the Theory of Social Behaviour, 51*, 215–231.

Moghaddam, F. M. (2022). *How psychologists failed: We neglected the poor and minorities, favored the rich and privileged, and got science wrong*. New York: Cambridge University Press.

Moghaddam, F. M. (2023). *Political plasticity: The future of democracy and dictatorship*. New York: Cambridge University Press.

Moghaddam, F. M. (2023). Political plasticity and possibilities for political change. *Possibility Studies & Society, 1*, 152-156.

Moghaddam, F. M., & Breckenridge, J. (2011). The post-tragedy "opportunity-bubble" and the prospect of citizen engagement. *Homeland Security Affairs, 7*, 1–4.

Moghaddam, F. M., & Covalucci, L. (2018). Macro, meso, micro creativity: The role of cultural carriers. In I. Lebuda & V. P. Glaveanu (Eds.), *The Palgrave handbook of social creativity research* (pp. 721–741). London: Palgrave Macmillan.

Moghaddam, F. M., & Riley, C. J. (2005). Toward a cultural theory of human rights and duties in human development. In N. J. Finkel & F. M. Moghaddam (Eds.), *Human rights and duties: Empirical contributions and normative commentaries* (pp. 75–104). Washington, DC: APA Press.

Moghaddam, F. M., & Stringer, P. (1986). "Trivial" and "important" criteria for social categorization in the minimal group paradigm. *Journal of Social Psychology, 126*, 345–354.

Moghaddam, F. M., & Studer, C. (1998). *Illusions of control: Striving for control in our personal and professional lives*. Westport, CT: Praeger.

Mok, F. K. T. (2020). *Civilian participants in the Cultural Revolution*. London: Routledge.

Molinari, L. (2004). Revising the revolution: The festival of unity and Shelley's "Beau Ideal." *Keats-Shelley Journal, 53*, 97–126.

More, T. (1965). *Utopia*. (Trans. P. K. Marshall). New York: Washington Square Press.

Mullaney, M. M. (1984). Women and the theory of "revolutionary personality": Comments, criticisms, and suggestions for further study. *The Social Science Journal, 21,* 49–70.

Namboodiripad, E. M. S. (1976). Mao Tse-Tung's contribution to theory and tactics of revolution. *Social Scientist, 5,* 57–66.

Naraghi, A. (2015). Ayatollah Khomeini's theory of government. In A. Milani & L. Diamond (Eds.), *Politics and culture in contemporary Iran: Challenging the status quo* (pp. 15–32). Boulder, CO: Lynne Rienner Publishers.

Nichol, L. (2010). Introduction. In L. Trotsky, *The permanent revolution & results and prospects* (pp. 7–28). Seattle, WA: Red Letter Press.

Noueihed, L., & Warren, A. (2012). *The battle for the Arab Spring: Revolution, counter-revolution and the making of a new era.* New Haven, CT: Yale University Press.

Osbeck, L., Moghaddam, F. M., & Perreault, S. (1997). Similarity and intergroup relations. *International Journal of Intercultural Relations, 21,* 113–123.

Osborn, R. (2007). On the path of perpetual revolution: From Marx's millenarianism to Sendero Luminoso. *Totalitarian Movements and Political Religions, 8,* 115–135.

Osborne, D., Sengupta, N. K., & Sibley, C. G. (2018). System justification theory at 25: Evaluating a paradigm shift in psychology and looking toward the future. *British Journal of Social Psychology, 58,* 340–361.

Pace, J. L. (2005). *Classroom authority.* New York: Routledge.

Panning, W. H. (1983). Inequality, social comparison, and relative deprivation. *The American Political Science Review, 77,* 323–329.

Pareto, V. (1935). *The mind and society: A treatise in general sociology.* (4 vols.). New York: Dover.

Pareto, V. (1971). *Manual of political economy.* New York: Augustus M. Kelly. (Translated from the French edition of 1927.)

Pepper, S. (1999). *Civil war in China: The political struggle 1945–1949.* Oxford: Rowman & Littlefield.

Pérez-Stable, M. (2012). *The Cuban revolution: Origins, course, and legacy.* New York: Oxford University Press.

Pesaran, E. (2008). Towards and anti-Western stance: The economic discourse of Iran's 1979 Revolution. *Iranian Studies, 41,* 693–718.

Pettigrew, T. F., Allport, G. W., & Barnett, E. O. (1958). Binocular resolution and perception of race in South Africa. *British Journal of Psychology, 49,* 265–278.

Petty, R. E., Cacioppo, J. T., & Schumann, D. (1983). Central and peripheral routers to advertising effectiveness: The moderating role of involvement. *Journal of Consumer Research, 10,* 135–146.

Piketty, T. (2014). *Capital in the 21st century.* (Trans. A. Goldhammer). Cambridge, MA: Belknap Press.

Pincus, A. L., & Lukowitsky, M. R. (2010). Pathological narcissism and narcissistic personality disorder. *Annual Review of Clinical Psychology, 6,* 421–446.

Pincus, S. C., & Robinson, J. A. (2011). *What really happened during the Glorious Revolution?* (No. w17206). Cambridge, MA: National Bureau of Economic Research.

Pipes, R. (1990). *The Russian revolution.* New York: Knopf.

Plato (1987). *The republic.* (Trans. D. Lee). Harmondsworth: Penguin.

Power, S. A. (2018). The deprivation–protest paradox: How the perception of unfair economic inequality leads to civic unrest. *Current Anthropology, 59,* 765–789.

Power, S. A., Madsen, T., & Morton, T. A. (2020). Relative deprivation and revolt: Current and future directions. *Current Opinions in Psychology, 35,* 119–124.

Price, M. (2002). *The fall of the French monarchy: Louis XVI, Marie Antoinette and baron de Breteuil.* London: Macmillan.

Pyszczynski, T., Solomon, S., & Greenberg, J. (2004). *In the wake of 9/11: The psychology of terror.* Washington, DC: American Psychological Association Press.

Rabbie, J. M., & Horwitz, M. (1969). Arousal of ingroup-outgroup bias by a chance win or loss. *Journal of Personality and Social Psychology, 13,* 269–277.

Radcliffe, E. (1994). Saving ideals: Revolution and benevolence in "The Prelude." *The Journal of English and German Philology, 93,* 534–559.

Rahimzadeh, A. (2020). Fraternal polyandry and land ownership in Kinnaur, Western Himalaya. *Human Ecology, 48,* 573–582.

Razavi, R. (2009). The cultural revolution in Iran, with close regard to the universities, and its impact on the student movement. *Middle Eastern Studies, 45,* 1–17.

Read, C. (2005). *Lenin.* Oxford: Routledge.

Reda, A. A., Sinanoglu, S., & Abdalla, M. (2021). Mobilizing the masses: Measuring resource mobilization on Twitter. *Sociological Methods & Research,* 1–40, https://doi.org/10.1177/0049124120986197.

Reed, S. (2015). Cathedral of light: The Nuremberg party rallies, Wagner, and the Theatricality of Hitler and the Nazi Party. *HOHONU, 13,* 74–80.

Rhodes, M., & Baron, A. (2019). The development of social categorization. *Annual Review of Developmental Psychology, 1,* 359–386.

Richards, M. D. (2004). *Revolutions in world history.* London: Routledge.

Ringwald, W. R., Manuck, S. B., Marsland, A. L., & Wright, A. G. C. (2022). Psychometric evaluation of a Big Five personality state scale for intensive longitudinal studies. *Assessment, 29,* 1301–1319.

Robinson, D. J. (1990). Liberty, fragile fraternity and inequality in early-republican Spanish America: Assessing the impact of French Revolutionary ideals. *Journal of Historical Geography, 16,* 51–75.

Rock, M. T. (2009). Corruption and democracy. *The Journal of Development Studies, 45,* 55–75.

Rothgerber, H. (1997). External intergroup threat as an antecedent to perceptions in in-group and out-group homogeneity. *Journal of Personality and Social Psychology, 73,* 1206–1212.

Runciman, W. G. (1966). *Relative deprivation and social justice.* London: Routledge Kegan Paul.

Salisbury, H. E. (1992). *The new emperors: China in the era of Mao and Deng.* New York: Avon.

Saney, I. (2009). Homeland of humanity: Internationalization within the Cuban Revolution. *Latin American Perspectives, 36*, 111–123.

Sargent, T. J., & Velde, F. R. (1995). Macroeconomic features of the French Revolution. *Journal of Political Economy, 103*, 474–518.

Schaffner, B. (1948). *Father land: A study of authoritarianism in the German family.* New York: Columbia University Press.

Schama, S. (1989). *Citizens: A chronicle of the French Revolution.* New York: Vintage Books.

Schinz, A. (1923). Review of "The Ideals of France." *The Modern Language Journal, 7*, 248–253.

Schock, K. (2013). The practice and study of civil resistance. *Journal of Peace Research, 50*, 277–290.

Scully, M. J., & Levitt, B. (1990). Injustice and the legitimation of revolution: Damning the past, excusing the present, and neglecting the future. *Journal of Personality and Social Psychology, 59*, 281–290.

Selbin, E. (1993). *Modern Latin American revolutions.* New York: Routledge. 2nd ed.

Selznick, P. (1952). *The organizational weapon: A study of Bolshevik strategy and tactics.* New York: McGraw Hill.

Setiawan, T., Scheepers, P., & Sterkens, C. (2020). Applicability of the social identity model of collective action in predicting support for interreligious violence in Indonesia. *Asian Journal of Social Psychology, 23*, 278–292.

Shakespeare, W. (1993). *King Lear.* Folger Shakespeare Library. New York: Simon & Schuster.

Sharlet, R. (1984). Dissent and the "contra-system" in the Soviet Union. *Proceedings of the Academy of Political Science, 35*, 135–146.

Sharp, G. (1973). *The politics of nonviolent actions* (3 vols.). Boston, MA: Porter Sargent.

Shepperd, J., Malone, W., & Sweeny, K. (2008). Exploring causes of self-serving bias. *Social and Personality Psychology Compass, 2*, 895–908.

Sherif, M. (1951). A preliminary experimental study of intergroup relations. In J. H. Rohrer & M. Sherif (Eds.), *Social psychology at the crossroads* (pp. 388–424). New York: Harper and Brothers.

Sherif, M. (1956). Experiments in group conflict. *Scientific American, 195*, 54–58.

Sherif, M. (1966). Group conflict and cooperation: Their social psychology. London: Routledge & Kegan Paul.

Sherif, M., & Sherif, C. W. (1953). *Groups in harmony and tension.* New York: Harper and Brothers.

Sherif, M., & Sherif, C. W. (1969). *Social psychology.* New York: Harper and Row.

Sherif, M., Harvey, O. J., White, B. J., Hood, W. R., & Sherif, C. W. (1961). *Intergroup conflict and cooperation: The Robber's cave experiment.* Norman, OK: University Book Exchange.

Sherif, M., White, B. J., & Harvey, O. J. (1955). Status in experimentally produced groups. *American Journal of Sociology, 60*, 370–379.

Shirk, S. L. (1984). The decline of virtuocracy in China. In J. L. Watson (Ed.), *Class & social stratification in post-revolution China* (pp. 56–83). New York: Cambridge University Press.

Sidanius, J., & Pratto, F. (1999). *Social dominance: An intergroup theory of social dominance and oppression*. Cambridge: Cambridge University Press.

Sidanius, J., Pratto, F., van Laar, C., & Levin, S. (2004). Social dominance theory: Its agenda and method. *Political Psychology, 25,* 845–880.

Simms, A., & Nichols, T. (2014). Social loafing: A review of the literature. *Journal of Management Policy and Practice, 15,* 58–67.

Skocpol, T. (1976). France, Russia, China: A structural analysis of social revolutions. *Comparative Studies in Society and History, 18,* 175–210.

Skocpol, T. (1979). *States and social revolutions: A comparative analysis of France, Russia, and China.* Cambridge: Cambridge University Press.

Skocpol, T. (1985). Cultural idioms and political ideologies in the revolutionary reconstruction of state power: A rejoinder to Sewell. *The Journal of Modern History, 57,* 86–96.

Smeaton, A. A. (1993). French scientists in the shadow of the Guillotine: The death roll of 1792–1794. *Endeavour, 17,* 60–63.

Smith, H., Pettigrew, T. F., Pippin, G., & Bialosiewicz, S. (2012). Relative deprivation: A theoretical and meta-analytic critique. *Personality and Social Psychology Review, 16,* 203–232.

Smith, K. B. (1985). Seeing justice in poverty: The belief in a just world and ideas about inequalities. *Sociological Spectrum, 5,* 17–29.

Smith, L., Moa, S., Perkins, S., & Ampuero, M. (2011). The relationship of clients' social class to early therapeutic impressions. *Counselling Psychology Quarterly, 24,* 15–27.

Smith, S. A. (2017). *Russia in revolution: An empire in crisis.* New York: Oxford University Press.

Söllner, L. (2013). Rewriting revolutionary myths: Photography in Castro's Cuba and Tania Bruguera's Tatlin's Whisper#6. *Culture, 4,* 59–64.

Somin, I. (2018). *Stillborn crusade: The tragic failure of Western intervention in the Russian civil war.* New York: Routledge.

Sorkhabi, N., & Mandara, J. (2013). Are the effects of Baumrind's parenting style culturally specific or culturally equivalent? In R. E. Larzelere, A. S. Morris, & A. W. Harrist (Eds.), *Authoritative parenting: Synthesizing nurturance and discipline for optimal child development* (pp. 113–135). Washington, DC: American Psychological Association Press.

Stiglitz, J. E., & Bilmes, L. J. (2008). *The three trillion dollar war: The true cost of the Iraq war.* New York: W. W. Norton.

Stites, R. (1989). *Revolutionary dreams: Utopian vision and experimental life in the Russian Revolution.* New York: Oxford University Press.

Stoppard, T. (2006). *The coast of utopia: Voyage, shipwreck, salvage.* London: Faber & Faber.

Stouffer, S. A., Suchman, E. A., De Vinney, L. C., Star, S. A., & Williams, R. M. (1949). *The American soldier: Adjustments during army life.* (Vol. 1). Princeton, NJ: Princeton University Press.

Strug, D. L. (2009). Why older Cubans continue to identify with the ideals of the Revolution. *Socialism and Democracy, 23,* 143–157.

Suny, R. G. (1993). *The revenge of the past: Nationalism, revolution, and the collapse of the Soviet Union.* Stanford, CA: Stanford University Press.

Swaab, R. I., Lount Jr., R. B., Chung, S., & Brett, J. M. (2021). Setting the stage for negotiations: How superordinate goal dialogues promote trust and join gain in negotiations in teams. *Organizational Behavior and Human Decision Processes, 167,* 157–169.

Swatos, W. H. (1981). The disenchantment of charisma: A Weberian assessment of revolution in a rationalized world. *Sociological Analysis, 42,* 119–136.

Tackett, T. (2000). Conspiracy obsession in a time of revolution: French elites and the origins of the Terror, 1789–1792. *The American Historical Review, 105,* 691–713.

Tackett, T. (2015). *The coming of the Terror in the French Revolution.* Cambridge, MA: The Belknap Press of Harvard University Press.

Tajfel, H. (1959). Quantitative judgement in social perception. *British Journal of Psychology, 50,* 16–29.

Tajfel, H. (1970). Experiments in intergroup discrimination. *Scientific American, 223,* 96–102.

Tajfel, H. (Ed.) (1984). *The social dimension.* (2 vols.). Cambridge: Cambridge University Press.

Tajfel, H., & Turner, J. C. (1979). An integrative theory of intergroup conflict. In W. G. Austin & S. Worchel (Eds.), *The social psychology of intergroup relations* (pp. 33–47). Monterey, CA: Brooks/Cole.

Tajfel, H., & Wilkes, A. J. (1963). Classification and quantitative judgement. *British Journal of Psychology, 54,* 101–113.

Tajfel, H., Flament, C., Billig, M. G., & Bundy, R. F. (1971). Social categorization and intergroup behaviour. *European Journal of Social Psychology, 1,* 149–177.

Takano, Y., & Osaka, E. (2018). Comparing Japan and the United States on individualism/collectivism: A follow-up review. *Asian Journal of Social Psychology, 21,* 301–316.

Tan, L. H. (1984). The Khmer Rouge: Beyond 1984? *Index on Censorship, 13,* 3–5.

Tanter, R., & Midlarsky, M. (1967). A theory of revolution. *The Journal of Conflict Resolution, 11,* 264–280.

Taylor, D. M., & McKirnan, D. J. (1984). A five-stage model of intergroup relations. British *Journal of Social Psychology, 23,* 291–300.

Taylor, D. M., & Moghaddam, F. M. (1994). *Theories of intergroup relations: International social psychological perspectives.* Westport, CT: Praeger. 2nd ed.

Taylor, G. E. (1936). The powers and the unity of China. *Pacific Affairs, 9,* 532–543.

Teets, J. C., & Hasmath, R. (2020). The evolution of policy experimentation in China. *Journal of Asian Public Policy, 13,* 49–59.

Teiwes, F. C., & Sun, W. (1999). *Mao, central politicians, and provincial leaders in the unfolding of the Great Leap Forward, 1955–1959*. New York: M. E. Sharpe.

Telios, T., Thoma, D., & Schmid, U. (Eds.) (2020). *The Russian revolution in ideal and practice*. Cham: Palgrave Macmillan.

Tennen, H., & Affleck, G. (2000). The perception of personal control: Sufficiently important to warrant careful scrutiny. *Personality and Social Psychology Bulletin, 26*, 152–156.

Terhune, V., & Matusitz, J. (2016). The Uighurs versus the Chinese government: An application of realistic conflict theory. *Journal of Applied Security Research, 11*, 139–148.

Thomas, E. F., Mavor, K., & McGarty, C. (2016). Social identities facilitate and encapsulate action-relevant constructs: A test of the social identity model of collective action. *Group Processes & Intergroup Relations, 15*, 75–88.

Thomas, E. F., McGarty, C., & Mavor, K. (2016). Group interactions as the crucible of social identity formations: A glimpse of the foundations of social identities for collective action. *Group Processes & Intergroup Relations, 19*, 137–151.

Thomas, E. F., Zublielevitch, E., Sibley, C. G., & Osborne, D. (2020). Testing the social identity model of collective action longitudinally and across structurally disadvantaged and advantaged groups. *Personality and Social Psychology Bulletin, 46*, 823–838.

Tilly, C. (1973). Does modernization breed revolution? *Comparative Politics, 5*, 425–447.

Timasheff, N. S. (1955). The anti-religious campaign in the Soviet Union. *The Review of Politics, 17*, 329–344.

Tocqueville, A. de (1955). *The old regime and the French revolution*. (Trans. S. Gilbert). New York: First Anchor Books. First published in 1856.

Trenta, L. (2013). The champion of human tights meets the King of Kings: Jimmy Carter, the Shah, and Iranian Illusions and rage. *Diplomacy & Statecraft, 24*, 476–498.

Trimberger, E. K. (1978). *Revolution from above: Military bureaucrats and developments in Japan, Turkey, Egypt, and Peru*. New Brunswick, NJ: Transaction Books.

Trotsky, L. (2005). *Literature and revolution*. (Trans. R. Strunsky). Chicago, IL: Haymarket Books. First published in 1923.

Trotsky, L. (2010). *The permanent revolution & results and prospects*. Seattle, WA: Red Letter Press. First published in 1906.

Tsai, W. (1999). Mass mobilization campaigns in Mao's China. *American Journal of Chinese Studies, 6*, 21–48.

Tyler, T. R. (2001). A psychological perspective on legitimacy of institutions and authorities. In J. T. Jost & B. Major (Eds.), *The psychology of legitimacy: Emerging perspectives on ideology, justice, and intergroup relations* (pp. 416–436). New York: Cambridge University Press.

Tyler, T. R. (2006). Psychological perspectives on legitimacy and legitimation. *Annual Review of Psychology, 57*, 375–400.

Van Bezouw, M. J., van der Toorn, J., & Becker, J. C. (2021). Social creativity: Reviving a social identity approach to social stability. *European Journal of Social Psychology*, *51*, 409–422.

Van den Berghe, P. (1987). *The ethnic phenomenon*. New York: Praeger.

Van der Toorn, J., Tyler, T. R., & Jost, J. T. (2011). More than fair: Outcome dependence, system justification, and the perceived legitimacy of authority figures. *Journal of Experimental Social Psychology*, *47*, 127–138.

Van Dick, R., Tissington, P. A., & Hertel, G. (2009). Do many hands make light work? How to overcome social loafing and gain motivation in work teams. *European Business Review*, *21*, 233–245.

Van Zomeren, M., Postmes, T., & Spears, R. (2008). Toward an integrative social identity model of collective action: A quantitative research synthesis of three social-psychological perspectives. *Psychological Bulletin*, *134*, 504–535.

Vance-Cheng, R., Rooney, I. C., Moghaddam, F. M. & Harré, R. (2013). Waging war, talking peace: A positioning analysis of storylines used to interpret "war for peace" rhetoric. In R. Harré & F. M. Moghaddam (Eds.), *The psychology of friendship and enmity: Relationships in love, work, politics, and war. Vol. 2: Group and intergroup understanding* (pp. 11–36). Santa Barbara, CA: Praeger.

Vanek, M., & Mücke, P. (2016). *Velvet revolution*. New York: Oxford University Press.

Vince, N. (2020). *The Algerian war, the Algerian revolution*. Cham: Palgrave Macmillan.

Volkova, E. V., & Rusalov, V. M. (2016). Cognitive styles and personality. *Personality and Individual Differences*, *99*, 266–271.

Voss, Z, G., Cable, D. M., & Voss, G. B. (2006). Organizational identity and firm performance: What happens when leaders disagree about "who we are"? *Organizational Science*, *17*, 741–755.

Wagoner, B., Moghaddam, F. M., & Valsiner, J. (Eds.) (2018). The psychology of radical social change: From rage to revolution. Cambridge: Cambridge University Press.

Walster, E., Walster, G. W., & Berscheid, E. (1978). *Equity: Theory and research*. Boston, MA: Allyn & Bacon.

Walton, C. (2009). *Policing public opinion in the French Revolution: The culture of calumny and the problem of free speech*. New York: Oxford University Press.

Wang, Y. (2021). The political legacy of violence during China's Cultural Revolution. *British Journal of Political Science*, *51*, 463–487.

Watson, J. L. (1984). Introduction: Class and class formation in Chinese society. In J. L. Watson (Ed.), *Class & social stratification in post-revolution China* (pp. 1–15). New York: Cambridge University Press.

Weede, E., & Muller, E. N. (1998). Rebellion, violence and revolution: A rational choice perspective. *Journal of Peace Research*, *35*, 43–59.

Welzel, C., & Inglehart, R. (2008). The role of ordinary people in democratization. *Journal of Democracy*, *19*, 126–140.

Wigell, M. (2021). Democratic deterrence: How to dissuade hybrid interference. *The Washington Quarterly*, *44*, 49–67.

Willner, A. R. (1984). *The spellbinders: Charismatic political leadership.* New Haven, CT: Yale University Press.

Wilson, E. O. (1975). *Sociobiology: The new synthesis.* Cambridge, MA: Harvard University Press.

Wolf, C. (2008). How secularized is Germany? Cohort and comparative perspectives. *Social Compass, 55,* 111–126.

Wood, E. J. (2003). *Insurgent collective action and civil war in El Salvador.* New York: Cambridge University Press.

Wood, W., Quinn, J. M., & Kashy, D. A. (2002). Habits in everyday life: Thought, emotion, and action. *Journal of Personality and Social Psychology, 83,* 1281–1297.

Woodward, B., & Costa, R. (2021). *Peril.* New York: Simon & Schuster.

Wright, S. C., Taylor, D. M., & Moghaddam, F. M. (1990). Responding to membership in a disadvantaged group: From acceptance to collective action. *Journal of Personality and Social Psychology, 58,* 994–1003.

Xu, Y. (2022). Fragile fortune: State power and concentrated wealth in China. *Politics & Society.* https://doi.org/10.1177/00323292221124408.

Yadav, V., & Mukherjee, B. (2016). *The politics of corruption in dictatorships.* New York: Cambridge University Press.

Yan, H., Bun, K. H., & Siyuan, X. (2021). Rural revitalization, scholars, and the dynamics of the collective future in China. *The Journal of Peasant Studies, 48,* 853–874.

Zald, M. N., & McCarthy, J. D. (2002). The resource mobilization research program: Progress, challenge, and transformation. In J. Berger & M. Zelditch (Eds.), *New directions in contemporary sociology* (pp. 147–171). Lanham, MD: Rowman & Littlefield.

Zárate, M. A., Garcia, B., Garza, A. A., & Hitlan, R. T. (2004). Cultural threat and perceived realistic group conflict as dual predictors of prejudice, *Journal of Experimental Social Psychology, 40,* 99–105.

Zhou, X., & Xie, Y. (2019). Market transition, industrialization, and social mobility trends in postrevolution China. *American Journal of Sociology, 124,* 1810–1847.

Zimbalist, A. (2018). *Cuban political economy: Controversy in Cubanology.* New York: Routledge. First published in 1988.

Index

Adorno, Theodore, 148
Afghanistan, 59
Ahmadinejad, Mahmoud, 62
Algerian Revolution, 7, 41
Allen, Woody, 146
Altemeyer, Bob, 150
American Revolution, 7, 26, 53, 93, 159
    French support for, 77
Anderson, John, 128
anti-dictatorship revolutions, 65
Arab Spring, 2, 6, 64, 65, 76, 159
Arendt, Hannah, 150
Argentina, 189
Aron, Leon, 60
Assad, Bashar, 26
authoritarian personality, 148
authority, 71
Awad, Sarah, 64, 187
Axworthy, Michael, 68

Bahrain Revolution, 6
Beetham, David, 92
behavioral continuity, 3, 9, 94, 99, 101, 102, 107,
    129, 131, 135, 182
    "Who will guard the guards themselves?", 107
Beissinger, Mark, 6
Ben Ali, Zine el-Abidine, 22, 64
Berman, Greg, 96
Bochner, Stephen, 140
Bolivian Revolution, 6
Brenton, Tony, 79
Brinton, Crane, 3
Buchner, George, 143
built environment, 5, 110, 171
Bullock, Alan, 81, 126
Burke, Edmund, 174

Cambodia
    Khmer Rouge, 105, 107, 119
    Pol Pot, 96

capitalism
    and psychological assumptions, 33
Carter, President Jimmy, 39, 189
    Tehran US Embassy hostage taking, 39
Castro, Fidel, 39, 54, 86, 96, 133, 141, 177
Chamberlain, William, 174
charisma
    and revolutionary leadership, 141
Chinese Revolution, 7, 9, 72, 77, 90, 93, 95, 96,
    119, 130, 136, 157, 175, 184
class consciousness. *See* Marx, Karl
cognitive dissonance theory, 23
collective action, 4, 17
collective mobilization, 22, 87
collective movements, 4
collectivization, 118, 121, 163, 176, 184
Color Revolutions, 7
conflict graffiti, 187
conformity, 93
conspiratorial thinking and revolutions, 147
corruption, 124, 182
Corruption Perception Index, 182
craving for power
    and revolutionary leaders, 138
creativity during revolutions
    micro, meso, macro, 187
Cromwell, Oliver, 119, 183
Cuban Revolution, 6, 7, 65, 72, 90, 92, 93, 96, 119,
    130, 176, 184
cultural carriers, 10, 99, 119, 126, 128, 129, 131
Cultural Revolution, 9, 95, 103, 105, 113, 118, 175
    and universities in Iran, 104
    similarities between cultural revolutions in
    Iran and China, 114
cyclical model of revolution, 1, 153
Czechoslovakian Revolution, 80

Dahlum, Sirianne, 158
Darwin, Charles, 25, 27
David, Jacques-Louis, 82

For EU product safety concerns, contact us at Calle de José Abascal, 56–1°,
28003 Madrid, Spain or eugpsr@cambridge.org.

www.ingramcontent.com/pod-product-compliance
Ingram Content Group UK Ltd.
Pitfield, Milton Keynes, MK11 3LW, UK
UKHW020354140625
459647UK00020B/2456